FOREIGN INVESTMENT, DEBT AND ECONOMIC GROWTH IN LATIN AMERICA

Also by Antonio Jorge and Jorge Salazar-Carrillo
EXTERNAL DEBT AND DEVELOPMENT STRATEGIES IN LATIN
   AMERICA
FOREIGN DEBT AND LATIN AMERICAN ECONOMIC DEVELOPMENT
TRADE, DEBT AND GROWTH IN LATIN AMERICA

Also by Jorge Salazar-Carrillo
THE BRAZILIAN ECONOMY IN THE EIGHTIES

Foreign Investment, Debt and Economic Growth in Latin America

Edited by
Antonio Jorge
and
Jorge Salazar-Carrillo

both Professors of Economics
Florida International University

St. Martin's Press   New York

© Antonio Jorge and Jorge Salazar-Carrillo 1988

First published in the United States of America in 1988

Printed in Hong Kong

ISBN 0–312–00936–4

Library of Congress Cataloging-in-Publication Data
Foreign investment, debt, and economic growth in Latin America
edited by Antonio Jorge and Jorge Salazar-Carrillo.
    p.   cm.
Proceedings of the Fourth Annual Conference on Key Problems of
Latin America, held Dec. 3–4, 1985 in Miami, Fla., organized by
Florida International University.
Includes bibliographies and index.
ISBN 0–312–00936–4 : $30.00 (est.)
1. Investments, Foreign—Latin America—Congresses. 2. Debts,
External—Latin America—Congresses. 3. Latin America—Economic
conditions—1945– —Congresses. I. Jorge, Antonio, 1931– .
II. Salazar-Carrillo, Jorge. III. Conference on Key Problems of
Latin America (4th : 1985 : Miami, Fla.) IV. Florida International
University.
HG5160.5.A3F675   1987
332.6′73′098–dc19   87–18808
                                                              CIP

Typeset by Latimer Trend & Company Ltd, Plymouth

To our parents

Contents

Contents

Preface

The Fourth Annual Conference on Key Problems of Latin America took place on 3 and 4 December 1985 in Miami, Florida. Florida International University was the organiser of the Conference. The three previous economic conferences were undertaken in February 1982, March 1983, and February 1984. The Department of Economics at Florida International University has been a sponsor of all of them, with Wharton Econometrics a co-sponsor of the Second Conference. The First Conference dealt with foreign debt and economic growth in Latin America. The second emphasized the area of trade, growth and debt in these countries. The third stressed the strategy of economic development, within the purview of the external debt problem in the Western Hemisphere. This last conference focused on foreign investment and economic growth in Latin America. As can be seen, these conferences weave a pattern descriptive of the changing character of the short-run economic problems afflicting Latin America.

During the conferences, a free and vibrant exchange between key Latin American policy makers (at the ministerial level), major Latin American academic advisors to Latin American institutions and/or academicians from these countries, government officials from the United States, businessmen from the United States and Latin America, and members of the academic community in the US and Europe took place. This frank exchange has been particularly pregnant with solutions that eventually have been adopted by the policy-making world to deal with the Latin American crisis. The major policy conclusions in chronological order have been the following:

1. In February 1982 we signalled the imminence of the debt crisis that was about to erupt in August of that year. In being the prophets of the coming of the debt crisis, we have to acknowledge that our words fell on to deaf ears, and against our advice the financial institutions abruptly stopped all international credit to Latin America after the explosion, without understanding the relationship between debt, growth, and development in the region.
2. By the time of our Second Conference in March 1983, our original message was beginning to gain wider acceptance. The

bankers increasingly saw the debt as a long-run problem. A new dimension which was added in our conference was that a requirement for the passage of the debt in the short-run was to insure that the Latin American countries could substantially increase their exports to the developed world and be allowed to restrict their imports from it, this being a necessary condition for the region to generate the trade surpluses required to transfer back the resources implicit in the debt to the creditor nations.

3. Our Third Conference worked over the theme of the first one, but with the reputation we had gained by our now-accepted policy prescriptions with respect to international trade and the long-run analysis of debt. We pointed out that it was impossible to insist on the adjustment process for debt repayment in Latin America as it was stopping the wheels of growth in those countries in the short term. We stressed that the long-run solutions already accepted meant that in order to successfully repay the debt, Latin America had to renew economic growth and could not continue to waste time in adjusting its economy. Both objectives, debt repayment and economic growth and development in Latin America, had to be complied with simultaneously.

4. The conclusions of our Fourth Conference have also been dramatic. We have agreed that foreign investment is not a short-term panacea that could solve the financial stringencies affecting Latin America, but rather that an effort to increase internal savings and to assure a greater efficiency of investment are the essential immediate objectives that would allow Latin America to continue growing, and at the same time to repay its debt.

ANTONIO JORGE
Miami, Florida   JORGE SALAZAR-CARRILLO

Acknowledgements

Listing acknowledgements is always a less than equitable process which most academics dread to engage in. Our remote indebtedness to a colleague or professor explicitly named may be much heavier than the proximate help received from a recent collaborator.

In a volume of this nature, characterized by an intense level of interaction among a relatively large number of people proceeding from rather different but complementary professional approaches, the task becomes a nearly impossible one. We have simplified our responsibility by reducing our immediate indebtedness to two names: Mr Robert Schwarzreich and Ms Teresita Pedraga.

All that needs to be said is that their work was essential to the production of this book. Without their untiring labour the reader would not have had the opportunity to pass judgement on the piece now in his/her hands.

A.J.
J.S.-C.

Notes on the Contributors

Florencio Ballestero is an economist with the Inter-American Development Bank in charge of studies on the Latin American external sector and industrialized countries' economies. Previously, he was a researcher at the Center for Economic Research of the Instituto Torcuato Di Tella and Senior Economist for the Organization of American States.

Richard L. Bernal is Lecturer in the Department of Economics at the University of the West Indies, Mona. Previously, he worked in the Research Department of the Bank of Jamaica and the Macro-Economic Division of the National Planning Agency. Mr Bernal has published extensively in the fields of trade, external debt, balance of payments adjustment and IMF stabilisation programmes.

Mario I. Blejer is Chief of the Special Fiscal Studies Division of the International Monetary Fund, and Professional Lecturer in International Economics at the School of Advanced International Studies at Johns Hopkins University. He has previously taught at the University of Jerusalem, Boston University and New York University. He has written in the fields of international trade and finance, economic development and Latin American economies.

Compton Bourne is Professor of Economics at the University of the West Indies, St Augustine. He has co-authored two books, edited four collections of essays, and authored numerous technical articles on the economics of the financial sector.

Helson C. Braga is Professor of Economics at the Federal University of Rio de Janeiro and Senior Economist at the Institute of Economic and Social Planning of the Barzilian Ministry of Planning.

Andres Dauhajre is Chairman of the Department of Economics at the Universidad Catolica Madre y Maestra in Santiago, Dominican Republic. He obtained his PhD from Columbia University in 1982. His recent publications have been in the area of financial and exchange-rate policies.

Adalberto Garcia Rocha is Professor of Economics at El Colegio de Mexico, that country's leading post graduate institution. He authored a book on income distribution in Mexico, *La Desigualdad Economica*, which earned the National Award in economics for 1986. His PhD is from Stanford University.

Manuel Gollas is Professor of Economics at El Colegio de Mexico. He previously served as Planning Director of the Mexican National Council of Science and Technology. Mr Gollas is the author of *La Economia Desigual: Empleo y Distribucion en Mexico*, as well as numerous articles on the Mexican economy.

Henry Gomez-Samper is founding Professor and President of the Instituto de Estudios Superiores de Administracion (IESA), and President of the Consejo Latinoamericano de Escuelas de Administracion (CLADEA). Previously he taught at the University of Indiana, the Universidad Catolica Adres Bellow and New York University. In 1965, he obtained his PhD in economics from the latter university. He is the author of various books and articles in the fields of management, economics and marketing.

Antonio Jorge is Professor of Political Economy at Florida International University. He has previously taught at the University of Miami, Merrimack College and Villanova University of Habana, Cuba. From January 1959 to March 1960 he was Chief Economist of the Cuban Ministry of Finance. He has written numerous works on economic development and the Latin American economies. He has authored and edited several volumes on the Latin American economies, including *Integracion y Cooperacion en America Latina*. In addition, he is the author of *Competition, Cooperation, Efficiency, and Social Organization: An Introduction to the Political Economy of Competition and Cooperation.*

Markos J. Mamalakis is Professor of Economics at the University of Wisconsin, Milwaukee. He has previously taught at the University of Gottingen, Yale University and the University of Chile. He has written extensively in the areas of economic development and economic history, focusing, in particular, on Latin American economies. His works include a three-volume edition entitled *Historical Statistics of Chile, as well as The Growth and Structure of the Chilean Economy* and *From Independence to Allende.*

Alberto Martinez-Piedra is the US Ambassador to Guatemala. Prior to his current appointment, he served as Senior Policy Advisor and US Representative to the Economic and Social Council of the OAS, for the Department of State. His academic career was spent primarily at the Catholic University of America, where he held the positions of Director of the Latin American Institute and Chairman and Professor of the Department of Economics. He has written numerous articles on the Latin American economies.

Raul Moncarz is Professor of Economics at Florida International University, and for the last several years he has also been Professor of Banking at the Central American Banking School in Honnduras. He is the author of *Moneda y Banca en America Central* and has written numerous articles on the economics of Central America.

Barbara W. Newell is Regents Professor, Florida State University and Visiting Lecturer at Harvard University. She was, until 1985, Chancellor of the State University of Florida. Prior to her appointment as Chancellor, she was respectively, US Ambassador to UNESCO and President of Wellesley College. She began her academic teaching career in the field of economics at the University of Illinois and Purdue University.

Andres Passicot is the Vice-President of the publicly owned Banco del Estado, the largest bank in Chile. Prior to his current position, he was respectively Minister of Economics and Head of the National Institute of Statistics for the government of Chile. He was formerly Professor of Economics at the University of Chile. In addition, Mr Passicot has served as a consultant to CEPAL, OAS and AID.

Felipe Pazos is Economic Adviser to the President of the Central Bank of Venezuela. He developed the famous Pazos–Simonsen model of inflation used as a framework for recent anti-inflationary policies in Latin America. He was a member of the Committee of Nine ('Wise Men') which gave intellectual leadership to the Alliance for Progress. Earlier he had been the founder and President of the Cuban Central Bank.

Jorge Salazar-Carrillo is Chairman and Professor of Economics at Florida International University and concurrently non-resident Staff Member of the Brookings Institution. Previously he was Acting

General Coordinator of ECIEL and Senior Fellow of the Brookings Institution. In addition, he has served as a consultant to the United Nations, the Inter-American Development Bank and the Organization of American States. He had written extensively in the areas of Latin American economic development and purchasing power parity. He has authored and edited numerous volumes on the Latin American economies, including, most recently, *The Brazilian Economy in the Eighties*. Dr Salazar-Carrillo is the author of the forthcoming work, *Methodologies and Regional and International Comparisons of Purchasing Power Parities and Real Income*.

Larry A. Sjaastad is Professor of Economics at the University of Chicago. Since 1978, he has also held a Chair at the Institut Universitaire de Hautes Etudes Internationales, University of Geneva. He has had considerable experience as an adviser to governments and central banks in Latin America. Most notably, he was engaged as a consultant to the Ministry of Planning and Economic Development in Panama for a period of ten years. He was also a consultant to the governments of Uruguay and Chile and an adviser to the Central Bank of Uruguay. He has written extensively in the area of economic development in Latin America.

Francisco Thoumi is head of the International Economics Section at the Inter-American Development Bank and teaches Latin American economic development at the Catholic University of America. Mr Thoumi has recently contributed chapters and co-edited *State and Society in Contemporary Colombia: Beyond the National Front*. In addition, he has written numerous articles in the areas of economic development and Latin American economies.

Julian Villalba is Associate Professor of Business at the Instituto de Estudios Superiores de Administracion (IESA). His current research interests centre on policy for public enterprises and the role of government as entrepreneur and regulator in the economy. He has published articles in the areas of industrial organization, technology transfer and government economic policy.

Juan A. Yañes is President of Management Associates International. Previously, he held various positions with the Exxon corporation, the most recent of which was Chief Executive Officer for Esso Caribbean and Central America.

Clarence Zuvekas is International Economist, Bureau for Latin America and the Caribbean, at the US Agency for International Development (AID). From 1971 to 1976 he was Associate Professor of Economics and Coordinator of Latin American Studies at Moorhead State University. He is the author of *Economic Development: An Introduction* and co-author of *Income Distribution and Poverty in Rural Ecuador, 1950–1979*. In addition, he has written numerous articles on Latin American development.

Part I
Introduction

1 An Introductory Overview

Antonio Jorge and Jorge Salazar-Carrillo

During the last few years, the countries comprising Latin America and the Caribbean, as a region, have experienced severe economic distress. As a result of the deteriorating economic conditions, which offer bleak prospects for renewed growth in the near future, a re-evaluation of the need for foreign investment to augment the forces of economic growth has taken place. This volume addresses the role that foreign investment can play in the reactivation of the economies of this region, through a mixture of papers that explore this issue in general, on a country-by-country basis, and those that are regional in approach.

It opens with two brief remarks, the former by Barbara Newell, who focuses on the increased significance of the international component to the economic growth of Florida, and the latter by J. A. Yañes, who emphasises the important role that direct foreign investment can play in restoring health to the Latin American economies.

The first paper by Felipe Pazos, 'Foreign Investment Revisited', discusses the course of foreign investment (in particular US) in Latin America since 1950, with the objective of analysing the contribution that an increase in foreign investment could have on the alleviation of the debt crisis in Latin America. He points out that, for the period 1950–83, US foreign investment would have proceeded at the healthy rate of 4.6 per cent per annum had it not been for disinvestment which was caused by the unprofitability of public utility holdings, the expropriations in Cuba and the nationalisation of the copper and petroleum industries in Chile and Venezuela. This would seem to indicate that, although government policies did not substantially discourage new foreign investment in Latin America, apparently foreign investment was, in part, discouraged as economic growth proceeded at a rate of 5.5 per cent per annum, higher than that for foreign investment. None the less, Pazos indicates that it is unlikely that increased amounts of foreign investment would have significantly augmented the rate of growth in Latin America for this time period, as it was very near the maximum average that could have been

3

attained. In conclusion, he argues that the liberalisation of current regulations governing foreign investment would probably not significantly increase foreign investment, and as such would contribute little to the alleviation of the foreign debt burden of Latin America.

Markos Mamalakis, in his contribution 'Foreign Investment and Unilateral Transfers', offers a largely unexplored line of analysis in regard to long-term economic development in Latin America. He argues that unilateral transfers have been received, in the main, by the privileged and semiprivileged rather than the underprivileged poor, causing distortions that are inimical to sustained economic growth. Since 1973, foreign banks have played a major role by providing loans to national customers. This seemed to be an unlimited source for unilateral transfers in Latin American nations, as they could absorb and distribute the funds that banks were willing to lend. However, ultimately they lacked the capacity to repay them. Mamalakis notes that in this era of very limited lending on the part of foreign banks, Latin American nations are being forced to curtail what had become an uncontrolled distribution of unilateral transfers. By reducing unilateral transfers to their original and proper function, that is, to assist the neediest, a major and an important necessary step will be taken in restoring incentives and the optimal use of resources to the Latin American economies.

Richard Bernal, in his paper 'Default as a Negotiating Tactic in Debt Rescheduling Strategies of Developing Countries: A Preliminary Note', focuses on deliberate default, which is a suspension of repayment of the loan, leaving open the possibility of repayment at some time in the future, as a legitimate debt policy option open to debtor nations. The objectives of default are to either force creditors to commence refinancing and/or rescheduling negotiations in a meaningful fashion, or to force an improvement in the terms of refinancing and/or rescheduling. He then discusses the costs and benefits of the policy of deliberate default and in the final section analyses the experience of three developing nations that pursued such a strategy. He reaches two conclusions. First, deliberate default by developing countries has proved successful in accelerating the process of debt negotiation and in obtaining more favourable terms for the rescheduled debt and, secondly, given the appropriate circumstances and effective implementation, deliberate default can be used as an effective tactic to bring about more purposeful negotiations and better terms.

Florencio Ballestero and Francisco Thoumi, in their paper 'The Instability of Intra-Latin American and Caribbean Exports and

Exchange Rates', develop a model based on which the concept of instability can be discussed and estimations of the instability of intra- and extra-regional exports and relevant exchange rates made. They found the instability of exports of the Latin American and Caribbean countries (LAC) to be much higher than that of the exports of the US and other industrialised countries. The instability of intra-LAC exports was found to be a great deal higher than that of LAC exports in general. An analogous result was obtained in regard to real exchange rates. Further, the exchange rate instability of the LAC countries explained a significant proportion of the intra- and extra-regional export instability. They conclude with a policy implication drawn from their results, namely, that if the countries of the region can co-ordinate their real dollar exchange rate policies in a way that would lessen real dollar exchange rate fluctuations, then intra-regional trade would be facilitated.

Mario Blejer, in his paper 'Growth, Investment, and the Specific Role of Fiscal Policies in Very Small Developing Economies', discusses the major economic characteristics of these economies, namely, their small size and high degree of openness. These characteristics result in two important consequences for these nations. First, a very high degree of export dependence leading to extreme vulnerability to international market fluctuations. Secondly, highly ineffective monetary and exchange rate policies as domestic prices are heavily dependent on foreign price developments. He then elaborates on the role and functions of fiscal policy in developing countries in general, and discusses the specific role that fiscal and other macroeconomic policies can play in the smallest of developing nations. He indicates that it is important for very small economies to be particularly concerned with preventing budgetary excesses that generally lead to domestic credit policies inconsistent with long-term monetary and exchange stability. He stresses the need for policies which promote the mobilisation of savings. In the absence of capital markets, he suggests that government has the option of providing a proxy for a capital market, in which credit incentives financed by budgetary surpluses would be a crucial component of fiscal policy. In conclusion, Blejer indicates that through the use of this instrument, resources can be mobilised for investments deemed to have high social significance.

In his contribution, 'The Economic Crisis in Central America', Clarence Zuvekas details the nature and causes of the severe economic contraction in each of the five Central American nations. He indicates that it will be at least the end of the decade before previous levels of Gross Domestic Product (GDP) per capita can be restored in the region. This, in fact, may be a somewhat optimistic appraisal as the prospects for economic recovery in Latin America are not, at present, particularly bright. New sources of foreign exchange need to be made available to the region in order that it may help meet its debt service obligations and allow for the increased flow of imported inputs necessary for economic recovery. He points to increased assistance from bilateral and multilateral organisations and the export of non-traditional products to markets outside the region, as possible sources of foreign exchange. To some extent the former is occurring through increased US assistance to the region, and the latter is facilitated by the expansion of the number of goods that can enter the US duty free, as a result of the Caribbean Basin Initiative. However, in order for the region to benefit from this, reforms within the structure of the Central American Common Market (CACM) are needed that would encourage more efficient production, leading to a more competitive pricing structure. However, the success of this export-led strategy, even if these reforms are undertaken, depends on, at least, moderately rapid growth in the industrialised countries.

Raul Moncarz, in his paper 'Financial and Capital Flows in Central America in the 1980s', focuses attention on the Central American economies during the last five years. These countries have been characterized by a deepening crisis of the external sector. The crisis has led to a significant downturn in economic activity to the point, for instance, where the 1983 GDP per capita income in Nicaragua and El Salvador was at the level achieved 20 years ago, thus undoing 15 years of steady and rapid growth. He reviews the recent developments in the region, particularly with regard to the external sector and domestic savings. Professor Moncarz concludes by noting several measures which might help remedy the current crises:

1. Obtaining long-term purchase agreements at fixed prices for primary commodities.
2. The procurement of long-term loans at low interest rates.
3. Increased US commitment to the region, particularly in terms of technical financial flows to at least maintain the viability of these countries.
4. Following domestic policies which would, secondarily, discourage foreign intervention.
5. The adoption of policies that maintain positive real interest rates and realistic exchange rates.

6. The higher rate of utilisation of existing production capacity.

In his paper, 'The Economy of Guatemala: Recent Developments', Alberto Martinez-Piedra chronicles the decline of the Guatemalan economy during recent years, one which, until the late 1970s, had been one of the most stable of the less-developed countries. This severe contraction can be attributed to the world economic recession, the political conditions prevailing in the region, and serious internal political violence. He then provides detailed discussions of the developments in sectorial production; aggregate expenditures; employment, wages and prices; the public sector; and the external sector. He indicates that a reversal of this negative economic growth may be in the offing as the country returns to a constitutional government in January 1986. To achieve this end, however, the new government will have to convince the people of the vital need to establish and carry out fiscal and monetary reforms, without which the country cannot regain economic health. Estimates of the 1986 Guatemalan GNP indicate that the new government has achieved some limited success in reversing the trend of negative economic growth.

Compton Bourne, in his contribution 'Financial Deepening, Domestic Resource Mobilisation and Economic Growth: Jamica 1955–82', focuses on the role of the financial sector in domestic resource mobilisation and economic growth, analysing, in particular, the case of Jamaica. He begins with a description of the major trends in economic growth and aggregate savings and investment behaviour for the period under study. Professor Bourne then examines the process of financial deepening and shallowing, as well as the relationship between financial deepening and aggregate domestic savings and investment rates. He presents econometric results of his analysis of these issues. Finally, he draws the following policy implication from his conclusions – although a regime of positive real interest rates is likely to strengthen the financial sector, it is necessary to direct the credit policies of financial intermediaries in order that financial growth be accompanied by growth of the nation's capital stock.

Andres Dauhajre, in his paper 'Some Warnings Concerning Possible Financial Reform in the Dominican Republic', argues that the often made recommendation by the International Monetary Fund (IMF) to developing countries with severe balance of payments disequilibria, of increasing the rate of interest on time deposits may, in fact, have very negative effects on economic activity. He demonstrates that for a country, such as the Dominican Republic, where the informal market interest rates is tied to the international interest rate plus expectations of depreciation of the parallel market exchange rate, financial liberalisation, in the form of an increased rate of interest on time deposits, may lead to higher rates of inflation. He does so through the use of a dual exchange market model with incomplete segmentation that allows for the existence of a fragmented financial system. He concludes that, at the present, a programme of financial reform in the Dominican Republic would have negative impacts on the economy, and should not be considered until the authorities have first achieved equilibrium in public finances and an orderly exchange rate system.

In their paper, 'A Venezuelan Paradox: The Prospects for Attracting (or Repatriating) Foreign Investment', Henry Gomez-Samper and Julian Villalba discuss the prospects of restoring Venezuelan economic growth, based on the repatriation of foreign-based savings and the attraction of new foreign investment. They are not optimistic in regard to the former for a variety of reasons, of which the threat that exchange controls may be imposed is the predominant factor making the repatriation of Venezuelan savings abroad unlikely. However, they suggest that, in light of new legislation planned to liberalise the regulations governing foreign investment, the high level of consumer purchasing power, and political and economic stability, Venezuela is now emerging as an attractive site for renewed foreign investment. Further, they indicate that once this foreign investment is in place, it could act as a catalyst to the economic recovery of Venezuela.

In his 'Comments on the Mexican Economy in 1984', Manuel Gollas reviews the major developments during the past year, highlighted by the renegotiation of the country's external debt in August 1984. Although this agreement gave Mexico some immediate economic leeway, the burden of the debt has not been lightened, but merely transferred to the medium-term future. The year 1984 marks the reversal of a two-year decline in GNP. However, the outlook for continued recovery is marred by stagnant consumer demand, a high rate of unemployment, an unstable government deficit and the possible return of higher interest rates due to efforts to stimulate the economy. In fact, expansion slowed to 2.7 per cent in 1985, and estimates for 1986 indicate a contraction of about 4 per cent.

Adalberto Garcia Rocha, in his contribution 'Inequality and Growth in Mexico', draws attention to the failure of economic policy in Latin America to incorporate the poor into the benefits of economic growth. In recent years this problem has been exacerbated in many countries by negative rates of growth. He indicates that, while taxation is generally considered the most important policy instrument to reduce inequality, the impacts of both taxation and government spending on income redistribution need to be simultaneously evaluated. In fact, government spending in Mexico is most probably regressive in nature. In regard to public policy, he strongly suggests that the goal of reducing inequality should not be added to all policy investments, but rather that specific instruments need to be designed to achieve this important societal objective.

Larry Sjaastad, in his paper 'Latin America and the World Economy', attributes the Latin American recession, in large measure, to the international effects that have accompanied the recovery of the US dollar since 1980. The appreciation of the dollar depressed dollar prices of internationally traded commodities, then transmitting deflationary pressures, particularly to those nations that heavily relied on primary commodity trade. It also resulted in extremely high real rates of interest on foreign debt denominated in dollars, which was, in turn, transmitted to domestic currency assets. Adverse consequences were also felt in terms of trade for many Latin American countries. Further, he points out that the net debt of $125 billion for the four largest debtor countries in the region is not an onerous burden, since the GDP of these nations (Brazil, Mexico, Argentina and Venezuela) exceeds $500 billion. However, he points out that the debt is owed by the public sectors, whereas the foreign savings are owned by private individuals.

Helson Braga, in his contribution 'The Role of Foreign Direct Investment in Economic Growth: The Brazilian Case', provides a detailed discussion of this role in the Brazilian economy during the post-Second World War era, with particular emphasis on the post-1974 period. He provides an in-depth analysis of the treatment of foreign direct investment. He discusses the registration of foreign direct investment, the Profit Remittance Law and the foreign transfer of technology. Professor Braga then evaluates the Brazilian regulatory scheme, focusing on distortions that need to be removed. First, legislation that encourages foreign investors to register their investment as debt, instead of as equity. Secondly, the Profit Remittance Law does not allow for an indexation to compensate for the devaluation of the currency in which the capital registration was made. Thirdly, the setting of a simple ceiling for the percentage of remittance on the invested capital does not allow for variations in gross earnings of different activities. Finally, he notes that efforts to promote better co-ordination between the different governmental agencies involved, and more stable rules of the game, would be highly desirable. In conclusion, he notes that, despite the important role foreign investment can play in fostering growth in the Brazilian economy, and the positive impact this would have on the debt problem, he raises some doubts remain about the effectiveness of a more liberal treatment of foreign investment.

In his paper, 'Foreign Investment and Development: The Experience of Chile 1974–84', Andrcs Passicot discusses the impact of foreign investment on the Chilean economy in an era marked by the liberal treatment of foreign investment. He demonstrates that, due to the policy changes affecting foreign investment (which he discusses in detail), Chile moved from a discretionary to a standard treatment of investment, which today treats foreign and domestic investors alike. Although this resulted in a significant increase in the value of foreign investment, it has not had a decisive impact on capitalisation in Chile, representing only 6.9 per cent of total investment for the period 1974–83. He points out that only 27.8 per cent of authorized foreign investment effectively entered the Chilean economy for this period. In conclusion, he suggests the need for investment banks as an adjunct to the traditional banking structure; the need for development policies to move further away from protectionist practices; and the need to conduct a steady economic policy, instead of one in which the rules of the game are forever changing.

2 Some Comments on International Activities and the Economic Development of Florida

Barbara W. Newell

Florida government has spent much time looking at questions of its own economic development and investment. Florida was the poorest of the 48 US states at the turn of the century. It was viewed as a sand spit, with sun, mosquitoes and no natural resources. Outside investment in Florida's railroads brought expansion and an economy based on tourism, sophisticated farming, and the retired. But the state has found this base volatile, and in need of diversification. However, Florida has a fragile environment which is easily ruined by inappropriate development. As a result there has been a conscious decision to develop service industries, and those in the knowledge-based and high technology fields.

To attract these industries the state found it needed to enhance the educational base of both the elementary and secondary schools, as well as the universities, in order to obtain the kind of skilled work force needed for these industries. Additionally, the state looked to the universities for research and to develop a true partnership with industry. Florida has placed a special emphasis on the international component of development. This is reflected in:

1. State government and business are looking abroad to joint partnerships, with the expectation of production abroad and Florida becoming the point of entry for the products;
2. every major Florida city has established free trade zones; and
3. the Florida governor has augmented President Reagan's Caribbean initiative by initiating his own scholarships and trade missions.

Florida's push for economic development fascinates me, not only as a partner in the state enterprise, as Chancellor, but as an economist. I began my own study of economic development in the 1950s when the profession had ideological answers. For example, one must socialise production, or establish heavy industry, or redistribute land and one would find a panacea for development. Today economists are more modest. We all recognise the complexity and interdependency of economic development, public health, transportation, capital formation, and so on. Increasingly, economists look towards pragmatic solutions to the problems of development, with a much keener awareness of cultural and institutional differences.

3 Some Comments on Direct Foreign Investment in Latin America

J. A. Yañes

It is important to focus attention on direct foreign investment in Latin America, because this topic has long been overshadowed by numerous financial schemes when discussing solutions to the present debt crisis in Latin America. This significance has been echoed by, among others, President Reagan in a recent meeting with the International Monetary Fund (IMF), when he said that countries will have to rely less on external debt, and more on direct private investment, both foreign and domestic.

Additionally, World Bank President Clausen indicated in a September, 1985 address that reviving private and public capital flows is essential to the restoration of the development momentum and long-term prospects of the developing economies. Also, Argentine President Alfonsin, in a forum for US and Argentine businessmen in November, 1985, urged US investors to have confidence in the democratic process and increase investment in that country.

Given this trend in recognising the important role direct foreign investment can play, it is ironic to see that there is little concrete evidence of firm steps being taken toward policies required to increase foreign investment. This impression has been corroborated by the recently released survey of the Council of the Americas. It showed that US investments in Latin America are currently well below their levels of four years ago, and that most of the US firms surveyed are not contemplating an expansion of their Latin American operations in the future.

What is additionally distressing is that, with the poor growth trend projected for the region, the question for some US companies is not whether to invest in the future, but rather whether to reduce stake or withdraw. The investment policies of the host government that discouraged foreign investment were tolerable in the past because the growth climate was favourable, but they are not so now.

Easing credit terms alone will not alleviate the debt burden, nor will raising the threat of social chaos improve perception of the business climate. What everyone must recognise is that direct foreign investment can have a substantial positive impact on these countries, particularly in the current environment; and that work must be done towards creating conditions attractive to foreign investment.

For examples of positive host government policies and their effects, we only need to look at South Korea, Taiwan, Singapore or other developing countries in South-East Asia. These countries suffered from the same worldwide hardships, such as the oil price shocks and economic recession. However, their development models were based on open economies, and encouraged the inflow of foreign capital. In these countries, direct foreign investment has produced a high level of funds and jobs, which are helping to meet their financing and development needs.

Some areas that need to be explored include – reasons governments do not welcome direct foreign investment, such as distrust and loss of control; responses to these concerns; and conditions needed to attract foreign investment, such as less government intervention and changes in foreign exchange and remittance regulations.

Latin Amercia, in the world of today, needs to move in this direction and adopt policy measures designed to attract direct foreign investment. Hopefully, the result of this would be to ease the burden of the debt crisis.

Part II
General

4 Foreign Investment Revisited

Felipe Pazos

In 1957 I wrote a paper on foreign investment for a meeting of the International Economic Association,[1] and in 1965 another one, also for the IEA;[2] but since then my attention has been devoted to other problems, and it is only in recent weeks, owing to the invitation to this conference, that I have looked at the subject again. In spite of my lesser interest in the subject, only partially recovered, I have obviously enjoyed revisiting a place in which I had not been in 20 years, since I was curious to see how much it had changed, which has been somewhat more than I expected.

The objective of the 1957 and 1965 papers was to evaluate the advantages and disadvantages, or benefits and costs if you prefer, of private direct foreign investment on one side, and international public loans on the other, as channels to transfer additional resources to developing countries. The objective of the present paper is closely related to that of the former ones, since it is to examine the contribution that an increase in direct foreign investment could make to alleviate the current debt crisis in Latin America. This paper makes therefore liberal use of the findings and conclusions of the old ones, but in the light of the evolution of private capital movements since then. For this purpose, the paper examines the net value of US investment abroad in 1950 and 1982, by groups of countries and by industries, and compares the Latin American figures with those in other developing countries and with those in fully industrialised nations.

FINDINGS AND CONCLUSIONS OF THE PREVIOUS PAPERS

The 1957 and 1965 papers analysed the nature, functions and characteristics of the different types of international capital flows, and reached some conclusions that may be summarised as follows:

1. In the international sphere, as well as the national, equity capital (direct investment) and loan capital play different, though closely supplementary, roles. Equity capital finances the basic share of the costs of new plant and equipment of enterprises (private or public) that produce for the market, whereas loans finance: (i) the remainder of such costs and (ii) all or part of the costs of public overhead capital (roads, public schools, public hospitals, hydroelectric dams, public office buildings, and so on).

2. Both equity and loan capital may originate in the private or in the public sector, and may be invested in either one. Private equity capital originates in private savings and finances private enterprises; private loan capital originates in private savings and may finance private investment or may be lent to the Government to cover public needs; and public loans originate in public savings but may be used by the Government, by public organisations or by private enterprises. Both private and public loans may be channelled through private or public intermediaries.

3. In countries where all marketable goods and services are produced by private enterprises, private equity capital finances about 40 per cent of total investment, and loans the other 60 per cent. When public utilities are government owned, the ratios change to 30 per cent equity capital and 70 per cent loans. In order to keep a balanced allocation between foreign capital inflows and domestic savings, the share of direct investment in foreign inflows should not exceed the proportion of total equity capital in total investment. Otherwise, the share of foreign capital in the ownership of the country's means of production would increase.

4. Direct investment flows to countries where it can promote the expansion of exports or the production of import substitutes: it flows to countries that are rich in natural resources or have large and expanding markets.

5. Direct investment is an entrepreneurial activity more than a financial transaction. It is generally carried out by large corporations that have all the facilities (organisation, experience, technical and managerial skills, patents, trade-marks, marketing channels, and so forth) to establish new production units, and to expand the existing ones, with a very high probability of success. Direct investment brings to a country what we might call 'prefabricated' industries, ready for use and guaranteed to operate satisfactorily.

6. The main weakness of direct investment as a development agent is

a consequence of the complete character of its contribution. As it brings enterprise, management and technology to the country, it may inhibit the emergence and formation of local personnel and local enterprises to perform these essential functions.[3] On the other hand, it strengthens existing local enterprises and encourages the creation of new ones through its expanding effects on income, through its training of local personnel, through its purchases in the country (Hirschman's backward linkage effects) and through its production of more abundant supplies of inputs (forward linkage effects). In countries that are experiencing rapid development, foreign investment probably induces the creation of more local enterprises than it potentially displaces; and it certainly trains and employs many more administrators and technicians than it brings from abroad. But the actual and potential effects of foreign direct investment on local entrepreneurs, managers and technicians should be constantly borne in mind, not only for economic reasons, which are very important in themselves, but also on account of sociological and political considerations.

UNITED STATES DIRECT INVESTMENT ABROAD 1950–82

Having completed the above summary of the functions and characteristics of direct investments and loans, we may examine the evolution of the former in the last three decades in Latin America, in other developing countries and in industrial nations. However, we do not have good statistics on direct investment originating in countries other than the United States. Therefore we will have to limit ourselves to work only with US direct investment figures on which we have a great wealth of detailed, comparable and reliable data, representing a large percentage of the total, possibly as much as 70 per cent of all direct investment.

International flows of equity capital are not normally measured at constant prices, owing to the difficulty of finding appropriate price indices with which to deflate the nominal figures. The difficulty is even greater when we measure the flows by the differences in book values at different dates, because existing assets are usually kept at their original values and are not adjusted for current price movements. But in order to know the rate at which direct investment really flows, and to compare the real amounts going to different countries or regions, we need figures at constant prices, which need not be very precise if we are interested in approximate rates of change, and not in exact absolute figures. We have chosen as a deflator the price of equipment goods in the US wholesale price index, which yields figures that look reasonable. In any case, all groups of countries have been adjusted by the same deflator and, thus, the comparison between them can be relied upon.

Table 4.1 registers the value of US direct investment abroad in 1950 and 1982, by groups of countries and by industries, deflated by the US index of equipment prices. Table 4.2 shows the composition of investment as a percentage of the total for each year. As can be readily seen in Table 4.1, total US direct investment in Latin America increased at an annual rate of 1.6 per cent, whereas in other developing countries it rose at 4.1 per cent per annum, and in developed nations at 6.2 per cent. The rapid growth of US investment in Europe after the Second World War is a well-known fact of which I was fully aware before compiling the table, but the slow growth of direct investment in Latin America has been a great surprise to me. The increase has been much lower than in industrial nations, and also considerably lower than in other developing countries. This makes it necessary to ask whether Latin American countries have discouraged foreign investment: whether the fear to rely excessively on foreign investment has induced the adoption of too strict a set of regulations governing foreign investment. This, however, does not seem to be the explanation, or at least the main explanation, since there are other factors that account for the slow growth. The principal causes of this slowness seem to be the following:

1. In 1950 there were large amounts of US capital invested in public utilities in Latin America, one-third of which were confiscated by Castro in 1960, and the other two-thirds were willingly sold to governments during the period, because they had become unprofitable owing to inflation. US investment in public utilities in Latin America fell from $927 million in 1950 to a small amount, not separately registered, in 1982. Outside Latin America, the United States had only small amounts invested in public utilities and, therefore, there was no drastic reduction in this type of investment in other regions.
2. In 1950, there were large amounts of capital invested in agricul-

Table 4.1   US direct investment in 1950 and 1982 (in millions of 1950 dollars)

	1950	1982	1982/ 1950	Annual rate of increase (%)
Latin America				
Mining and smelting	628	422	0.67	—
Petroleum	1 233	1 133	0.92	—
Manufacturing	780	3 512	4.50	4.8
Trade	242	680	2.81	3.3
Finance	71	1 159	16.32	9.1
Miscellaneous*	1 491	343	0.23	—
Total	4 445	7 249	1.63	1.6
Other Developing Countries				
Mining and smelting	145	235	1.62	1.6
Petroleum	1 207	3 483	2.89	3.4
Manufacturing	92	966	10.50	7.7
Trade	48	606	12.63	8.2
Finance	4	137	34.25	11.7
Miscellaneous*	262	874	3.34	3.8
Total	1 758	6 301	3.58	4.1
Developed Countries				
Mining and smelting	360	872	2.42	2.8
Petroleum	950	8 336	8.77	7.0
Manufacturing	2 959	16 611	5.61	5.5
Trade	472	5 054	10.71	7.7
Finance	350	5 472	15.63	9.0
Miscellaneous*	496	1 579	3.18	3.7
Total	5 587	37 924	6.79	6.2

*Mainly agriculture and public utilities.

Sources: 'US Business Investment in Foreign Countries', Table 3, US Department of Commerce, 1960; 'US Direct Investment Abroad, 1982', Table 12, *Survey of Current Business*, August 1983.

ture in Latin America, especially in sugar and banana plantations. Those in Cuba, representing one-half of the total, were confiscated in 1960, and the other half diminished rapidly owing to the decision of US corporations to sell the land to their former tenants and workers and continue to operate mainly as buyers and exporters. US investment in agriculture in Latin America thus fell from $520 million in 1952 to a small amount in 1982, again not separately registered. Outside Latin America, US

Table 4.2   US direct investment in 1950 and 1982
(in per cent)

	1950	1982
Latin America		
Mining and smelting	14	6
Petroleum	28	16
Manufacturing	17	48
Trade	5	9
Finance	2	16
Miscellaneous*	34	5
Total	100	100
Other Developing Countries		
Mining and smelting	8	4
Petroleum	69	55
Manufacturing	5	15
Trade	3	10
Finance	—	2
Miscellaneous*	15	14
Total	100	100
Developed Countries		
Mining and smelting	6	2
Petroleum	17	22
Manufacturing	53	44
Trade	8	13
Finance	6	14
Miscellaneous*	10	5
Total	100	100

*Mainly agriculture and public utilities.

Sources: 'US Business Investment in Foreign
Countries', Table 3, US Department of Commerce,
1960; 'US Direct Investment Abroad, 1982', Table 12,
Survey of Current Business, August 1983.

investments in agriculture were very small and thus could not
experience large reductions.
3. In 1950, US investment in Cuba amounted to $642 million and in
1982 to zero. Although a large part of this amount has already
been accounted for in the previous paragraphs, $108 million were
in fields other than public utilities and agriculture.
4. In 1950 the US had $351 million invested in copper in Chile, that
was nationalised in full agreement with the owners in 1965, and
$857 million in petroleum in Venezuela, that was sold to the

Government in 1976, also with full satisfaction to the owners.
These two voluntary transfers added up to $1,208 million.

Of the four types of foreign disinvestment described, those originating in the loss of earning power of public utilities and those provoked
by expropriations cannot be attributed to government policies (in
countries other than Cuba); and those consisting in sales of land to
local farmers were not induced by government pressure. Only the
nationalisation of copper and petroleum, with full compensation to
the owners, was caused by deliberate government policies. These were
nationalistic actions, but not anti-foreign, as evidenced by the fact
that the new government enterprises, both in Chile and Venezuela,
have received ample technical assistance from the large foreign
corporations that formerly owned and operated these businesses.
Strictly speaking, none of these disinvestments, that to a large extent
explain the slow net growth of US investment in Latin America, can
be imputed to anti-foreign policy except, of course the expropriations
in Cuba. If the disinvestments had not taken place, US investment in
Latin America would have increased during the period at a 4.6 per
cent rate, or somewhat faster than in other developing countries.
Based on these facts, it might be considered that government policies
have not discouraged foreign investment in Latin America; but a
more detailed analysis indicates that there has been some discouragement of foreign investment, although not necessarily harmful from a
sociological and political point of view.
Given the higher degree of economic and institutional development
in Latin America than in other agrarian and semi-industrial countries,
and its closer political and cultural ties with the United States, this
nation's investment in Latin America should have been much higher
than in other developing countries. Besides, during this period economic growth in Latin America averaged 5.5 per cent per year, or
more. Assuming a constant capital-output ratio, total investment
would have increased at that rate, which is significantly higher than
the rate of growth of foreign investment (after disinvestments are
deducted).
Restraints have mainly taken the form of limitations on the
percentage of foreign ownership of enterprises, and of prohibitions to
enter certain fields, for instance mining, banking, steel, petrochemicals, and so forth, which are reserved for the Government or for
private domestic capital. Before the nationalisation of mining and
petroleum, discouragement resulted mainly from the heavy taxation

of foreign enterprises in these fields, not because they were foreign but because they were a rich source of fiscal revenues.

Another source discouraging foreign investment, to which most people attribute more importance than those previously mentioned, is the legislation regulating foreign investment, as that agreed to by member countries in Decision 24 of the Andean Pact. However, I firmly believe that the effect of these regulations has been greatly exaggerated. A study of the effects of Decision 24 on the flow of investment to the countries that are members of the Andean Pact, shows that these flows did not diminish after the regulations were enacted.[4]

ECONOMIC AND POLITICAL EFFECTS OF THE MODERATE RESTRAINT OF FOREIGN INVESTMENT

Between 1950 and 1982 Latin American countries grew economically at a very fast sustained pace that may be estimated at 5.5 per cent per year, or more. This figure is very near the maximum average rate that could have been attained by a large group of countries in a 32-year period. It is thus hard to imagine that a larger inflow of private equity capital would have raised this rate of growth by any significant amount.

There are, however, some instances where more foreign investment would have brought about an increase of production and income. In the 1950s and 1960s, lower taxes, and a commitment to the transnationals to renew their concessions, might have induced higher copper and petroleum investments in Chile and Venezuela, and a higher level of production and exports. These pro-foreign investment policies might have slowed down the development of copper in Africa and of petroleum in the Middle East, but geological considerations would have induced these developments even in the absence of policies discouraging foreign investment in Latin America.

It should also be noted that Bethlehem Steel would have erected and operated the Guyana steel plant more efficiently than the Government, but it is doubtful whether Bethlehem Steel would have invested in such a large steel operation in Venezuela. But outside these instances, and a few others of this type, I do not think that a greater flow of direct foreign investment would have promoted faster or sounder development in Latin America.

It might be contended that more direct investment would have reduced foreign borrowing and consequently the growth of Latin America's debt; and also that it would have increased exports and brought about a more outward-oriented development pattern. But both contentions are weak: given the great eagerness of banks to lend (owing to the enormous increase in their available resources), governments would have borrowed as much as they did even if more equity capital had entered the country; and, in fact, more capital did not enter because governments could borrow abroad to finance new government industries or to relend the proceeds to local private entrepreneurs. The second contention is more valid, but only to a certain extent: more direct investment would have brought about more primary exports and more re-exports of articles brought to the country for further processing, but not more sales abroad of manufactures entirely produced in the country. The bulk of 'real exports of manufactures' from Latin America is generally produced by domestically-owned enterprises.

Most sociological and political effects of the moderate restraining policy applied to foreign investment are not quantifiable and, hence, their evaluation has to be based on purely subjective grounds. There are socioeconomic facts that can be quantified, such as the proportion of a country's productive facilities owned by foreigners, and the importance of foreign-owned facilities in the country's economy; but the psychological, sociological and political repercussions of these facts are not quantifiable, and their evaluations depend on the sentiments and beliefs of the person that analyses them. Therefore, I can only express my personal opinion that in countries where the key industry and a large number of other enterprises are owned and managed by foreigners, the nationals develop feelings of inferiority and of silent hostility towards foreigners that are not politically or sociologically healthy. The population develops feelings that are akin to those of political dependence, though much less intense. An economic system cannot be considered as politically sound when foreigners are the employers and nationals the employees. A capitalist system owned by foreign corporations can be labelled as capitalism without capitalists, and cannot be considered as a sound and stable regime.

If I am not utterly wrong, the consensual nationalisation of the public utilities, copper and petroleum, that have taken place in Latin America in recent decades, together with the faster growth of domestic investment relative to foreign investment, are highly desirable developments that have enhanced the self-esteem of the people of

Latin American countries and substantially heightened their feelings of friendship with the United States.

POSSIBLE CONTRIBUTIONS OF FOREIGN INVESTMENT TO THE ALLEVIATION OF THE CURRENT CRISIS

As previously mentioned, the purpose of this paper is to inquire into the contribution that direct foreign investment could make to alleviate the grave economic and financial crisis currently faced by Latin American countries; and, we may now add, to discuss the policy that countries should follow towards foreign equity capital: whether governments should maintain the policy of moderate restraint that has just been described, or should liberalise current regulations and apply a policy strongly encouraging foreign investment. The answer to this question depends to a large extent, though not entirely, on whether less regulation and more incentives would considerably increase the flow of private capital.

Before discussing the effects of a policy change, we must remember that both in the national and international spheres private investment is primarily motivated by the prospects of selling the goods that will be produced with the new plant and equipment, that is, by the actual and prospective levels of aggregate demand. Private investment is not an independent variable that can be used as a policy instrument to reduce the intensity of cyclical fluctuations, but is a dependent variable that follows the cycle very closely. As can be seen in Table 4.3, private investment flows to Latin America have drastically fallen in recent years.

Table 4.3   Private investment flows in four countries, 1981–83 (in millions of dollars at current prices)

	1981	1982	1983
Argentina	944	257	183
Brazil	2 313	2 534	1 373
Mexico	2 537	1 399	496
Venezuela	184	253	− 62

Source: International Financial Statistics, November 1984.

Until the current regional depression reverts into a new expansion, foreign corporations will not have to increase investment in Latin American countries in order to supply additional demand for the goods and services they produce because, until then, additional demand will not develop. The most important policy that would lend to increased private foreign investment in Latin America in the immediate future would be to apply effective measures to solve the current financial and economic crisis.

It could be argued that, as present restrictions are liberalised, foreign capital might invest in the purchase of domestic shares of the enterprises which they partially own, or of domestic enterprises operating in fields in which they cannot now enter, or in the creation of new industries in these fields. However, it is highly doubtful that foreign corporations would invest on the basis of policies that could change in the future, when the political pendulum could swing again in the direction of more nationalistic attitudes. It is thus highly improbable that direct foreign investment would increase before aggregate demand increases again and economic growth is resumed. The liberalisation of current regulations would probably not stimulate an increase in foreign private investment in any significant amount, and much less in the amounts needed to make a dent in the current crisis.

The above conclusions do not mean that present Latin American policies on foreign investment are perfect and cannot be improved. They could and should be improved in the sense of eliminating restrictions on foreign capital entering fields that could be covered much better by them than by domestic enterprises, and by simplifying or eliminating unnecessary bureaucratic regulations. The above conclusions only mean that such policy improvements could not make a significant contribution to overcome the current crisis.

Notes

1. 'Private versus Public Foreign Investment in Underdeveloped Areas', in Howard S. Ellis and Henry C. Wallach (eds) *Economic Development for Latin America* (London: MacMillan, 1961).
2. 'The Role of International Movements of Private Capital in Promoting Development', in J. H. Adler (ed.) *Capital Movements and Economic Development* (New York: St Martin's Press, 1967).
3. For a fuller discussion see Albert O. Hirschman, 'How to Divest in Latin America, and Why', Essays in International Finance No. 76, Princeton

University, 1969; and Gene M. Grossman, 'International Trade, Foreign Investment, and the Formation of the Entrepreneurial Class', *American Economic Review*, Vol. 74, No. 4, 1984.

4. C. Michael Aho and Jose Núñez del Arco, 'United States Investment in Latin America, 1966–1976: an Empirical Analysis of the Impact of the Andean Code (Decision 24)', mimeograph.

5 Foreign Investment and Unilateral Transfers

Markos Mamalakis

INTRODUCTION

The relationship between foreign investment and unilateral transfers is a multifaceted one. It is necessary to analyse this relationship because it is one of the most important and least examined relationships determining long-term economic development in Latin America.[1] Unilateral resource transfers are a pernicious disease afflicting major segments of the society, economy and political system of the majority of Latin American countries. The pervasive presence of unilateral transfers in developing countries is a critical factor that separates them from the present day developed countries during their corresponding early stages of growth. While the discussion of capital and interest rates formed the foundation of classical economic thinking, it is the origin, size, and distribution of unilateral transfers that implicitly form *the*, or at least *a*, major foundation of modern development thinking.

HOW UNILATERAL TRANSFERS HAVE LED TO THE FOREIGN DEBT PROBLEM

International distribution of unilateral transfers

Unilateral transfers first arise as an integral part of a North–South battle over real or perceived resource surpluses. According to the centre-periphery, metropolis-colony, dependency and Marxist theories, there is a resource surplus which belongs to developing countries, but is appropriated by developed countries. Part of the resource surplus of the South, it is alleged, becomes a unilateral transfer to the North. The resource surplus of the South is generated, in part, by private foreign investment which also acts as the mechanism for transferring this surplus to the North. Within this analytical and ideological framework, foreign investment is not only a source of income and wealth in developing countries, but also the tool used by developed countries to obtain unilateral transfers from the developing ones.

National distribution of unilateral transfers

Once the distribution of the resource surplus of the South between itself and the North is determined, that is, once the international distribution problem of resource transfers has been solved, the national or domestic distribution issue arises. Having determined how large the retained national resource surplus will be, a battle arises between the state and the private sector with each trying to maximise its share. This second step determines how much of the national resource surplus will become a unilateral transfer to the state, that is, will be retained by its military and civilian segments, and how much will be shared by the private sector.

The role of foreign investment in this second stage of the resource distribution process can, once again, be pivotal. To the extent that the resource surplus arises in foreign-owned sectors, and because of foreign ownership, the conversion of income generated by foreign capital into unilateral transfers to the state or the private sector through taxation or other means can kill the proverbial goose that lays the golden egg, namely foreign investment. Furthermore, to the extent that government converts the income generated by foreign investment into unilateral transfers to national privately-owned enterprises, a serious conflict may arise between the foreign- and nationally-owned segments of the private sector. Such a conflict may not only weaken the privately-owned segment of the economy as a whole, but also reduce over-all economic growth.

Consumption, investment and unilateral transfers

Examined from a third angle, the retained national resource surplus can be appropriated either by government or households for consumption or by firms for investment. The hypothesis advanced here is that C, consumption, G, government expenditure, and/or I, investment, in developing countries can exceed the levels determined by the natural productivity of national labour, land and capital by an amount equal to the portion of the resource surplus generated by foreign investment which they receive in the form of unilateral transfers.

Parallel to the money and capital markets and, sometimes, even as an 'integral' part of them, there operates under such circumstances a market of unilateral transfers. Households, firms and government may participate on the demand and/or supply side of the unilateral transfer market. Unilateral transfer markets exist whenever economic agents spend more than what they earn and do not rely on capital markets to bridge their expenditure/income gap. In some, but by no means all, instances the permanent expenditure of households, firms and government exceeds their permanent income by an amount equal to the net resource surplus generated by, and contributed to, them in the form of unilateral transfers by foreign investment.

Who receives unilateral transfers: the poor? the rich?

Unilateral resource transfers from the government to the poor are hardly new. Centuries ago the English Poor Laws attempted to both define and control them. What is new in many developing countries of Latin America is that there exist at least three labour groups, namely, the underprivileged, the semiprivileged and the privileged, and that the primary competition for unilateral transfers is not among the underprivileged poor but between (and within) the privileged and semiprivileged, on the one hand, and the underprivileged poor on the other side.[2]

During the industrial revolution in England, Germany and the United States, the pole of attraction was industrial employment, and work and savings were the main sources of income and wealth. Nations competed in terms of production and strategic industrial growth. In contrast, in many less developed countries the manna that feeds the hope and shapes migratory movements has, as a major ingredient, the unilateral transfers of governmental welfare, tax holiday, transport, food, child, utility and other subsidy programmes.

In addition, there are sectoral as well as regional dimensions to this issue. Unilateral resource transfers accrue to selective segments of urban industry and services where most members of the privileged and semiprivileged classes are employed, and where they are least needed.

The aforementioned discussion explains why the strongest and most irrational antagonism against foreign investment frequently comes from the privileged classes, especially those of the public sector. With welfare of these groups affected by the resources generated by foreign investment, they frequently follow the short-sighted policy of trying to extract maximum resources (unilateral transfers) in the short-run through nationalisation, taxation and so forth. Flight of foreign capital, reduced income and resource surplus are likely consequences of such policies.

The origin of unilateral resource transfers

The origin of unilateral resource transfers has already been discussed *in passim* in the earlier sections. A further, in-depth, analysis of the many interrelated sources is needed.

A primary source of such transfers in Latin America, Africa and Asia has been the surplus (short-period rents) generated by agricultural and mineral export sectors, often with the help of direct foreign investment. A second source of unilateral transfers is the agricultural food surplus. Since agriculture and this surplus have only limited links to foreign investment I will deal with it only briefly.

If and when export generated resource surpluses stabilise, fall or evaporate, as in the aftermath of Peru's guano and Chile's nitrate boom, those previously receiving unilateral resource transfers experience a reduction in welfare due to a fall in their transfer-funded expenditure level. Accustomed to the status of preferred recipients of unilateral transfers, they seek out new donors. Agriculture and public utilities provide ideal targets. Unilateral transfers are obtained through the time-honoured strategy of seeking maximum salary, wage and fringe benefit increases while keeping prices of agricultural goods and public services low or fixed for 'social' reasons.

Whether for Latin America, other developing economies, or industrialised countries, the term 'social' has to be defined in terms of unilateral transfers. In practice, what is 'social' and socially desirable to the group receiving a unilateral transfer is antisocial and undesirable to the donor group generating it. And, while during export booms or when foreign investors generate transitory bonanzas of resource surpluses there may be a resource surplus pie large enough to feed all the 'hungry', be they rich, middle class or poor, during periods of normal growth or contraction, giving to one group unilateral transfers generally requires confiscating part of another group's legitimate income. This brings us to the modern and most recent case of foreign investment in Latin America, Africa and Asia.

Impact of unilateral transfers on internal donors

The negative effects of unilaterally extracting resources from agriculture, transportation, mining, public utilities and so forth are so pervasive that the underlying policies are, sooner or later, modified or abandoned. Output prices of the sectors being discriminated against are liberalised and, as market forces come into play, unilateral transfers shrink or even disappear. This ushers in a new state of affairs.

International distribution reversed: receiving transfers from abroad

With the 'safety valve' of internal unilateral transfers recognised as unsafe, counterproductive and full of disincentives to investment, effort and productivity, external unilateral transfers become the new, sought-after, *deus ex machina*. The game is simple: the nation spends more than it produces, runs a deficit in the current account of its balance of payments and the excess of the gross domestic expenditure (GDE) over gross domestic product (GDP) augments the welfare of some or all consumers. It also leads to levels of consumption, investment and government expenditure not otherwise attainable.

For this game to be played, trusting partners are needed. These are the foreign 'investors', most recently the foreign creditors. By definition, GDE cannot exceed GDP unless foreigners either invest (become equity owners), lend (become debt owners) or donate (provide unilateral resource transfers) resources to the nation under consideration.

Like in any other partnership, there is a demand and supply side. It would be a mistake to argue that the 'investors', 'lenders' or 'donors' to Latin America during 1973–83 were forced to cover its GDE–GDP gaps. To the contrary, they were willing, even eager partners. Awash with petro-dollar surpluses, banks in developed nations were eager, even desperate, to unload their petro-deposits to petro-importers, to petro-dollar demanders.

As oil prices rose, most petro-nations had a limited investment, consumption and government expenditure absorptive capacity. What they had in almost unlimited supply, at least in the short run, was the capacity to save much more than domestic investment could absorb, and to deposit their surpluses in the international money and capital markets. They became the world's prime lenders. And the global financial system worked just too well. Oil-importing nations were besieged by the global financial system with easy credits to finance any, not just oil, imports. And if they, willingly or unwillingly, waved the flag of private enterprise, free markets and open trade, as did Argentina, Uruguay, and Chile, they were inundated by foreign bankers who looked for, and were absorbed by, slogans, but ignored hard facts.

It is under these circumstances during 1973–83 that we experienced the golden age of mingling between money and capital on the one hand, and unilateral transfer markets on the other hand. Foreign banks played a new role, namely that of providing bilateral loans to nation-customers that had a capacity to absorb unilateral transfers, but lacked the capacity to repay bilateral foreign loans.

WAYS OUT OF THE FOREIGN DEBT PREDICAMENT[3]

The extended mutual conditionality principle[4]

Foreign bankers, especially American ones, have greatly reduced since 1983 their new loans abroad, especially to Latin America, as their supply of funds to lend dried up. Furthermore, whenever they provided new funds it was under the condition that the International Monetary Fund, the World Bank and the US Treasury co-lend and co-insure their old, as well as their new loans, and vice versa. However, this limited co-operative agreement or 'mutual-lending-conditionality' between bankers, the IMF and the US Treasury is not sufficient to neutralise the foreign debt problem. What is also needed is an 'extended co-operative agreement' or 'extended-credit-transfer-conditionality', where borrowers accept foreign credit under the condition that nations with permanent current account surpluses use part of them to amortise the non-repayable debt of the nations with current account deficits.

Efficient global capital markets will exist only if and when they are separated and distinguished from the unilateral transfer ones. The large portion of post-1973 loans, which in reality was unilateral transfers, needs to be amortised through a superfund established primarily through contributions from nations with current account surpluses. And in the future an international monetary authority must ensure that nations without credit repayment capacity, either do not run deficits in their current account, or have them funded through unilateral transfers.

The need for more direct foreign investment

Animosity against direct foreign investment and multinationals explains in part the shift towards debt or portfolio, indirect 'investment', in developing countries. However, under stable and mutually fair rules of the game, direct private or public investment is superior to debt lending because it guarantees a higher increase in production. More specifically, in the case of 'direct foreign investment', it is *almost impossible to have* a unilateral transfer component, except in situations of *ex post* confiscation. In contrast, in the case of credits to, financial 'investment' in, or portfolio loans to developing countries, it is *almost impossible not to have* a unilateral transfer component, possibly a significant one.

Thus, direct foreign investment, which involves ownership, and I emphasise that it can be both private and public, has the advantage over 'indirect' investment or purchase of bonds which does not involve ownership, that it minimises the role of undesirable, unplanned and unpredictable unilateral transfers.

Up to now I have used the terms foreign investment and foreign saving in a general way without always providing specific definitions. In order to gain a better understanding of the issues in the ongoing debate I am presenting in the next section some of the basic concepts.

SOME BASIC ISSUES IN SHARPER FOCUS

Foreign saving versus foreign investment[5]

Foreign saving, S_f, is that portion of domestic saving, S, funded from abroad. By definition, it is equal to the deficit of the nation on current account. S_f is a financial national accounts concept. The sum of foreign, S_f, and national saving, S_n, equals total saving, that is, $S_f + S_n = S$.

In constrast, foreign investment is an ownership concept. And there are at least four concepts of it. First, foreign investment, I_{f1}, stands for that portion of annual gross investment owned by foreigners. Statistics of this concept are either difficult to find or non-existent. According to a second notion, foreign investment, I_{f2}, is synonymous with foreign capital and is defined as the absolute amount or percentage share of a nation's real capital stock owned by foreigners. According to a third notion, I_{f3}, foreign investment is measured by the absolute or relative amount of equity financial ownership by foreigners. Finally, according to the broadest notion, I_{f4}, foreign investment is defined as the absolute or relative amount of portfolio *and* equity, corporate and unicorporate financial ownership by foreigners.

Whatever the contributions of foreign investment and debt, their long term growth depends on the ability of a nation to attract them, service and repay them. The following two concepts are therefore important in formulating a strategy concerning foreign investment, foreign debt, foreign saving and unilateral transfers.

Foreign investment absorption and repayment capacity

The notion of foreign investment repayment capacity is important because it measures the capacity of a nation to service and repay the obligations that arise from direct foreign investment. The foreign investment repayment capacity is determined, on the one hand, by the productivity of specific foreign investment projects, and, on the other hand, by the over-all productive use of all financial resources imported by a nation.

Thus, ultimately, it is the productivity of, or foreign investment absorption capacity of, a nation which determines, other things being equal, the repayment capacity. With developed and unconstrained money, capital, labour and bond markets, and with unilateral markets separate from the capital ones, the absorption determines the repayment capacity and vice versa. The foreign investment absorption capacity of the public and private enterprises also determines their repayment ability. And, their repayment ability is taken as an indicator of their absorptive capacity.

The foreign debt absorption and repayment capacity

The foreign debt repayment capacity is determined by the over-all productive use of foreign resources. This, in turn, is shaped by the distribution of foreign saving, S_f, between (a) unilateral transfers, (b) household accumulation of human and other forms of capital, (c) direct foreign investment, I_{f1}, (d) the portion of I_{f1} in the export sector, and (e) national investment, I_n.

The first choice and decision that Latin America has had to make was that of dividing foreign saving between bilateral loan contracts and unilateral transfers. It is here, where a competition between money-and-capital markets on the one hand, and unilateral transfer markets on the other hand develops, and direct foreign investment plays a critical role. Because direct foreign investment is an integral, inseparable part of the money and capital markets, its presence tilts foreign saving towards the capital markets and productive uses and away from the unilateral transfer markets.

The second choice, and consequently competition, is between investment and consumption both for capital and unilateral transfer market funds. Since unilateral transfer funds do not have to be repaid, they tend to be used primarily for consumption. In contrast, direct foreign investment tilts the balance in favour of investment and away from consumption because neither is it, nor is it regarded, as a free good. Thus, direct foreign investment assumes under these circumstances the double function of maintaining and strengthening the integrity of the financial markets on the one hand, and of promoting investment rather than consumption on the other hand. Direct foreign investment bypasses the intermediation steps that can divert internal and external funds away from investment. In both instances foreign investment increases the foreign debt repayment capacity. In contrast, unilateral transfers reduce this capacity by weakening the capital markets, reducing investment and hurting exports.

Put in a summary and explicit form, the debt repayment capacity of a nation is inversely related to the share of foreign saving that has been used to finance unilateral transfers. The higher the share of S_f going into unilateral transfers, the lower the productivity of imported saving, the lower the nation's foreign saving absorptive capacity, and ultimately the lower its foreign debt repayment capacity.

The unilateral transfer absorption capacity: is it matched by a willingness to give?

A nation's aggregate unilateral transfer absorption capacity has three components: the government, business and household ones. All three agents may and often do profess unlimited capacities to receive, but normally reveal only limited or negative capacities to give, unilateral transfers. What I have argued in this paper is that the unilateral transfer supply and absorption (demand) capacities need to be taken explicitly into account when formulating development strategies, because they can infringe upon money and capital markets, national and foreign savings and investment and, ultimately, growth.

CONCLUSION

Foreign savings and investment have assumed special significance in recent decades because Latin America has suffered from the Medusa-like distortions of ever present unilateral transfers; if and when Latin America can restore health and efficiency in its financial markets, the pivotal role of foreign resources is likely to decline.

The enemy of Latin America is uncontrolled unilateral transfers, not foreign investment. By being forced to choose between foreign investment and unilateral transfers, Latin American nations may curtail such transfers sufficiently to let the true choices emerge. One of these true choices is between foreign investments, I_f, and national investment, I_n. While foreign investment is a hands down winner when unilateral transfers are its competing alternative, we cannot presume that I_f can and will win a clear-cut superiority over I_n if financial markets operate efficiently.

Filling the GDE > GDP, $M > X$ (M = imports, X = exports) and $I > S_n$ gaps, or reversing them, is an ongoing challenge to Latin America. These gaps are likely to disappear or be funded by absorbable foreign resources if unilateral transfers are reduced to their original and proper function. This is to assist the needy, especially the poorest of the poor, acquire or augment their capacity to contribute to output and escape from poverty. In this way, the unilateral transfers will be transformed from the current negative or zero sum game to a growth promoting positive sum game, in which the benefits the poor will receive will not cause the rich and middle class to lose, but, in fact, will allow them to benefit as well. This may not guarantee immediate prosperity, but it will definitely be a major and necessary step forward in restoring incentives, financial services and an optimum use of scarce resources.

Notes

1. There was never any intention to provide detailed statistical information on growth, foreign debt, foreign investment and unilateral transfers in Latin America. Such background information can be found in T. O. Enders and R. P. Mattione, *Latin America: the Crisis of Debt and Growth*; E. V. Iglesias, 'A Preliminary Overview of the Latin American Economy during 1983'; A. Jorge, J. Salazar-Carrillo and E. Sanchez (eds) *Trade, Debt and Growth in Latin America*; A. Jorge, J. Salazar-Carrillo and R. Higonnet (eds) *Foreign Debt and Latin American Economic Development*; Inter-American Development Bank, *Economic and Social Progress in Latin America – Economic Integration*; M. J. Mamalakis, *Historical Statistics of Chile: Money, Income and Prices*, Volume 4; World Bank, *World Development Report 1984*; and World Bank, *Brazil, Financial Systems Review*.
2. For the hypothesis and evidence concerning plural labour markets in Latin America, see M. J. Mamalakis, 'Overall Employment and Income Strategies', in V. Urquidi and S. Trejo Reyes (eds) *Human Resources, Employment and Development*, Volume 4.
3. A wide spectrum of corrective strategies is suggested by W. R. Cline, 'International Debt: From Crisis to Recovery?', and M. J. Mamalakis, 'A North–South Dilemma: The Need and Limits of Conditionalities in the Americas'.
4. For the discussion of conditionalities, M. J. Mamalakis, 'A North–South Dilemma: The Need and Limits of Conditionalities in the Americas', and J. Williamson (ed.) *The IMF Conditionality*.
5. For a comprehensive discussion of the underlying national accounts concepts and methodological background see M. J. Mamalakis, *The Growth and Structure of the Chilean Economy: From Independence to Allende*, chapter 13, and M. J. Mamalakis, *Historical Statistics of Chile: Money, Income and Prices,* chapters 1,2, and 8 to 10.

References

Cline, W. R., 'International Debt: From Crisis to Recovery?', *American Economic Review*, Vol. 75, No. 2, 1985, pp. 185–90.
Comisión Económica para América Latina y el Caribe (CEPAL), 'El Mercado del Trabajo en la Actual Coyuntura—Análisis del PREALC (Programa Regional de Empleo para América Latina y el Caribe)', Notas sobre la Economía y el Desarrollo, No. 403 (Santiago, Chile: CEPAL, United Nations, 1984).
Enders, T. O. and R. P. Mattione, *Latin America: The Crisis of Debt and Growth* (Washington, DC: The Brookings Institution, 1984).
Iglesias, E. V., 'A Preliminary Overview of the Latin American Economy during 1983', *CEPAL Review*, 22 (April 1984) pp. 7–38.
InterAmerican Development Bank (IDB), *Economic and Social Progress in Latin America – Economic Integration* (Washington, DC: IDB, 1984).

40   *Foreign Investment and Unilateral Transfers*

Jorge, A., J. Salazar-Carrillo and R. P. Higonnet (eds) *Foreign Debt and Latin American Economic Development* (New York: Pergamon Press, 1983).

Jorge, A., J. Salazar-Carrillo and E. Sanchez (eds) *Trade, Debt and Growth in Latin America* (New York: Pergamon Press, 1984).

Mamalakis, M. J., *The Growth and Structure of the Chilean Economy: From Independence to Allende* (New Haven, Conn.: Yale University Press, 1976).

Mamalakis M. J., 'Overall Employment and Income Strategies', in V. Urquidi and S. Trejo Reyes (eds) *Human Resources, Employment and Development*, Volume 4, *Latin America* (Proceedings of the Sixth World Congress of the International Economic Association, Mexico City, 1980) (London: Macmillan, 1983).

Mamalakis, M. J., *Historical Statistics of Chile: Money, Income and Prices*, Volume 4 (Westport, Conn.: Greenwood Press, 1983).

Mamalakis, M. J., 'A North–South Dilemma: The Need and Limits of Conditionalities in the Americas', *Journal of InterAmerican Studies and World Affairs*, Vol. 27, No. 1, 1985, pp. 103–21.

Williamson, J. (ed.) *The IMF Conditionality*, Papers presented at Conference of Institute for International Economics, Airlie House, Va: 22-26 March 1982 (Cambridge, Mass.: MIT Press, 1983).

World Bank, *World Development Report 1984* (New York: Oxford University Press, 1984).

World Bank, *Brazil, Financial Systems Review* (Washington, DC: World Bank, 1984).

6 Default as a Negotiating Tactic in Debt Rescheduling Strategies of Developing Countries: A Preliminary Note

Richard L. Bernal

INTRODUCTION

The last decade has witnessed the exponential escalation of the external debt of developing countries to alarming levels, which constitute a serious problem for the international financial system. During the 1980s there has been a sharp increase in the number of defaults by developing countries and rescheduling exercises, involving both private and official creditors. Rescheduling debts has been by negotiations, which in many instances have been acrimonious affairs in which the debtors have had limited bargaining power, indeed, the only leverage has been that derived from default. This raises the crucially important issue of the use of default by an individual country as a tactic in debt rescheduling negotiations.

This brief preliminary note examines the deliberate use of default on external debt by a government of a developing country as a tactic in a strategy to manage its debt situation. The objective is to ascertain in what circumstances, if any, would it be advantageous for a government of a developing country to employ a policy of default. This analysis requires:

1. a discussion and definition of the term default;
2. a review of the history of default by developing countries;
3. an outline of the objectives of a deliberate default;

4. an explanation of the costs and benefits of default; and
5. an examination of the experience of developing countries which have deliberately defaulted during the post-war period.

On this basis it will be possible to draw some conclusions about the circumstances in which a deliberate default can be an effective and advantageous component in a debt policy.

DEBT POLICY OPTIONS

There are four debt policies which constitute the options of the governments of developing countries. We shall discuss each of them in turn.

Repayment

The government can, if it has the necessary foreign exchange, repay the country's external debt on the existing repayment scheduling. The benefit of this option is that it enables the country to retain its reputation of not ever defaulting. It will also permit the country to maintain its credit rating. This may not be very significant since the indebtedness of many developing countries already excludes them from further commercial borrowing. The cost of maintaining the current repayment schedule is that repayment will use such a large share of foreign exchange that import capacity will be sharply curtailed, which will be deflationary, adversely affecting growth of output, exports and employment.

Refinancing

A developing country may be able to roll-over its external debt by converting repayment of principal and/or interest falling due over some future period, into a new loan. This is an option only for loans from transnational commercial banks, which are those which are most onerous, as they have the shortest maturity and bear the highest rates of interest. However, this possibility depends principally on factors outside the control of the government and which influence the willingness of transnational commercial banks to provide refinancing.

The advantage of refinancing is that it provides relief, but has the disadvantage of costing more since the risk charge has increased. The 'lead bank' also profits by charging fees for arranging refinancing.

Rescheduling

Rescheduling is an agreement between lenders and the borrower to lengthen the repayment schedule of principal and/or interest. Both private and official lenders have concluded rescheduling pacts with increasing frequency since the mid-1970s.

Default

There are different ways in which the term default is used, these include:

1. 'in default' – the lender declares that the borrower has failed to comply with some stipulation of the loan agreement. Three variations can be distinguished:

    (a) 'actually in default' – failure to meet requirements of the loan agreement relating to the schedule of repayment.
    (b) 'legally in default' – a borrower is only in default when the lender declares that this is so. This is the legal prerogative of the lender. In some cases a country has missed a payment or is accumulating arrears and is therefore actually in default but the lenders, in the expectation that the interruption in servicing is temporary, will avoid the drastic step of calling the borrower 'legally in default'.
    (c) 'technically in default' – the borrower may be on schedule with repayments but may be in breach of some stipulation of the loan agreement. For example, transnational commercial banks, through the 'cross-default clauses'[1] of their loan agreements, require a government to be 'in good standing' with the IMF, that is to be eligible to use its resources. A government which has failed to meet the quantitative performance criteria of an IMF agreement is 'technically in default'.

2. 'to default' – when a borrower fails to fulfil the stipulations of the loan agreement, relating to interest and/or amortisation. This paper is focussed on deliberate default which is a suspension of repayment, leaving open the possibility and recognising the obligation to repay the debt at some time in the future. Default is therefore temporary and must be distinguished from repudiation, which is a termination of repayment with a declaration of not ever repaying the outstanding debt. Repudiation is usually undertaken when the government no longer recognises the legitimacy of the debt and is therefore permanent.

It should be noted that each of the four policy options are not exclusive, in fact, they are frequently combined, for example, refinancing and rescheduling.

HISTORY OF DEFAULT[2]

Defaults on foreign debts have a long history, involving both developing and developed countries and involving governments and private corporations. The earliest recorded cases of default on external debt were those of the Greek city states in the fourth century B.C. Another notable incident in antiquity was in 1327 when Edward III of England renounced his debts causing the collapse of the Bardi and Peruzzi banks. Some countries made a regular practice of default, for example, Dammers records that France ceased payments on its debt on the average once every 30 years between the sixteenth and nineteenth centuries.

There have been four major waves of defaults in modern history, starting with the defaults of the newly-independent Latin American republics' default on international bond issues during the years 1822 to 1825. The second wave of defaults involved Turkey, Egypt and several Latin American countries in the 1870s. The third wave occurred during the 1930s when several European and nearly all the Latin American countries defaulted. The fourth wave has been taking place since the beginning of the 1980s and encompasses African and Latin American countries.

OBJECTIVES OF DELIBERATE DEFAULT

Developing countries experiencing extreme difficulty in servicing their external debt have sought to negotiate with their creditors refinancing and/or rescheduling agreements. The leverage of the debtor government is usually limited to the use of default, that is, a deliberate default as against a default due to inability to meet repayments on schedule. The latter may occur when the country does not have sufficient foreign exchange to meet its external debt payment or when cash flow problems disrupt the repayment schedule. A deliberate default is a situation in which the debtor government decides that the social, political and economic cost of servicing the external debt are excessive, whether they be in the form of increased unemployment or shortages of essential imports such as basic foods and oil, and ceases repayment. The objectives of a deliberate default are:

1. to force creditors to commence negotiations about refinancing and/or rescheduling or to pursue ongoing negotiations meaningfully with regard to the duration of negotiations and the terms offered.
2. to force an improvement in the terms of refinancing and/or rescheduling. Specifically, this could refer to the consolidation period, the percentage consolidated, the grace period, the repayment period, interest charges, fees, or new loans.

The use of deliberate default has often been prompted by the intransigence of the creditors regarding the willingness to reschedule and the terms of rescheduling. It is often difficult to reach mutually acceptable terms by amicable negotiations because the interests and objectives of the debtor and creditor are diametrically opposed. The debtor wants to reschedule if possible with the addition of a new loan and on the least onerous terms. The creditor prefers not to reschedule, certainly not accompanied by the extension of a new loan,[3] and on terms which provided the most rapid repayment on the most profitable basis.

COST AND BENEFITS OF DEFAULT

The costs

The costs of a default consist of (i) imposed costs, that is, punitive costs which do not result from the retaliatory actions of creditors. There are ten retaliatory measures which lenders may resort to in the event of a deliberate default or a debt repudiation. Most of these sanctions can be applied directly by the lending institution, while those requiring governmental action or authorisation can be engineered by political pressure. Transnational commercial banks are influential in the foreign economic policy of the United States,[4] and often work closely with the International Monetary Fund.[5]

Punitive measures include the following:

1. Termination of lending
2. Acceleration
3. Default interest
4. Termination of trade credit
5. Withdrawal of insurance for exports
6. Curtailment of aid
7. Import ban
8. Legal action
9. Seizure of foreign assets
10. Economic blockage.

In the case of a default the first six measures can be applied, the first five being directly imposed by the lending institution and the sixth by political pressure of the home government. All ten measures can be imposed in a situation of debt repudiation, but the last four apply only to debt repudiation.

Termination of lending

In the event of a default or repudiation, transnational commercial banks would immediately stop considering new loans and would suspend further draw-downs of the undisbursed portion of existing loans. This may not be an effective penalty since a country which defaults or repudiates debt is most likely already not able to get new loans from the banks. Multilateral and bilateral aid agencies may be more tolerant, for example, the World Bank has only on rare occasions exercised this remedy although it is entitled to under section VI of its General Conditions.[6]

Acceleration

The lender can declare the outstanding portion of the loan to be immediately due and payable, that is, the borrower is obliged to repay the balance of the principal and accrued interest at once.

In practice, it is recognised that no borrower is likely to be able to satisfy this obligation. However, the power to render the repayment obligation current is needed by the banks, with no grace period in order that they may speedily take any necessary action against the borrower or any of its assets so as to protect their position.[7]

Default interest

Loan agreements stipulate a rate of interest to be paid on all sums defaulted on, whether or not the loan is accelerated. The rate of default interest is usually 1 or 2 per cent per annum above the rate of interest charged on the loan. This is justified by the banks on the grounds that they incur additional costs in time and money when there is a default.[8]

Termination of trade credit

Most of world trade is financed by credit from the transnational commercial banks and their initial reaction to a default or debt repudiation is to terminate trade credit to pressure the offending country. If there is a deliberate default but debt negotiations have commenced, then the banks are more likely to roll-over trade credits at the existing level so as to avoid exacerbating an already difficult situation. The banks in different regions of the developed world may react differently, for example, when US banks terminated trade credits to Chile during the Allende administration, Chile was able to shift trade financing to European banks.

Withdrawal of insurance for experts

Creditor countries can withdraw insurance of exports to the debtor country thus discouraging exports to that country, for example, the case of Ghana.[9]

Curtailment of aid

Most countries have punitive legislation which can apply to countries in default to its government or private financial institutions. Legislation in the United States imposes penalties on any country that:

has taken steps to repudiate or nullify existing contracts or agreements with any United States citizen or any corporation, partnership, or association not less than 50 per cent beneficially owned by United States citizens ... any such country ... fails within reasonable time ... to take appropriate steps which may include arbitration, to discharge its obligations under international law.[10]

Countries in violation of these statutes are prohibited from receiving foreign aid, excluded from the generalised system of trade preferences and Caribbean Basin Initiative, and the US representative will vote against loans from the World Bank and the InterAmerican Development Bank. The United States is notorious for terminating bilateral aid and blocking loans from multilateral aid institutions and has taken this action on numerous occasions on a variety of economic and political pretexts.

Import ban

A creditor country may prohibit imports from the debtor country.

Legal action[11]

Legal recourse against a government which has defaulted or repudiated its debt is extremely limited, although the few international cases to date have ruled that a State cannot plead economic hardship as 'force majeure' to refuse to honour its loan commitments.[12] Legal action in cases of default are almost unheard of since they are costly, time consuming and the rulings are ineffective. The courts may decide not to hear the case on the basis of upholding the doctrine of 'sovereign immunity'.[13] A vindication of the right to be paid may be completely ineffective. In 1982 the US District Court in Birmingham, Alabama, ruled that the People's Republic of China should pay US$41.3 million plus interest to 280 holders of 5 per cent Hukuong Railways Sinking Fund Gold Loan. These bonds were issued in 1911 and defaulted on in the 1930s. The Chinese government refused to be involved in the case, pointing out that US Courts do not have jurisdiction over China. The Chinese Foreign Ministry in a diplomatic note to the Court warned that if the court attacked Chinese property in the US in settlement of the debt, it reserved the right 'to take corresponding measures' in China.[14]

Seizure of foreign assets

The government of a creditor country could authorise the seizure and sale of the debtor country's foreign assets. A recent reminder of this possibility was the US government's freezing of an estimated US$8 billion of Iranian assets in November 1979. The Iranian assets frozen included US$6 billion in bank deposits in US commercial banks.[15] Seizure of foreign assets is a frequently voiced threat but is an extreme action unlikely to be used unless all possibilities of a negotiated settlement have been exhausted. In the case of the United States, Section 1611(b)(i) of the Foreign Sovereign Immunity Act of 1976, stipulates that the property of foreign Central Banks is immune from 'Pre-Judgement Attachment' (Seizure).[16]

Economic blockage

The lending country or countries could impose an economic blockage on the borrowing countries, thus severing all economic relations. This kind of action is most unlikely, but is a possibility as demonstrated by US intervention in the Caribbean and Central America in the inter-war period, and more recently the financial blockage of the Allende government in Chile.[17]

The costs incurred other than those imposed by the creditors are:

1. Loss of credit rating, which may already be so low that the country cannot raise new commercial loans.
2. It creates uncertainty among foreign investors who perceive an increase in the risk of expropriation, nationalisation, inability to repatriate profit and lack of foreign exchange to meet foreign obligations.
3. There will be a loss of international political goodwill which may seriously damage the willingness of other governments to provide loans or technical assistance.

The benefits

The benefits of a deliberate default are in the short run, the immediate debt relief which may free as much as 20–40 per cent of foreign exchange earnings. This could restore a corresponding increase in imports which could alleviate shortages and stimulate output and employment. In the medium term it could result in securing negotiations on rescheduling external debt and even better terms for rescheduled debt.

EXPERIENCE OF DEVELOPING COUNTRIES WHICH DELIBERATELY DEFAULTED

Deliberate defaults have been implemented either by themselves or accompanied by a repudiation of existing debt. Repudiation may be permanent or temporary, and may be used as the ultimate bluff. Permanent debt repudiation would produce effects which would amount to an economic embargo which would constitute enforced autarchy. Autarchy is an unsustainable position for developing countries whose economies are characterised by a high degree of openness, that is, having a foreign trade/Gross Domestic Product ratio of over 50 per cent, or foreign capital inflows accounting for over 30 per cent of gross investment. If a debt repudiation takes place, the country must be prepared to do without trade credits, foreign aid and loans from the transnational commercial banks. This would apply not only to new loans, but to drawing the undisbursed portion of existing loan commitments. The termination of external financing could cause a collapse in a small, open economy, especially given the extremely low levels of inventories of imported items and the inability to produce import substitutes in the short run.

Faced with this kind of situation, a country would have to be prepared to re-orient its international economic relations from the capitalist world economy to the Socialist Bloc. This would be possible only if the socialist countries are convinced that the country is seriously committed to, and actively implementing, a transition to socialism. Cuba repudiated some of its external debt in 1961 and was able to re-orient most of its foreign trade with the sugar purchase of one million tons by the Societ Union between 1960 and 1964, and US$357 million import credits granted by the COMECON countries and China between February 1960 and August 1961.[18] The severe disruptions in production and consumption during this transition period may be very difficult to handle politically in a two-party democracy. Cuba has been able to carry on a significant portion of its external trade with non-socialist countries (excluding the US) – about one-fifth of total trade[19] and borrowed over US$400 million in the

Eurocurrency markets.[20] Both the Cuban[21] and Rhodesian experiences demonstrated that economic embargoes by industrialised capitalist economies have not been able to engineer an economic collapse. Most bankers believe that developing countries will not resort to deliberate default because of the adverse effect on their trade and the difficulty of returning to credit-worthiness.[22]

The basis for debt repudiation is often a change of government where the new administration disclaims responsibility for loans owed by the previous regime, as in the case of the Soviet Union and China. Creditors persist in their attempts to recover the repudiated debt.[23] Probably the longest standing dispute is between British bondholders and the State of Mississippi. Mississippi passed a constitutional amendment in 1875, disclaiming its obligations. But the Council of Foreign Bondholders formed in 1868 is reported to be still pursuing compensation for the Mississippi bonds, as well as Tsarist Russian bonds. New York investment firm, Carl Marks & Co., is involved in a suit seeking US$619 million from the Soviet Union for two debt issues by the Imperial Russian Government in 1916 and repudiated by the Soviet government. In 1984 an Alabama Court dismissed a suit to recover US$43 million of Ching Dynasty Railway Bonds.[24]

In examining the experience of developing countries which have deliberately defaulted as a bargaining tactic to induce creditors to open debt rescheduling negotiation and to obtain better rescheduling terms, this paper concentrates on three cases. These are Ghana in the early 1970s, Nicaragua in the late 1970s and Mexico in the early 1980s. These countries were selected on the basis of (a) certainty that default was a negotiating tactic, and (b) the availability of information. While three case studies may not be a large sample of deliberate defaults and while it may be a limited basis for generalisations, the three cases are very different and do provide useful insights. A further limitation is that in the three cases the resort to deliberate default achieved the objectives of initiating and/or expediting debt restructuring negotiations and attaining better terms, and therefore unsuccessful cases, if any, are not considered.

The case of Ghana

Ghana is a small, open, underdeveloped economy with a high import content in industrial production and relies almost exclusively on the export of cocoa for foreign exchange. It accumulated large debts to official agencies especially trade credits and infrastructure loans during the early 1960s under the Nkrumah government. The National Liberation Cuncil and the Busia administration were involved in a constant round of negotiations with creditors to reschedule short-term and medium-term debts. The NLC on assuming power announced categorically that it considered repudiation immoral and stated that it intended to honour its debt obligations to the full, and expected to arrive quickly at a reasonable arrangement with all its creditors.[25] Several agreements were reached but collapse resulted in a hardening of the creditors' position. In January 1972 Colonel Acheampong seized power in a military coup and established the National Redemption Council which immediately announced a repudiation of external debt. All debts incurred by the Nkrumah administration were to be examined and where questionable would be repudiated. Short-term debts to be honoured would be paid when the foreign exchange position permitted it. Long-term debts were to be unilaterally rescheduled on terms of a 40-year repayment period with a 10-year grace period. 'Formally, the creditors ... looked upon the Acheampong measures as proposals rather than a fait accompli' and a counter-proposal, more generous than previous offers, was made in October 1972. After long complex negotiations, Ghana and its creditors reached an agreement on rescheduling in March 1974.[26]

The case of Nicaragua

Nicaragua is a small, underdeveloped economy whose main exports consist of primary products and which is self-sufficient in basic food items. Following the removal of the Somoza dictatorship, the Sandinista government repudiated 'debts contracted by Somoza-owned companies for dubious purposes'[27] and defaulted on its external debt. The default was partly tactical and partly due to the almost complete depletion of foreign exchange reserves. Nicaragua was able to negotiate a rescheduling of its debts to transnational commercial banks on the most generous terms provided to any country in recent years (see Table 6.1) and without signing a stand-by arrangement with the IMF.[28] Another development worthy of note is that, during its first three years, the Sandinista government was able, despite its stand on external debt, to raise US$1200 million in external finance, of which 32 per cent came from developed capitalist countries[29] in spite of US efforts to discourage such flows.

The case of Mexico

Mexico is a large, industrialising, developing country and is one of the largest debtors to the international banking system. While it was known that Mexico's external debt was excessive and debt servicing was at an unacceptable level, and that a long-term default would have the most serious effects for transnational commercial banks, it was felt that a responsible country like Mexico would not default. This perception was assiduously encouraged by Mexico which then suddenly and deliberately defaulted and immediately initiated serious negotiation for debt rescheduling. The terms achieved by Mexico were better than the average terms provided by recent rescheduling arrangements and involved the provision of new loans (see Table 6.1).

The results

The terms of recent commercial bank reschedulings have been consolidation periods of one year, with 80–100 per cent of total principal payments rescheduled. The maturity of the new loans were typically 7–8 years with a grace period of 2–3 years, fees of 1–1½ per cent of the amount rescheduled, and rates of interest of 1¾–2¼ per cent above London Inter-bank Offered Rate (LIBOR).[30] Rescheduling of official debts recently have involved a consolidation period of one year and 90–100 per cent of total principal and interest payments. The maturity period was usually 7–9 years, including a grace period of 3–4 years.[31] The terms achieved by Nicaragua and Mexico are significantly better than the average terms (see Table 6.1).

It could be argued that these cases represent special circumstances, for example, Ghana and Nicaragua had experienced major political upheavals and were virtually bankrupt and could not pay. This, however, could not have been the decisive factor since several other developing countries have been in comparable political turmoil and economic collapse. It could be suggested that Mexico's terms reflect their importance to the international banking system and their political importance to the United States, but Brazil and, to a lesser extent, Argentina are very large debtors and are politically strategic to the United States, yet the terms of new loans and rescheduling are not as favourable as those extended to Mexico.

Table 6.1 Terms and conditions of bank debt restructurings, 1978–early October 1983

Country, date of agreement, and type of debt rescheduled	Basis	Amount provided (US$ million)	Grace period (In years)	Maturity (In years)	Interest rate (In percent; spread over LIBOR US Prime)
Nicaragua					
Agreement of December 1980					
Arrears on interest or due up to December 1980	75% of arrears and amount due	90	—	5	
Arrears on principal as of December 1979	100% of arrears on principal	252	5	11	
Due after December 1979	100% of principal	240	5	12	$\frac{3}{4}$–1$\frac{1}{4}$, but with deferred interest payment provision and interest recapture clause
Agreement of September 1981					
Accumulated arrears	90% of interest and principal	180	1	10	
Due after September 1981 (debt of nationalized banks)	100% of principal		5	10	
Agreement of March 1982					
Accumulated arrears	90% of interest and principal	55	—	10	
Due after March 1982 (debt of nationalized businesses)	100% of principal		5	10	$\frac{3}{4}$–1$\frac{1}{4}$, but with deferred interest payment provision and interest recapture clause

Rescheduling in process					
Interest and principal payment between June 1983 and June 1984	—	—	—	—	—
New loan	New financing	150	—	—	—
Mexico					
Agreement of 27 August 1983					
Mexico's public sector short-, medium-, and long-term debt due from 23 August 1982 to 31 December 1984	100% of principal	20 000	4	8	$1\frac{7}{8}$–$1\frac{3}{4}$
Syndicated loan	New financing (net)	5 000	3	6	$2\frac{1}{4}$–$2\frac{1}{8}$
Official financing	New financing	2 000 to 2 500			
Settlement of interest in arrears on private sector's debt	—	1 000 to 1 500	—	—	1–$1\frac{7}{8}$

Source: 'Recent Multinational Debt Restructuring with Official and Bank Creditors', Occasional Paper No. 25 (Washington, DC: IMF, December 1983) pp. 37–8.

CONCLUSIONS

There are two conclusions:

1. Deliberate default by developing countries has been a successful tactic in achieving the objectives of (a) initiating or accelerating the process of debt rescheduling negotiation, and (b) securing more favourable terms for rescheduled debts.
2. Given the 'right' conditions and effective implementation, a deliberate default can be employed to achieve more purposeful negotiation and better terms. Therefore, a more in-depth analysis encompassing as many case studies as feasible should be undertaken to establish how developing countries can best use a policy of deliberate default and in what circumstances.

Notes

1. Richard L. Bernal, 'Transnational Banks, the International Monetary Fund and External Debt of Developing Countries', *Social and Economic Studies*, Vol. 31, No. 4, 1982, pp. 85–8.
2. Clifford Dammers, 'A Brief History of Sovereign Defaults and Rescheduling', in D. Suratgar (ed.), *Default and Rescheduling: Corporate and Sovereign Borrowing* (London: Euromoney Publications, 1984) p. 77; and Rene P. Higonnet, 'Latin American Debt: More Rescheduling?', in Antonio Jorge, Jorge Salazar-Carillo and Rene P. Higonnet (eds) *Foreign Debt and Latin American Economic Development* (New York: Pergamon, 1983) pp. 61–76.
3. Since 1982 much of the new commercial bank lending to developing countries has been 'involuntary', often as part of rescheduling packages (see Stephany Griffith-Jones, *International Finance and Latin America* (London: Croom Helm, forthcoming) pp. 73–4).
4. Christopher Elias, *The Dollar Barons* (New York: Macmillan, 1973).
5. Richard L. Bernal, 'Transnational Commercial Banks, the International Monetary Fund and Capitalist Crisis in Jamaica, 1972–1980', in Jaime Eztevez and Samuel Lichtenszetjn (eds) *Nueva fase del capital financiero. Elementos teoricos y experiencias en America Latina* (Mexico City: ILET/CEESTEM, Editorical Nueva Imagen, 1981) pp. 281–334.
6. Georges R. Delaume, 'Special Risk and Remedies of International Foreign Loans', footnote 22, p. 98, in D. Suratgar (ed.) *Default and Rescheduling: Corporate and Sovereign Borrowing* (London: Euromoney Publications, 1984).
7. Keith Clark and Andrew Taylor, 'Events of Default in Eurocurrency Loan Agreements', *International Financial Law Review*, September 1982, pp. 12–15 (see p. 14).
8. Ibid.

9. Andrzej Krassowski, *Development and the Debt Trap. Economic Planning and External Borrowing in Ghana* (London: Croom Helm, 1974) p. 133.

10. Johathan Eaton and Mark Gersovity, 'Poor Country Borrowing in Private Financial Markets and the Repudiation Issue', Princeton Studies in International Finance, No. 47, June 1981, pp. 32–3.

11. There are many unresolved issues in the laws pertaining to international loans – see Zouhair A. Kronfol, 'The Proper Law of International Loans', *Journal of World Trade Law*, Vol. 10, No. 2, 1976 pp. 129–44.

12. George R. Delaume, 'Special Risk and Remedies of International Foreign Loans', footnote 19, p. 98 in D. Suratager (ed.) *Default and Rescheduling: Corporate and Sovereign Borrowing* (London: Euromoney Publications, 1984).

13. William Tudor John, 'Sovereign Immunity', in Lars Kalderen and Qamar S. Siddiqi (eds) *Sovereign Borrowers, Guidelines on Legal negotiations with Commercial Lenders* (Uppsala: Dag Hammarskjold Foundation, 1984) pp. 144–55.

14. Barry Kramer, 'Federal Judge in Alabama Orders China to Pay Off Imperial Government Bonds', *Wall Street Journal*, 9 September 1982, p. 39.

15. Harvey D. Shapiro, 'The Fallout From Iran', *Institutional Investor*, March 1980, pp. 69–70.

16. 'Is Debt Repudiation Out of the Question?' *International Currency Review*, Vol. 15, No. 5, 1983, pp. 27–30.

17. James Petras and Morris Morley, *The United States and Chile* (New York: Monthly Review Press, 1975) Chapter 5.

18. Archibald R.M. Ritter, *The Economic Development of Revolutionary Cuba. Strategy and Performance* (New York: Praeger, 1974) pp. 87–91.

19. Estimate based on *Highlights of Cuban Economics and Social Development 1976–80 and Main Targets for 1981–85* (Havana: Banco Nacional de Cuba, January, 1981) p. 6, and Cuba Cifras Estadisticas, Legundo Congreso del Partido Comunista de Cuba, Diciembre, 1980, p. 94.

20. Carmelo Mesa-Lago, *The Economy of Socialist Cuba: A Two-Decade Appraisal* (Albuquerque: University of New Mexico Press, 1981) p. 106.

21. Donald L. Losman, 'The Embargo of Cuba: An Economic Appraisal', *Caribbean Studies*, Vol. 14, No. 3, 1974, pp. 95–119.

22. M.S. Mendelsohn, *Commercial Banks and the Restructuring of Cross-Border Debt* (New York: Group of Thirty, 1983) p. 9.

23. Anthony Sampson, *The Money Lenders: Bankers in a Dangerous World* (London: Hodder & Stoughton, 1981) pp. 55–6.

24. 'China: Modernising a Rail System', *Newsweek*, 12 November 1984, p. 39.

25. Andrzej Krassowski, *Development and the Debt Trap: Economic Planning and External Borrowing in Ghana* (London: Croom Helm, 1974).

26. Ibid., p. 134.

27. 'Nicaragua. Preparing to settle with the banks', *World Business Weekly*, 1980, p. 51.

28. Richard S. Weinert, 'The Rescheduling of Nicaragua's External Debt', in D. Suratgar (ed.) *Default and Rescheduling: Corporate and Sovereign*

Borrowing (London: Euromoney Publications, 1984), and 'Nicaragua's Debt Renegotiation', *Cambridge Journal of Economics*, Vol. 5, No. 2, 1981, pp. 187–94.

29. *The Philosophy and Policies of the Government of Nicaragua* (Managua: Nicaragua Libre, March 1982) p. 13.

30. 'Recent Multilateral Debt Restructuring with Official and Bank Creditors', Occasional Paper No. 25 (Washington, DC: International Monetary System, December 1983) pp. 25–6.

31. Ibid., p. 10.

7 The Instability of Intra-Latin American and Caribbean Exports and Exchange Rates

Florencio Ballestero and Francisco Thoumi

INTRODUCTION

One of the main justifications used to promote systems of economic integration in Latin America was the need to dampen the effects of the fluctuations of the value of the region's exports to the rest of the world. The advocates for economic integration expected that the Latin American regional market would provide a more stable base for development than the markets of the developed world, as export instability was deemed to cause a lower over-all volume of trade and thus, to affect the growth of the economy.

In this essay the instability of the intra-Latin American and Caribbean (LAC) exports and exchange rate is measured for the period 1960–82, and an estimate of the importance that the intra-LAC exchange rate instability has on the corresponding export instability is obtained.

The instability of exports and the exchange rate has been dealt with in the economic literature in two independent ways. The first one, which surfaced during the early 1950s, studied export instability. These works generally measured the instability of the volume, price and value of exports, and correlate it with macroeconomic variables such as the rate of growth of the economy, the income level, investment behaviours and so on. The literature in this field is abundant,[1] and focussed mostly on the underdeveloped countries.

The second way appeared first in the second half of the 1970s, and mostly deals with exchange rate instability in developed countries after the collapse of the Bretton Woods system. These studies relate this instability with export growth and other macroeconomic variables. However, there are no studies which relate exchange rate and export instability.

The empirical studies that relate export instability with its own rate of growth can be classified in two categories, those which study bilateral trade and those which deal with trade among several countries.[2] Among those of the first type, there is only one of a Latin American country (Brazil).[3] This study finds a negative and highly significant relationship between exchange rate instability and export growth. The second type of study uses cross-sectional regression techniques to estimate the average reaction of exports from the countries considered to the exchange rate instability.[4]

The second section of this essay discusses the instability concept used, while the third section summarises the relationship between the exchange rate instability and export instability; this is followed by estimations of the instability of intra- and extraregional exports and of the relevant exchange rates in the fourth and fifth sections respectively. Then, the importance of exchange rate fluctuations in determining those of trade flows is estimated. The essay ends with a summary of the conclusions obtained.

DEFINITION OF INSTABILITY

Instability is normally measured by comparing the observed values of a series of some predicted set of values. This is usually done utilising arithmetic square, geometric square or absolute value deviations.[5] The instability measure used here, for a time series for the 1960–82 period, is the variance of its annual deviations from the trend, and thus falls in the second of Brodsky's categories.

The following procedure was used to estimate these variances. Taking a time series X_t which covers a period of $n+1$ years ($t = 0, 1, \ldots, n$), the average growth rate for the period (r_x) is the geometric average of the rates of growth in each year (r_{xt}). That is:

$$(1 + r_x) = [\pi_t(1 + r_{xt})]^{1/n} = [\pi_t(X_{t+1}/X_t)]^{1/n} \tag{7.1}$$

for $t = 0, 1, \ldots, (n-1)$, where π signifies product.

r_x is then used to estimate the present value at year zero of each observation of the variable:

$$X^0_t = [X_t/(1+r_x)^t] \qquad \text{for } t=0, 1,\ldots, n. \qquad (7.2)$$

The average value for the variable at moment zero is then defined as the geometric average of the present values at moment zero of each of the observations:

$$X^0 = (\pi_t \, X^0_t)^{1/n+1} \qquad \text{for } t=0, 1,\ldots, n, \qquad (7.3)$$

This average value at moment zero and the rate of growth are used to estimate the dynamic average for the series which is defined as:

$$Y_{xt} = X^0(1+r_x)^t \qquad \text{for } t=0, 1,\ldots, n. \qquad (7.4)$$

The deviations of the series with respect to its dynamic average are then defined as a natural log of the ratio of the original value of the series to its dynamic average:

$$W_{xt} = \ln (X_t/Y_{xt}) \qquad \text{for } t=0, 1,\ldots, n. \qquad (7.5)$$

Notice that in this case, the average of the deviations for the whole period is zero.

Finally, the instability of the series during the period is defined as the variance of the deviations estimated above:

$$VW_x = \sum_{t=0}^{n} \frac{W^2_{xt}}{n+1}. \qquad (7.6)$$

Thus defined, the instability has the same time unit as the original series. Furthermore, the unit in which instability is measured is always the same (a log quotient), independently of the units of the original series. This permits the comparability of the instability of any kind of series.

THE RELATIONSHIP BETWEEN EXCHANGE RATE AND EXPORT INSTABILITY

To analyse this relationship it is assumed that the export supply is given by the following function:

$$X_t = [(P^e_{rxt} \cdot E_{rt})^\alpha \; Z^\beta_t] \cdot e^{\varepsilon_t} \cdot e^{aVW_x} \tag{7.7}$$

where X_t = volume supplied in the year t.

The first bracket of independent variables includes the traditional supply variables: P^e_{rxt} is the real export price in dollars, E_{rt} the real exchange rate, and α the price elasticity of supply measured in domestic currency.[6] Z_t is a scale variable which measures the installed capacity (real value of assets) in the export sector,[7] and β the elasticity of the supplied export volume with relationship to the scale.

The variable ε_t represents the effect that several minor variables such as the degree of commercial or financial organisation in the export sector; the level of export restrictions, the diversification of products and export markets, the weather conditions which affect the productive capacity of the agricultural sector, and so on, have on exports. During the period under consideration, it is assumed that this variable has an average μ and a variance δ.

Export instability (VW_x) during the period affects exports negatively. Its parameter reflects the perceived risk, based on historical experience, of working in the export sector.

The analysis done is restricted to the supply function, which implicitly assumes: (i) that the country studied is a small supplier which takes the price of its exports in the international markets as given, and (ii) that even though X_t and P^e_{rxt} affect the supply of foreign exchange, which in turn will determine E_{rt}, the effect of other variables such as the volume and real price of imports, the demand and supply of services, the capital flows and the movement of reserves which affect E_{rt} is so large, that the exporters of goods can take the value of E_{rt} as independent of supply factors, and also that the covariance between P^e_{rxt} and E_r is low.[8]

Applying to the supply function the methodology described above to measure instability, it is concluded that:

$$(VW_x) = \delta + \alpha^2 \, (VW_{prx}) + \alpha^2 \, (VW_{er}) + \text{covariances} \tag{7.8}$$

where VW_i is the instability of the variable i.

That is, the export instability can be explained by the instability of its real price measured in foreign currency, the instability of the real exchange rate and that of the effect of the minor variables and the covariances, whose value could be considered as very small. This equation is then utilised to estimate later on the effects of the exchange rate instability on exports.

EXPORTS INSTABILITY ESTIMATION

Table 7.1 shows the accumulated real value of exports and the export instability of each country of Latin America between 1960 and 1982. These data are broken down into total exports, exports to Latin America and exports outside Latin America.[9] The figures corresponding to the region as a whole, the United States, the industrialised countries, and the world, are also provided as reference benchmarks. The Latin American weighted average instability is the average of the one observed in each country, weighted by the accumulated real value of its exports between 1960 and 1982. The regional instability (Latin America, World, Industrialised Countries) is that of the total exports of each of those regions.

The instability of the total exports of each of the Latin American countries is generally quite high, almost always two times, or more, than that of the United States.[10] The Latin American weighted average is also very high: 17.0 compared to 9.4 for the United States.

The estimates for Brazil's exports to LAC, outside LAC and to the world are significantly lower than those of the other LAC countries. The instability of the last two export categories has a magnitude similar to that of the total exports of the United States. Paraguay is another exceptional case as it has very low total export instability although the instability of its intra- and extra-LAC exports is rather high, which suggests a high degree of substitution between intra- and extra-LAC markets for this country's exports.

The instability of the intra-Latin American exports of all of the region's countries is extremely high. The weighted average for these exports is 29.8, which is three-quarters higher than the weighted average of the instability of the exports to the rest of the world. Intraregional exports of several small countries have been extremely unstable, those of Ecuador have been over four times as unstable as its extraregional exports, and those of Bolivia, Costa Rica, Dominican Republic, El Salvador, Guatemala, and Surinam have shown instability measures about triple those of extraregional exports. The instability of intraregional exports of Colombia, Chile, Panama, Peru, and Uruguay has been about double the instability for their extraregional exports. It is remarkable that even countries that have

Table 7.1 Export instability of Latin American countries, 1960–82

	Total		EXPORTS Outside Latin America		To Latin America	
Country[1]	Real value[2]	Instability[3]	Real value[2]	Instability[3]	Real value[2]	Instability[3]
United States	2 998 060	9.4	—	—	—	—
Latin America						
Argentina	132 888	16.1	104 180	18.5	28 708	20.0
Bolivia	21 931	18.9	17 002	23.2	4 929	75.7
Brazil	236 522	9.7	203 960	9.6	32 562	17.4
Chile	63 687	12.5	52 707	14.1	10 980	26.6
Colombia	61 084	13.3	52 418	13.3	8 666	28.6
Costa Rica	17 785	19.8	11 791	14.6	3 994	48.5
Dominican Republic	19 489	26.6	18 887	26.5	603	79.3
Ecuador	36 517	21.3	28 064	14.2	8 454	58.3
El Salvador	17 353	15.6	12 458	13.1	4 895	42.0
Guatemala	20 609	14.7	14 793	17.1	5 817	54.9
Guyana	9 519	20.0	7 933	29.9	1 857	41.5
Honduras	12 349	21.9	10 369	26.2	1 979	22.8
Jamaica	22 367	19.9	20 926	20.8	1 442	34.2
Mexico	184 695	21.8	168 526	24.0	16 169	27.8

Panama	5 823	19.4	5 523	21.1	600	44.7
Paraguay	4 827	7.1	3 190	17.2	1 637	23.5
Peru	77 218	15.1	68 806	17.1	8 411	32.9
Surinam	8 681	31.2	8 392	31.4	289	88.5
Trinidad & Tobago	123 881	19.1	111 233	19.7	12 648	26.8
Uruguay	15 447	16.6	12 082	17.9	3 365	34.4
Venezuela	639 549	18.1	564 277	18.1	75 272	28.1
Latin America						
Weighted average[4]		17.1		29.8	—	—
Regions						
Latin America	1 741 894	7.9	1 506 961	9.3	234 933	9.7
World	26 676 800	9.4	—	—	—	—
Industrialized countries	17 229 700	8.3	—	—	—	—

1. Bahamas, Barbados, Haiti and Nicaragua are excluded because of missing data.
2. Millions of 1980 dollars. Accumulated value from 1960 to 1982.
3. The instability estimate is shown after multiplying it by 100.
4. Weighted by the real value of the accumulated exports from 1980 to 1982.

Source: IDB estimates based on IMF and ECLA data.

very low total and extraregional instability, such as Brazil, have a substantially higher instability in their exports to the region. This indicates that the factors which generate the instability in some of the Latin American countries affect the intraregional exports of globally stable countries such as Brazil. Only Honduras shows a lower instability for its intra than its extraregional exports.

The instability of the regionally aggregated exports and of the total exports of each of the countries are generally lower than the instability measures for the extra and intraregional exports.[11] This shows that changes in extraregional exports are compensated, at least partially, with changes of opposite sign in intraregional exports and vice versa. This phenomenon is likely to be explained by the differences in the timing and intensity of the dollar exchange rate variations in every country and by similar changes in other export stimuli. For example, a country could be devaluing in real terms with respect to the dollar, while the rest of the LAC countries will also be doing so but to a higher degree; thus, the first country revalues its currency with respect to the rest of the region. This country's extraregional exports will be stimulated by the devaluation, while its intraregional exports are discouraged by its revaluation relative to the LAC countries.

The instability of the total exports of Latin America as a region, is remarkably lower than the weighted average of the instability of exports for each country.[12] This total export instability is also lower than that of the United States, the industrialised countries and the world as a whole, as well as lower than that of each Latin American country individually. This indicates that the exports of the Latin American countries are asynchronic, that is, at a given point in time, the observed deviation of one country's exports relative to its trend tends to be compensated by a similar deviation in the opposite direction of another countries' exports. As a result of this, the aggregate series for all the countries is more stable than the individual ones.

The asynchrony found can be caused by several factors, for example, when one country has a bad crop and lowers its coffee exports, that induces an increment in the exports of a competitor country. A strike in a copper mine of a country lowers its exports, but also promotes those of a different country. The prices of primary commodities are also asynchronic.[13] Thus, when the real export price of a main product for one country falls, there is the likelihood that the main product for another country increases its price. As will be seen below, another factor is the lack of synchronisation among the region's countries when they devalue and revalue their currency in real terms with respect to the dollar. This phenomenon explains an important proportion of the relative stability of the aggregate exports of LAC relative to the stability of its components.

ESTIMATION OF THE EXCHANGE RATE INSTABILITY

Table 7.2 shows the estimates of the instability of the real and nominal exchange rates of each LAC country *vis à vis* the US dollar and the rest of the region.[14] The LAC countries are shown according to their real dollar exchange rate instability, beginning with those with higher levels.

Nominal exchange rate instability

The exchange rate experience of the Latin American countries between 1960 and 1982 shows great diversity (see columns 3 and 4, Table 7.2). There are countries with highly unstable nominal dollar exchange rates and high annual average devaluation rates such as Chile, Argentina, Brazil, Peru and Uruguay. Other countries have had absolutely stable nominal dollar exchange rates such as El Salvador, Dominican Republic, Panama, Honduras, and Guatemala. There is also a set of countries which represent intermediate cases. Half of the countries, as well as the weighted average for the region, show a much higher instability in the nominal dollar exchange rate than the one found in the nominal effective exchange rate of the United States with the industrialised countries;[15] while the other half of the LAC countries show a lower instability.

The differences in the behaviour of the nominal exchange rates of the Latin American countries mainly reflects the behaviour of their respective domestic money supplies. The country variations in the over-all average growth rate of the domestic money supply explain 96 per cent of the long-term variation in their rates of growth in the nominal dollar exchange rates (Table 7.2, column 4). The instability of the nominal dollar exchange rate of each country (Table 7.2, column 3) also reflects, to a great extent, its reaction to the instability of the domestic money supply. However, the explanatory power of this relationship is somewhat less than the one just described, as the

Instability of Exports and Exchange Rates

Table 7.2 Exchange rate instability in Latin America and the Caribbean, 1960–82

	EXCHANGE RATES				
	REAL		NOMINAL		
	US dollar rate	LAC rate[1]	US dollar rate		LAC rate[1]
Country	Instability $(I)^2$	$(I)^2$	Variation $(I)^2$	$(V)^3$	$(I)^2$
United States	*9.4*[4]	*6.5*[5]	*8.7*[4]	*−0.25*[5]	*26.0*[5]
Latin America					
Argentina	32.2	31.0	117.7	60.6	25.0
Costa Rica	20.0	28.0	42.2	9.0	63.4
Chile	17.8	21.0	144.2	63.3	16.9
Uruguay	17.8	18.5	37.7	38.5	79.6
Colombia	14.9	11.4	6.2	10.8	81.7
Venezuela	14.5	12.5	9.4	1.1	82.1
El Salvador	13.3	6.5	0.0	0.0	20.4
Peru	13.3	17.8	58.3	15.8	84.1
Ecuador	12.8	12.3	8.3	3.2	0.8
Paraguay	12.4	17.5	2.4	0.3	77.3
Guyana	12.3	8.6	4.7	2.5	19.7
Mexico	11.4	9.7	30.6	6.9	66.5
Bolivia	11.1	15.3	29.4	7.9	79.5
Trinidad & Tobago	10.0	3.9	5.4	1.5	16.8
Guatemala	9.9	5.2	0.0	0.0	19.5
Jamaica	9.0	10.2	16.8	4.2	32.8
Brazil	8.8	16.6	58.0	36.6	27.1
Dom. Republic	7.8	7.5	0.0	0.0	64.1
Honduras	5.6	6.9	0.0	0.0	20.4
Surinam	4.4	5.4	1.5	−0.2	27.9
Panama	3.3	5.7	0.0	0.0	56.0
Latin America Weighted Average[6]	*14.0*	*15.3*	*32.7*	*—*	*86.1*

1. Units of national currency per unit of currency of the rest of Latin America.
2. Instability estimates by 100.
3. Average annual variation rate between 1960 and 1982.
4. Effective US exchange rate with the industrialized countries.
5. Effective US exchange rate with Latin America.
6. Weighted by the real value of the accumulated exports of each country to the appropriate destination from 1960 to 1982.

Source: Authors' estimations based on IMF data. See the methodology in the Appendix.

variations in the instability of the money supply between the LAC countries explains only 81 per cent of the variation in the instability of their nominal dollar exchange rates. Since the time unit used to measure instability is a year, the relation between monetary and exchange rate instability measures the reaction of the latter to the former within the year. The lag in the short-term adjustment is thought to be explained by the fact that governments use international reserve fluctuations and foreign capital flows to postpone the full adjustments required.

It can thus be argued that the long-term variations in the nominal exchange rates of each country, with respect to the rest of the region, primarily reflect the difference in the variations of that country's monetary supply relative to one of the rest of the region. Further, it can be argued that the instability of the nominal exchange rate of each LAC country with respect to the rest of the region (Table 7.2, column 5) reflects, to a great extent, the relative instability of its monetary value *vis à vis* that of the monetary supply of the rest of the region. However, such instability also has a component which is determined by the complex interrelation of the effects of the country's policy of delaying, in the short run, the exchange rate adjustment required by the money supply variations.

Instability of the real dollar exchange rate

Prices of goods and services in any country adjust rather quickly to monetary pressures, while in the short run the nominal exchange rates are frequently restricted in their adjustment by the economic policies of the governments. The instability of the real dollar exchange rate (Table 7.2, column 1) takes place because, in the short run, the government does not allow the nominal exchange rate to adjust itself to monetary pressures, which, however, cannot be avoided in the long run. This failure to adjust results in the fact that the weighted average of the real dollar exchange rate of LAC has an instability which is 50 per cent higher than the one shown by the real effective exchange rate of the United States *vis à vis* the industrialised countries. Similarly, the weighted average of the real exchange rates of each of the countries of LAC with the rest of the region is 65 per cent more unstable than the exchange rate of the United States with industrialised countries.

Despite the fact that the lack of short-term adjustment of the nominal exchange rates constitute a generalised behaviour among the countries of the region, there are some which have a high instability in the nominal exchange rates, which allows for a quick adjustment and, consequently, achieve a relatively stable real exchange rate. Such is the case of Brazil, which has the fourth highest instability rate in LAC for its nominal exchange rate while it has the seventeenth highest one for its real exchange rate, a level which is lower than that of the United States to the industrialised countries.

In spite of the Brazilian case, there is a positive correlation between the instability of the nominal and real exchange rates. However, this trend is not too strong as the variation of the instability in the nominal exchange rate explains only 34 per cent of that of the real exchange rate. Notwithstanding the fairly low explanatory power of this regression, its value is significantly different from zero.[16] These results indicate that the higher the monetary instability, the higher the pressures on the nominal exchange rates, and the higher the propensity of the authorities to avoid and postpone short-term adjustment in the nominal exchange rates. Thus, monetary instability produces an environment conducive to the instability in the real exchange rate.

Generally, as will be seen below, since real exchange rate instability has important negative effects on export stability, a relevant economic policy conducive to increase export stability consists in allowing a rapid adjustment of the nominal exchange rate to the fluctuations in the monetary supply. A complementary policy of monetary stability would facilitate the real exchange rate stabilisation policy.

Instability of the real exchange rate of each country with the Latin American and Caribbean region

There are two ways to estimate the instability of the effective exchange rate of each LAC country with respect to the rest of the region: one is the weighted average of the instability of each series, and the other is the instability of the series' weighted average.[17] The method used here is the latter one.[18]

The LAC countries have their currencies tied to the dollar. Thus, the intra-Latin American exchange rate is determined implicitly by the dollar exchange rates of each of the countries of the region.

There is a high empirical correlation between the instability of these two exchange rates, as variations in the instability of the real dollar exchange rate explains 75 per cent of the instability of the intra-LAC real exchange rate. Therefore, the higher the instability in the real dollar exchange rate of a country, the higher the instability of its intra-LAC real exchange rate. In other words, LAC countries which try to increase their intra-LAC trade through a decline of the exchange rate instability, can achieve a substantial part of this goal through the stabilisation of its US real exchange rate. However, the countries that have the highest US dollar instability in the region tend to transmit that instability to the intra-LAC exchange rate of other countries of the area. This phenomenon is clearly illustrated in the example of Brazil and Argentina, countries which have the most important intraregional trade in the area. During the 1960–82 period Argentina had the highest instability of the real dollar exchange rate among the countries of the region, while Brazil had one of the lowest ones. However, the instability of Brazil's real intra-LAC exchange rate is twice that of its real dollar exchange rate, since the Argentinian instability is transmitted to the exchange rate of these two countries. Therefore, to achieve stability in the real intra-LAC exchange, a country requires the co-operation of its trading partners within the area.

Asynchrony of the dollar exchange rate variations among the Latin American and Caribbean countries

Asynchrony is also found in the case of the exchange rate. Table 7.2 shows that while the weighted average of the real dollar exchange rate instability for the LAC countries is 14.0, the instability of the real effective exchange rate of LAC with respect to the United States is only 6.5, a level more stable even than the effective real exchange rate of the United States with the industrialised countries.

This finding indicates that, while some of the LAC countries revalue in real terms relative to the dollar, others devalue their currency simultaneously. Therefore, the real effective exchange rate of LAC with respect to the dollar is more stable than that of each individual country. In as much as exchange rate instability affects export stability, this indicates that the exports of LAC as a region should be more stable than those of each individual country.

Exchange rate asynchrony also generates some instability in the intraregional trade as it sometimes stimulates exports of country A to country B and other times stimulates the opposite flows.

ESTIMATION OF THE IMPACT OF THE EXCHANGE
RATE INSTABILITY ON EXPORT INSTABILITY

Equation (7.8) provided the basis to measure the importance of the exchange rate instability as an explanatory variable for export instability. This equation was the basis for a cross-section regression utilising country data. The instability data used are those that appear in Tables 7.1 and 7.2. The instability of the real dollar exchange rate was used to explain extraregional export instability, and the instability of the real LAC exchange rate was related to the instability of intraregional trade.

Unfortunately, data availability does not allow any estimations of the instability of the real price of intra- and extra-Latin American exports separately. However, omitting this variable in the regression is not likely to make the estimation of the parameter biased and inconsistent, as the correlation between the instability of the real exchange rate and that of the real export price is likely to be quite low during the period covered.[19]

The observation of Table 7.1 suggests that there is a negative relationship between export instability and export volume, and also that this relationship is not proportional.[20] Therefore, the volume of exports was used as a proxy in the explanation of the instability constant δ. This was done incorporating the term $\delta_B (1/VE)$ in the regression.

In a cross-sectional regression, the estimated values for α are the average of the elasticities for the countries. Because of this, an attempt was made to determine which country groups and which export destinations had equation parameters in equation (7.8) which were significantly different. The results of this attempt produced regression (7.9) in which the dependent variable is the instability of total exports, and the explanatory variables are: the instability of the exchange rate (parameter α) broken down into twocountry groups (α_i and α_{ii}); the instability of the set of other variables (parameter δ), where three country groups were found (δ_{A1}, δ_{A2}, δ_{A3}) plus a differential for the instability of intra-Latin American exports ($\Delta\delta_{ALA}$); and finally, the instability attributed to the export volume ($1/VE$).

$$(VM_x) = \delta_{A1} + \delta_{A2} + \delta_{A3} + \Delta\delta_{ALA} + \delta_B(1/VE) + \alpha_i^2(VM_{eri}) + \alpha_{ii}(VM_{erii}) \tag{7.9}$$

It was found[21] that the relationship between exchange rate and export instabilities was significantly different for two groups of countries. One has low elasticity ($\alpha_i^2 = 0.17$) and is made up mainly for the larger Latin American countries and by countries with high nominal exchange rate instability: Brazil, Argentina, Mexico, Colombia, Chile, Uruguay, Costa Rica and Paraguay. Another group of higher elasticity ($\alpha^2_{ii} = 0.73$) is made up by the rest of the countries. No differences were found for the exchange rate elasticity for intra- and extra-Latin American trade.

The instability of other variables (δ) was found to differ in three types of countries. The first one is made up by Brazil which has the lowest extraregional export instability ($\delta_{A1} = 0$). The second group has a similar composition to that of the low elasticity countries mentioned in the previous paragraph. This group obviously does not include Brazil, but includes the countries mentioned above plus Peru, Venezuela, and Trinidad and Tobago ($\delta_{A2} = 10.5$). The third group is made up for the rest of the countries of the region ($\delta_{A3} = 19.8$).

Furthermore, it was found that the instability of the set of other variables on intraregional exports added a large constant factor to the extraregional exports ($\Delta\delta_{ALA} = 14.4$). This factor did not vary for the different country groupings.

The relationship between the volume of exports and export instability was statistically very significant. However, its incorporation into the regression did not permit the elimination of the constants of instability from the set of other variables. In spite of the high statistical significance, the numerical importance[22] in the explanation of the export instability is in general low. However, export volume is an important explanatory variable for the intraregional export instability of some small countries such as Surinam, Panama, Paraguay, Honduras, Dominican Republic, Jamaica and Guyana.

Multiplying the observed real exchange rate instability of each country by the estimated parameters for each kind of exports, one obtains an idea of the quantitative importance of the real exchange rate instability in the explanation of the export instability. The results of this exercise indicate that the export instability for the weighted average of LAC which is attributable to that of the real exchange rate is similar, in absolute terms, for intra- and extra-LAC trade (6.2 and 6.8 respectively). These values represent 21 and 38 per cent respectively of the weighted average of the observed instability of exports from the region. These are important, although not very high percentages given the great magnitude of the average observed instability of exports from LAC. However, in a comparison of the magnitude of the export instability, attributable to that of the real exchange rate with an international norm such as the instability of the world exports of the United States, one finds that the first are 66 and 71 per cent of the second, respectively.

To what extent does the exchange rate asynchrony explain the exports asynchrony? Considering extraregional trade, we found that the export instability of the weighted average of LAC which is attributable to the exchange rate instability is 6.8. On the other hand, the estimation utilising the effective real exchange rate instability of LAC with respect to the dollar (6.5, see Table 7.2) would be 2.6.[23] Thus, there is a 4.2 difference. The weighted instability of extraregional exports was 17.7 (see Table 7.1). The instability of the aggregate extraregional exports was 9.3; the difference between these two figures is 8.4. Therefore, it could be said that 50 per cent of the difference between the weighted average of each country's instability and the instability of the aggregate exports of the region can be attributed to the effect of the asynchronic movement in the real exchange rate of the different LAC countries.

Looking at intraregional exports one finds that the weighted instability of the countries' exports was 29.8, while that for the aggregate was 9.7 (see Table 7.1). There is a difference of 20.1. The effective exchange rate of LAC with itself is by definition equal to one with an instability equal to zero. Therefore, the estimation of the weighted instability of the intra-LAC exports attributable to the exchange rate (which was estimated to be 6.2) is the difference attributable to the effect of the exchange rate asynchrony. This constitutes 31 per cent of the total difference.

CONCLUSIONS

The instability of the exports of the LAC countries is much higher than that of exports of the United States and the industrialised countries. Furthermore, the instability of the intra-LAC exports is a great deal higher. Simultaneously, the instability in the real dollar exchange rate of almost all the LAC countries and that of the real exchange rate of each of the countries with LAC is much higher than that of the effective real exchange rate of the United States with respect to the industrialised countries.

The exchange rate instability of the LAC countries explains a substantial proportion of the high intra and extraregional export instability. Thus, the exchange rate instability creates an important financial risk which affects commercial activities and which should have a negative effect on the growth of intraregional trade. The elimination of this obstacle to the growth of intraregional trade requires that the region's countries co-ordinate their real dollar exchange rate policies, in such a way that the real dollar exchange rate fluctuations are brought down below historically observed levels.

Even though exchange rate instability is an important factor in the explanation of the intra and extraregional trade instability, there is a large margin in these trade instabilities which is explained by other factors not included in this exercise.

The accumulated value exports and real dollar exchange rate instability of the different countries of the region show a diversity of experience. Thus, there are countries with a high, medium, and low instability. Brazil is a notable case, because this country has achieved a stability in the value of extraregional exports which is comparable to that shown by developed countries. This country, however, has not achieved the same results with respect to the intraregional exports because the instability found in each of the region's countries is partially transmitted to its trading partners. This implies that a joint action among several countries is necessary to stabilise intraregional trade in the area.

Time asynchrony is found both in reference to the exports of the region and to the dollar exchange rate. Because of this, the aggregate value of exports of the region and the effective regional exchange rates are a great deal more stable than the exports and the exchange rates of each country. The greater stability in the aggregate regional exchange rates explains an important portion of the greater stability in the aggregate regional exports.

Appendix

DATA USED

1. **Exports**

The Directions of Trade Statistics of the International Monetary Fund (IMF) were used to obtain the value of total, extra and intraregional exports of each of the region's countries. The exports of the United States, industrialised countries, and the world, were taken from the International Financial Statistics of the IMF. All those data provide figures in current US dollars.

The total and extraregional exports of the LAC countries were deflated to 1980 dollars by using the total exports index estimated by the Economic Commission for Latin America (ECLA). The intraregional exports were also deflated by the same index due to the non-existence of a specific index for those exports. The exports of the United States, industrialised countries, and the world, were deflated to 1980 prices using the respective price indexes estimated by the IMF.

2. Exchange rate

(a) *Dollar exchange rate*

The nominal dollar exchange rates come from the International Financial Statistics of the IMF which were complemented with additional information from other sources. The values used correspond to an annual average.

Since in many of the countries of the region there have been multiple exchange rates systems, the exchange rate chosen was the one considered as the most representative by the IMF (the r.f. series, in the IMF's terminology).

(b) *Real exchange rates*

These were obtained by deflating the nominal exchange rates by the available price indexes of international and domestic goods and services. In the case of the United States and the other industrialised countries the implicit GNP deflator was used. In the case of the LAC countries, the consumer price index was used as it was the only one available for the 1960–82 period for all countries. The price indexes used also measure average annual price levels.

(c) *Intra-LAC exchange rates*

The intra-LAC exchange rate of country A with respect to another one in the area such as country B, is the ratio between the dollar exchange rate of country A and the dollar exchange rate of country B (E_{AB}). This measures the units of country A currency which are exchanged for a unit of country B currency.

(d) *Effective exchange rates*

The exchange rate of each LAC country with respect to the rest of LAC is known as the effective exchange rate. In the case of country A, in year t, this exchange rate (E_{At}) is the weighted average of the exchange rates of this country with respect to each of the other LAC countries in that year (E_{AJt}):

$$E_{At} = {}^{\pi}_{J} E_{AJt}{}^{a_{AJ}}$$

where $\Sigma a_{AJ} = 1$; J = all Latin American countries except A.

The weight values used (a_{AJ}) were obtained utilising the total real value of the sum of imports and exports between country A and country J during the period 1960–82. E_{At} and E_{AJt} have a base of a 100 in 1980. This index is measured in units of domestic currency of the particular country per unit of currency of the rest of LAC countries.

The exchange rate of the United States shown in Table 7.2, is also an effective exchange rate. It is the average of the US exchange rate with respect to the industrialised countries, weighted by its exports and imports of goods to those countries during 1960-82.[24] The index base year is also 1980 and it is measured in units of foreign currency per dollar.

The exchange rate of the United States with respect to LAC is a similar concept. Its base year is 1980 and measures the units of LAC currency per dollar.

Notes

The ideas expressed in this essay are those of the authors, and do not necessarily reflect any policies of the Inter-American Development Bank. The authors thank Simon Teitel for his comments to a preliminary draft, and Maria del Pilar Tovar for her patience and efficient typing.

1. For example, United Nations, *Instability of Export Markets of Underdeveloped Countries*; Joseph Coppock, *International Economic Instability, the Experience After World War II* and *International Trade Instability*; Benton Massell, 'Export Concentration and Fluctuations in Export Earnings, A Cross Sectional Analysis' and 'Export Instability and Economic Structure'; Alastair MacBean, *Export Instability and Economic Development*; Guy Erb and Salvatore Schiavo-Campo, 'Export Instability, Level of Development and Economic Size of Less Developed Countries'; Peter Kenen, 'Exchange Rate Variability – Measurement and Implications'; Peter Kenen and Constantine Viovadas, 'Export

78

Table 7.A1 Effects of the real exchange rate instability on the export instability of Latin America and the Caribbean (1960–82) (The following table shows the results of the regression based on equation (7.9) of the text.)

FE1	FE2	FE3	FEL1	FEL2	FEL3	VFE2	VFEL	XACUM	ICA	ICB	VICB	DW	σ	R^2	$\bar{R}^2$
0.198	0.105	0.000	0.343	0.250	0.144	−0.093	0.144	135.3	0.738	0.170	−0.568	1.73	0.186	62.1	57.0
(3.55)						(1.76)	(2.91)	(3.63)	(1.88)		(1.72)		(1.24)		
0.5						5.0	0.5	0.5	5.0		5.0		10.0		

Notes:

FEi is the instability of extraregional trade determined by the set of other variables ($i = 1, 2, 3$ are groups of countries).

FELi ibid., for intraregional trade.

VFEL is the incremental variation of the intraregional trade instability relative to that of extraregional trade, which is caused by the set of variables. This variable does not differentiate among the country groups as the regression results showed that their differences were not significantly different from zero.

VFE2 is the incremental variation of the extraregional trade of the countries in group 2 relative to those in group 1. In the regression shown the value of FE3 was assumed to be equal to zero. Experiments using regressions without this restriction showed that the absolute value of VFE3 and FE1 were almost equal.

XACUM is the value of the parameter of the inverse of the accumulated value of exports for the 1960–82 period.

ICJ is the real exchange rate instability ($J = A$; B denotes the corresponding groups of countries).

VICB is the incremental variation induced by the exchange rate effect in the countries of group B.

DW is the Durbin–Watson statistic. σ is the regression residuals autocorrelation parameter. The existence of autocorrelation of residuals does not have any economic meaning in our case as it depends on the arbitrary order in which the countries' data are listed. The method was used to eliminate the bias in the significance level of regression parameters caused by this autocorrelation.

R^2 is the correlation coefficient. $\bar{R}^2$ is the correlation coefficient corrected by the degrees of freedom of the regression.

The t values are shown in parenthesis. The figures below them show the parameters' degree of significance.
The variables for which the t values are shown were used as independent ones. The values assigned to the other variables were calculated implicitly.

Instability and Economic Growth'; Constantine Glezakos, 'Export Instability and Economic Growth: A Statistical Verification'; Odin Knudsen, and Andrew Parnes, *Trade Instability and Economic Development*; P. Yotopoulos and J. Nugent, *Economics of Development*; Leslie Stein, 'Export Instability and Development: A Review of Some Recent Findings'; Elio Lancieri, 'Export Instability and Economic Development: A Reappraisal', and Ricardo Ffrench-Davis, 'Antiguas y Nuevos Formas de Inestabilidad Externa en América Latina: Fuentes, Mecanismos de Transmisión y Políticas'.

2. See Victoria S. Farrell *et al.*, 'Effects of Exchange Rate Variability on International Trade and Other Economic Variables: A Review of the Literature'.

3. Donald Coes, 'The Crawling Peg and Exchange Uncertainty'.

4. See Peter Kenen, 'Exchange Rate Variability – Measurement and Implications'; Richard Abrahms, 'International Trade Flows under Flexible Exchange Rates', and Marie and Jerry Thursby, *The Uncertainty Effects of Floating Exchange Rates: Empirical Evidence on International Trade Flows*.

5. See David Brodsky, 'Decomposable Measures of Economic Instability'.

6. It is assumed that a one-year interval is long enough so that the exporters could respond to the price stimuli observed during that year.

7. Z is generally a stable variable which is assumed to grow constantly at its long term rate of growth. However, the annual rate of capital utilisation in the exports is unstable, and depends on price incentives $(P^e_{rxt}.E_{rt})$, so that the impact that the instability in the utilisation of installed capacity has on exports is incorporated in the effect on those exports generated by price instability.

8. In reference to extraregional trade of the LAC countries, it can be argued that the first assumption is violated in some cases. The second assumption is plausible, especially for short periods (that is, one year) during which the monetary authorities can keep the exchange rate fixed when the income generated by exports changes. This can be done by modifying the level of reserves, capital inflows and outflows, and changing import restrictions.

9. The first part of the Appendix shows how the data were used and which were their sources.

10. This result is consistent with those of Alistair MacBean, *Export Instability and Economic Development*, and Guy Erb and Salvatore Schiavo-Campo, 'Export Instability, Level of Development and Economic Size of Less Developed Countries'.

11. Except in Ecuador, El Salvador, and Costa Rica – small countries with very high intraregional instability. In Venezuela, Brazil and the Dominican Republic the difference between total and extraregional instability is quite small.

12. This result is consistent with what Ffrench-Davis (1984) found for the 1951–79 period. Notice that extra and intraregional aggregated exports are also a great deal more stable than those of each country and than their weighted average.

13. Ricardo Ffrench-Davis, 'Antiques y Nuevos Formas de Inestabilidad Externa en América: Fuentes, Mecanismos de Transmisión y Políticas'.

14. The exchange rate of each country with the rest of the region measures the currency units from that country which are exchanged for a unit of currency of the rest of Latin America (see Appendix).
15. The effective exchange rate is the average of the exchange rate of a country with a set of other countries.
16. The F statistic is equal to 10.47, therefore the regression is significant at a 1 per cent level of significance.
17. See Anthony Lanyi, and Esther Suss, 'Exchange Rate Variability: Alternative Measures and Interpretation'.
18. Since the observations are annual, this period is sufficiently large to allow each country to adjust its supply of exports to the annual variations in the exchange rate. The method used takes into account this adjustment.
19. P^*_{rxt} obviously has some impact in the determination of E_{rt}. However, in the short run during the period considered, other variables such as the movements in reserves, changes in capital flows and in financial service flows, and the price and volume of imports of P^*_{rxt} are likely to have been a great deal more important in the determination of E_{rt}.
20. In a similar sense, Benton Massell in 'Export Concentration and Fluctuations in Export Earnings, A Cross-Sectional Analysis', finds a negative correlation between the gross national product (GNP) of a country and the instability of its exports.
21. Table 7.A1 in the Appendix discusses in greater detail the results of the regression.
22. The estimated value of δ_B times $(1/VE)$.
23. The parameters of the effect of the exchange rate on equation (7.9) were weighted by the participation of group i countries (40.4 per cent) and group ii countries (59.6 per cent) in the volume of total extraregional exports during the 1960–82 period. The parameter thus obtained (α^2) utilised for this estimation was 0.39.
24. United Kingdom, Austria, Belgium, Denmark, France, Germany, Italy, the Netherlands, Norway, Sweden, Switzerland, Canada, Japan, Finland, Iceland, Ireland, Spain, Australia and New Zealand.

References

Abrahms, Richard K., 'International Trade Flows Under Flexible Exchange Rates', *Economic Review*, Federal Reserve Bank of Kansas City, March 1980.
Brodsky, David A., 'Decomposable Measures of Economic Instability', *Oxford Bulletin of Economic and Statistics*, Vol. 42, No. 4, 1980.
Coes, Donald V., 'The Crawling Peg and Exchange Uncertainty', in John Williamson (ed.) *Exchange Rate Rules: The Theory, Performance and Prospects of the Crawling Peg* (New York: St Martin's Press, 1981).
Coppock, Joseph D., *International Economic Instability, The Experience After World War II* (New York: McGraw Hill, 1962).

Coppock, Joseph D., *International Trade Instability* (Westmead: Saxon House, 1977).

Erb, Guy F. and Salvatore Schiavo-Campo, 'Export Instability, Level of Development and Economic Size of Less Developed Countries', *Oxford Bulletin of Economics and Statistics*, Vol. 31, No. 3, 1969.

Farrell, Victoria S. *et al.*, 'Effects of Exchange Rate Variability on International Trade and Other Economic Variables: A Review of the Literature', Board of Governors of the Federal Reserve System, Staff Studies no. 130, Washington, DC, December 1983.

Ffrench-Davis, Ricardo, 'Antiguas y Nuevas Formas de Inestabilidad Externa en América Latina: Fuentes, Mecanismos de Transmisión y Políticas', in Moshe Syrquin and Simon Teitel, *Comercio, Estabilidad, Tecnología y Equidad en América Latina*, Inter-American Development Bank, 1984.

Glezakos, Constantine, 'Export Instability and Economic Growth: A Statistical Verification', *Economic Development and Cultural Change*, July 1973.

Kenen, Peter B., 'Exchange Rate Variability – Measurement and Implications', Memorandum prepared for Consultive Group on International Economic and Monetary Affairs (US Treasury, Princeton, N.J.: Princeton University, Dept of Economics, International Finance Section).

Kenen, Peter B. and Constantine S. Viovadas, 'Export Instability and Economic Growth', *Kyklos*, Vol. 25, No. 4, 1972.

Knudson, Odin and Andrew Parnes, *Trade Instability and Economic Development* (Lexington: D.C. Heath & Co., 1975).

Lancieri, Elio, 'Export Instability and Economic Development: A Reappraisal', *Banco Nazionale del Lavoro Quarterly Review*, June 1978.

Lanyi, Anthony and Esther C. Suss, 'Exchange Rate Variability: Alternative Measures and Interpretation', *Staff Papers*, IMF Vol. 24, No. 4, 1982.

MacBean, Alastair I., *Export Instability and Economic Development* (London: George Allen & Unwin Ltd, 1966).

Massell, Benton F., 'Export Concentration and Fluctuations in Export Earnings, A Cross Sectional Analysis', *American Economic Review*, Vol. 54, No. 2, 1964.

Massell, Benton F., 'Export Instability and Economic Structure', *American Economic Review*, Vol. 60, No. 4, 1970.

Stein, Leslie, 'Export Instability and Development: A Review of Some Recent Findings', *Banco Nazionale del Lavoro Quarterly Review*, September 1977.

Thursby, Marie C. and Jerry G., *The Uncertainty Effects of Floating Exchange Rates: Empirical Evidence on International Trade Flows* (Colombus: Ohio State University Press, 1981).

Yotopoulos, P. and J. Nugent, *Economics of Development* (New York: Harper & Row, 1976).

United Nations, *Instability of Export Markets of Underdeveloped Countries* (New York, 1952).

8 Growth, Investments, and the Specific Role of Fiscal Policies in Very Small Developing Economies

Mario I. Blejer

This paper discusses some of the analytical aspects related to the implementation of fiscal and other related macroeconomic policies in the context of very small developing economies. The presentation is divided into three sections.

The first section discusses the economic characterisation of very small economies which differentiates them from other types of developing countries, and which conditions the effectiveness of their economic policies, as well as their ability to generate enough domestic investments and/or attract foreign capital.

The second section elaborates on the role and the functions of fiscal policies in developing countries in general, while the third considers the specific role that fiscal and other related macroeconomic policies can play in the smallest of the developing countries.

THE ECONOMIC CHARACTERISATION OF VERY SMALL ECONOMIES

Although many attributes can be used to define the economic concept of a small economy, it has been frequently argued that when the smaller of the developing countries are taken as a group, two main criteria stand out: population and the size of the country's gross domestic product (GDP). Since the size of the GDP is a variable that could widely fluctuate over time and across countries owing to valuation problems, as well as to oscillations in external terms of trade, it seems more proper to follow the population criterion and include in the group of so-called ministates those countries with a population of about one million inhabitants. Following such somewhat arbitrary criterion, many of the countries of the Caribbean region and of the Pacific Basin would qualify. We observe that many of those countries display a number of economic characteristics which may have important implications for the evaluation of their economic policies. Those implications may result in the need to use an economic framework of analysis which does not share the same features as the standard models applied to larger developing countries, and may call for the application of alternative concepts when designing and implementing economic policies.

In general, very small economies can be classified into a special category because they share a number of specific characteristics. For example, geographical isolation (particularly in the case of small island economies), an extremely narrow production base that results in marked diseconomies of scale, endowments of natural resources concentrated in a few commodities, and a relatively small base for the development of highly sophisticated financial structures. As a consequence of these conditions, ministates have been characterised by a number of common patterns in the nature of their economic development. The most prevalent is the *extremely high level of openness of both their goods and capital markets*. Indeed, very small economies have been shown to be largely open to international trade and to display a relatively large degree of capital mobility. This combination of small size and high degree of openness has had two notable consequences – an unusually large export dependence with an extreme vulnerability to international market fluctuations, and highly ineffective monetary and exchange rate policies. Such ineffectiveness is reinforced by the apparent optimality of adopting a policy of fixing or at least of keeping largely constant, the effective value of the exchange rate. The effects of these elements, for macroeconomic policies as well as for sustained economic growth, will be analysed following a discussion of some additional implications of a large degree of openness.[1]

Evidence of the openness of ministates on the trade side has been compiled by Galbis,[2] and this indicates that the ratio of imports to GDP in most ministates exceeds 50 per cent, a proportion far higher than that in larger countries of similar level of development. Evidence of the same type can be obtained for exports. In addition, it is observed that trade openness tends to increase with the level of development more quickly in ministates than in larger countries.

Such a high incidence of international trade has important consequences. In the first place, foreign influences have a large and rapid effect on domestic prices and domestic production. This is so because, in addition to the almost automatic effect of foreign prices on the price of tradables, further price repercussions will rapidly take place in other sectors through wage adjustments and direct substitution effects which affect the prices of nontradable goods. Therefore, movements in the aggregate price level will tend to be dominated, in the absence of exchange rate changes, by foreign price developments. Exchange rate changes will have effects similar to those of foreign prices, and will produce immediate and strong effects on domestic prices. A devaluation, for example, would immediately increase the price of tradables and, given the openness of the economy, would be swiftly transmitted to the aggregate price level. In other words, domestic prices in ministates would tend to be almost completely dependent on foreign price developments and would, fully and almost without delay, reflect the fluctuations in the nominal effective exchange rate.

With respect to their capital markets, the degree of openness of ministates is a less straightforward concept. The degree of capital market openness could be measured by calculating ratios of gross international capital flows into a country to its domestic financial flows or to some scale measure like GDP. A variety of evidence,[3] strongly suggests that small countries are more open to external capital flows than larger ones. Geographical location, historical links with large and advanced countries (resulting in long-term official capital inflows and also, in many cases, in direct foreign investments), as well as policies attempting to convert some of the ministates into off-shore financial centres appear to have determined the relatively high volume of capital flows in some of these countries. However, to a much larger extent than in the case of goods trade, domestic policies have been implemented with the stated objective of reducing free capital mobility. Exchange and capital controls have been prevalent in many small countries together with differential taxation of domestic and foreign assets. However, given the characteristics of these economies and their large dependence on foreign trade, the effectiveness of the controls has been low and, in practice, capital flows have been only negligibly discouraged.

A consequence of capital openness is that many ministates have shown a high degree of capital market integration with the rest of the world. Such integration is reflected in the lack of persistence of large differentials between domestic and foreign interest rates.[4] Two factors work, however, to prevent a perfect convergence of interest rates. One is the tendency of the domestic monetary authorities to establish domestic interest rate ceilings at artificially low levels. The other is the high incidence of capital market imperfections in ministates, reflected by the ability of financial institutions given the limited size, to form cartels with power to control domestic interest rates. Policies of interest rate repression have not been, however, very successful in attaining their objectives because capital flows are particularly difficult to control in ministates, with traditionally strong and developed links with international markets. Many of those policies were, in fact, abandoned under the pressure of market forces. Therefore, although not total or perfect, capital openness and capital mobility are central factors characterising the conditions, and to some extent the constraints, under which economic policy in ministates operates.

Two main consequences arise from the high degree of openness in goods and capital markets. In the first place, substantial trade openness is often accompanied, to a large extent, with export dependency and of export concentration in a few commodities, whose prices may be subject to large fluctuations in world markets. Export dependence tends to expose ministates to substantial real shocks which may have extremely serious effects on their economic activity. A change in production techniques in the rest of the world, for example, can reduce the demand and the prices of commodities in which ministates largely specialise, forcing them to restructure, sometimes under difficult circumstances, their own lines of production. Given the importance of the export sector, such external shocks can have serious effects which spread quickly throughout the over-all economy. Moreover, since external price and demand changes can be abrupt and unexpected, they may not leave too much time for adaptation, and therefore carry a high cost of adjustment. In addition, ministates may not be in a position to obtain sufficient external commercial financing which would enable them to carry out the adjustment process quite painlessly.

This high sensitivity of the over-all economy to external shocks makes the maintenance of a relatively higher level of international reserves, compared with larger countries, desirable. In larger and more diversified economies, the domestic impact of external shocks on employment and output is probably smaller than in ministates and therefore the social benefits of smoothing those shocks are lower. In ministates, the costs of holding foreign reserves, and of implementing

policies conducive to the preservation of an adequate level of creditworthiness which allows cheap and easy access to foreign resources,
should be weighed against the high social benefits of being able to
finance properly the adjustment to changing world conditions. In
other words, the importance of maintaining easy access to foreign
resources (either through own or borrowed reserves) is greater in
ministates than in larger countries, and such access should be maintained for precautionary reasons rather than for financing, even
temporarily, expansionary domestic financial policies.

A second important consequence of the economic openness of
ministates is the severe limitation that it imposes – particularly
because of their high degree of financial capital mobility – on their
ability to carry out effective monetary policies. This ineffectiveness is
largely compounded by the apparent optimality of adopting a fixed
exchange rate in ministates. Such optimality, or at least the empirical
preference of ministates to follow a policy of maintaining a rather
stable exchange rate is based, again, on a number of specific characteristics of small economies. In the first place, given the very high
incidence of foreign trade, changes in the domestic price of tradable
goods will rapidly feed back into the nontradable goods prices via
their effect on wages and other cost variables. Although such an effect
of exchange rate changes on nontradable prices is common in larger
economies as well, the magnitude of the effect is likely to be more
pervasive and faster in very open countries, given the higher *direct*
impact of the exchange rate on the aggregate price level and the higher
visibility of those changes. For instance, in situations of extreme
openness, labour unions tend to bargain for wage conditions in terms
of foreign currency values, thereby preventing the emergence of any
real-wage effect arising from a devaluation. In these circumstances,
exchange rate depreciations will mostly tend to affect the rate of
inflation with little or no gain in output.

Under these conditions, exchange rate policy has little effect on the
relative price of tradables versus nontradables, and is an inefficient
instrument for balance of payments adjustments. Large exchange rate
movements would be required in ministates to achieve a given
corrective result with the obvious negative impact on price stability.

In addition to the low efficiency of exchange rate policies in
attaining balance of payments objectives, there is in ministates a
strong argument, based on the thinness of their foreign exchange
markets, for fixed exchange rates. Such thinness, combined with the
high concentration of their export and financial markets, increases the

risk of destabilising speculative activities which may result in extremely wide and distorting exchange rate fluctuations.

The central outcome of this combination of economic openness and exchange rate inflexibility is the lack of independence, and therefore the high ineffectiveness, of monetary policy. Theory tells us that, under a fixed exchange rate system, perfect capital mobility renders monetary policy completely ineffective with respect to output and prices even in the short run, since all the effects of monetary policy leak through the balance of payments.[5] With less than perfect capital mobility, however, some effects may take place. An expansionary domestic credit policy, for example, may have some immediate domestic results even with a fixed exchange rate. Part of the increase in credit would leak to the balance of payments through capital outflows and imports, but the remainder would induce some expansion in domestic aggregate demand. The latter would probably induce domestic inflation, although output might also rise initially. This temporary gain in output, however, might be more than offset by a subsequent reduction, as adjustment policies would eventually have to be applied to arrest the ensuing loss of international reserves.[6]

The reduced scope for monetary policy in ministates arising from their high degree of openness, and their constraints to allow exchange rate flexibility, imposes on these countries a clear need for financial discipline and, in particular, for fiscal and budgetary restraint. This is one of the issues to be discussed in more detail in the last section. Here, it is important to stress the sources of the structural limitations that their small size imposes on macroeconomic policy management. These limitations are not easy to avoid.

Theoretically, by imposing measures that curtail capital mobility, the authorities could regain to some extent the effectiveness of monetary policy as a domestic stabilisation tool. But, as noted earlier, this would be practically unattainable in ministates because of their strong links with, and dependence on, the outside world, and because the effects of monetary policy measures would then tend to be offset by current account flows, a consequence of their high trade openness. Therefore, restricting capital mobility would, in fact, only shift the burden of adjustment to the current account and to the level of output. It follows that ministates would be ill advised to adopt restrictive policies and to introduce controls that attempt to reduce the degree of capital mobility in order to regain monetary policy independence.

THE ROLE OF FISCAL POLICY IN DEVELOPING COUNTRIES[7]

Generally speaking, fiscal policy should be designed with the purpose of attaining social objectives and of maximising social welfare. The priorities that the authorities attach to different possible aims should, therefore, reflect the choices which emerge from social consensus. However, when fiscal policies are actually implemented and analysed, more concrete concepts should be used. In this sense, it is possible to define four specific functions which can be fulfilled through the use of fiscal instruments: (a) allocation of resources; (b) redistribution of income; (c) macroeconomic stabilisation; and (d) the promotion of a high and sustainable rate of economic growth. Although the importance of each one of these functions may vary in different contexts, fostering growth can be regarded as the central and most important function of fiscal policy in developing countries. But growth cannot be achieved, nor sustained, without a stable environment. Therefore, the importance of fiscal policy in the context of stablisation efforts cannot be overlooked.

The justification for the implementation of fiscal policies for resource allocation was originally based on the recognition that society requires the provision of certain goods and services that the private sector is unwilling to supply because production, although socially valuable, is privately unprofitable. These are the so-called public goods which include defense, justice, public health, and so on. However, governments have been playing a much more active role in the area of resource allocation, either by directly using resources in specific areas of economic activity beyond the provision of public goods, or by creating the incentives which redirect privately-owned resources toward particular sectors in which governments have shown interest to develop.

Regarding the second role commonly attributed to fiscal policy, namely, the redistribution of income, it can be argued that it is not an intrinsic function of the government to play a role affecting the particular income distribution which would result from the free working of the economy. It is clear, however, that fiscal instruments are frequently applied to manipulate the outcome of market forces, promoting particular goals regarding the distribution of income or even wealth. This is so because, as mentioned above, fiscal policies are used to attain the objectives implied by the social consensus, including the desired distribution of national income.

When evaluating the role of fiscal policies in developing countries it can be argued, however, that both of the above-mentioned functions, resource allocation and income redistribution, should be related to the role of the government in promoting growth. One of the most important links between resource allocation and economic growth is found in the amount of total economic resources devoted to investments and to the accumulation of productive capital. Although the relationship between the level of investment and the rate of economic growth is by no means a straightforward one, it is quite well established that sustained economic development is not possible without sufficient capital accumulation. In this area, fiscal policy may have a two-fold role to play. As was previously mentioned, government policies could be designed to directly allocate resources toward selected uses but, further, they could also provide the environment and the incentives which would motivate the private sector to direct its own resources toward specific areas.

Clearly, direct public sector investment in infrastructure and in other types of public goods should be considered as beneficial, as a whole, within the context of economic development. However, in many cases, government investments may tend to reduce or discourage private sector investment. This is the so-called 'crowding out' phenomenon by which the private sector is effectively displaced from investment activities through a number of mechanisms. In a couple of recent studies,[8] a private investment function was derived which takes into account the effects of government policies, particularly in financial credit and government capital formation. The study attempts to make an empirical distinction between public investment, which is related to the development of infrastructure and which is likely to be complementary with private investment, and other types of government investment, which may in fact substitute for private capital formation. Empirical results indicate that (a), if the flow of domestic credit available for the private sector is reduced for whatever reason, including a larger absorption of credit by the public sector to finance budget deficits, private investment, and consequently growth prospects, would tend to decline and (b), an increase in the infrastructural component of government direct investment would raise private investment (probably by increasing its potential profitability), but similar increases in other types of government investment (such as in sectors producing marketable output) appear to crowd out, and therefore would reduce, the level of private sector investment.

With respect to the redistributional role of fiscal policy in the context of growth efforts, it is indeed possible to maintain that in some cases a more even distribution of income achieved through budgetary mechanisms will have a possible effect on the ability of an economy to increase and sustain its rate of economic growth. For example, a more even income distribution would mean a larger market for domestically produced industrial commodities. Moreover, a more equitable income distribution may increase productivity and incentives and even increase the total rate of private savings. This is, however, an empirical proposition.

With respect to the third role of fiscal policy, that is, stabilisation, it should be considered within a general macroeconomic framework of income determination. For many, stabilisation is the most important short-run objective of fiscal policy. In the developed countries the meaning of stabilisation is relatively unambiguous. For these countries, keeping the actual level of national income close to the potential is the most important economic objective. Potential output implies a relatively small level of frictional or structural unemployment and substantial price stability. Thus stabilisation policy is understood to be the manipulation of aggregate demand in order to achieve at the same time full employment and price stability. The balance of payments, although at times the object of some concern, is not generally the major objective of stabilisation (or short-run fiscal) policy. In developing countries, on the other hand, stabilisation as an objective loses the simple and well-defined nature that it exhibits in the developed countries. First, the concept of potential level of income is not easily definable since a substantial proportion of the labour force is underemployed, rather than openly unemployed. Secondly, for technological reasons there is not a clear correspondence between full employment of labour and full employment of capital. Thirdly, the balance of payments cannot be ignored as movements toward full employment may be stopped by limitations of foreign exchange. Finally, the evidence of many countries indicates that the implicit assumption of stabilisation policy – that prices will remain relatively stable as long as actual national income is lower than potential – simply does not hold.

It is possible, however, to relate stabilisation policies to the fiscal functions in the process of growth. In the first place, capital accumulation and growth can be maintained only in a stable environment, which conveys the credibility and confidence required to encourage domestic and foreign investments, as well as other types of financial commitments from the private sector. In this sense, fiscal policies designed to achieve and maintain macroeconomic stability play an indirect, but important, role in the process of development. In a more general sense, however, it is possible that stabilising fiscal policies directed primarily to correct temporary disequilibria may have long-run implications for the growth of the economy. Changing the level and composition of taxation to influence the level of aggregate demand is an example of a short-run stabilisation measure. This may, however, stimulate the demand for certain locally-produced commodities, and the enlargement of their market may bring about significant and long-lasting reductions in their average cost of production.

The last function, namely the direct promotion of economic growth, is probably the most important, particularly for the developing countries. As stressed by Tanzi,[9] fiscal policy can promote growth in a variety of ways. It can (a) increase the rate of savings, (b) channel these savings into more socially productive uses, (c) increase what has been called productive consumption, that is, education and health, (d) discourage nonproductive and extravagant consumption and investment, such as expensive cars, and luxury housing, (e) reduce inefficiency throughout the economy, (f) remove various bottlenecks, (g) reduce or eliminate growth-retarding distortions introduced by other public policies, and (h) eliminate, or at least reduce, distortions in the relative prices of the factors of production.

In many discussions about the role of fiscal policy with regard to growth, the emphasis has generally been on (a) the tax structure that would be the least damaging (or the most favourable) to growth, (b) the role of the government in providing the basic economic and social infrastructure for development, and (c) the role of the government in mobilising savings. The last role appears to be the most important, especially in the context of very small countries. Fiscal policy in developing countries should not be limited to creating economic and social infrastructures, but should be extended to insuring that the level as well as the quality of private investment, both domestic and foreign, be as high as needed. To attain this objective an appropriate level of savings must be generated, favourable conditions should be developed to provide the incentives for the internal reinvestment of savings, and lastly, a proper climate should be created to encourage foreign entrepreneurs to invest in the country. An important requisite for this to occur is the presence of proper functioning financial and capital markets. Without an efficient capital market, the government must aim at improving other mechanisms for attracting and channelling savings to productive investments.

It would certainly be desirable for the developing countries to have financial institutions that worked smoothly and efficiently to promote economic development. Unfortunately, many developing countries do not have the benefits of such institutions. There is then a particular and rather obvious role that the government of these countries can perform to alleviate some of the shortcomings associated with the absence of a capital market. First, the government can itself invest a rather substantial share of total savings, as has been done in Latin America in the past three decades. Secondly, it can construct some sort of proxy for the capital market. This particular role would provide an argument for a planned *budgetary surplus*. In other words, the government should aim to set its total tax revenues and its total expenditure (both current and capital) at a level that would yield an over-all surplus, which could then be made available on a competitive and nonconcessionary basis to the private sector, as well as to public enterprises. This would provide the government with a powerful and flexible tool that would facilitate, to a considerable extent, the allocation of private investment along efficient lines. That such an approach is possible is shown by the Japanese example in the decade after the Meiji Restoration (1868) and in the period following the Second World War. Thus, the availability of credit financed by surpluses in the government budget is an integral part of fiscal policy. But, unlike incentives and controls, it puts in the hands of the government an instrument that is exceedingly flexible. Through the use of this instrument, resources can be directed toward productive investments carried out by foreign and domestic private entrepreneurs and toward those with high social significance. In this way the government, in addition to increasing the level of savings, would stimulate entrepreneurship, could attract foreign resources, and thus affect the quality and not just the quantity of investment.

In fact, however, many developing countries have had substantial deficits that have generally been financed either by borrowing from the public (and more often from foreign institutions) or by borrowing from their central banks. These polcies have reduced the availability of resources which could be used for investment in the private sectors (financial crowding out) and often has had inflationary consequences that have distorted the financial structure of the countries, generated serious balance of payments difficulties, and retarded the development of a capital market. A relatively tight fiscal policy, together with a liberal monetary or credit policy, is likely to create the most favourable atmosphere for economic development.

CAPITAL INVESTMENT AND FISCAL POLICY IN THE SMALLEST OF DEVELOPING COUNTRIES

Although most of the roles that public sector policies could fulfil in the smallest of the developing economies do not differ in substance from the roles played in larger countries, the more specific problems and circumstances of the very small economies indicate that the importance of some fiscal policy functions, as well as the emphasis that they should receive, may certainly be different than in other developing countries.

The discussion in the second section concluded that by virtue of their high degree of trade and financial openness and of their constraints on exchange rate flexibility, very small economies are likely to benefit little, if at all, from carrying out an active monetary policy. Owing to the structural economic factors characterising the ministates, monetary policy, and particularly the attempts to manage the money supply, is practically ineffective either for stabilisation and adjustment or for allocative and distributional purposes.

In addition to this important limitation to the ability of the ministates to conduct economic policy, there are some deep-rooted structural conditions that exist, very much independently, of any macroeconomic policy that may be implemented. Very small open economies tend to be much more globally affected by exogenous developments in the commodity and financial markets of the large countries to which they are tied through trade and capital flows. Although open economies of all sizes are subject to, and have to absorb the impact of, external events, ministates are particularly vulnerable to supply shocks since the small size of their markets usually forces them to rely on a very reduced number of production and export activities. This sensitivity arising from the external sector is compounded by the technological characteristics of modern trade that require an extremely large and complex transport and communication infrastructure. Producers in very small countries do not have, in general, access to such technology (or it may prove to be economically nonviable given the share of the market that they may command) and, therefore, they are left at a competitive disadvantage in the world market.

To overcome their disadvantages as well as to reduce the impact that external shocks may have on the domestic economy, these countries must look for ways to diversify their economic activities into dynamic sectors where economies of scale play a less important role or where they have some type of natural resource advantage. This could include light manufacturing for export, creating export processing zones, developing tourism, and the setting up of off-shore financial centres.[10] But the diversification into these more dynamic sectors requires a substantial volume of new investments, given the need to develop a new productive base and to create a different trade infrastructure which includes credit systems, information and marketing networks, shipping arrangements, and so on. The problem is, however, that the small production scale allowed by domestic markets does not induce large investments in modern capital stock, because in many cases the domestic market serves as the basis for the development of export-oriented industries. But, probably, the most important problem is that, even in the presence of investment demand, very small economies may lack the proper capital market structure needed to mobilise domestic savings and, despite their openness, their smallness and remoteness may not be attractive to foreign investors. In addition, local entrepreneurs may not be able to mobilise enough venture capital in the international financial markets.

These two specific aspects of the very small economies, namely the very limited scope of monetary and exchange rate policies, and the importance of reducing the impact of external shocks by inducing sizeable capital investments needed to promote economic diversification, dictate a clear set of priorities for the management of fiscal policies.

The point of departure should be the recognition that monetary policy cannot be the centre-piece of any stabilisation or allocative effort. Very small countries should rely on stable effective exchange rates in their pursuit of domestic stabilisation goals and, therefore, they have to implement accommodating monetary policies designed to maintain the stability of the exchange rate. For that reason, ministates have to be especially careful to avoid large public sector deficits which will largely complicate, under their limitations, the proper conduct of exchange rate and monetary policies. Expansionary fiscal policies and substantial budgetary imbalances would lead to excessive external public sector borrowing or to the inability of the central bank to control the rate of growth of domestic credit, or both. A fixed exchange rate system, however, commits the authorities to moderate credit expansion to avoid balance of payments difficulties. Excesses in domestic credit creation arising from the need to finance fiscal deficits would rapidly leak through the trade and capital accounts, resulting in balance of payments deficits and in the loss of foreign reserves (or in an increase in foreign indebtedness). Ultimately, this would force the abandonment of the exchange rate rule leading to a vicious circle of currency depreciations and inflation with the consequent loss of international creditworthiness and its attending sequel: lack of flexibility to cope with future structural adaptation. It is, therefore, a fact arising from their structure that in the very small economies the link between budgetary imbalances, domestic credit expansion, and the balance of payments, is particularly strong. For that reason, governments in these countries are well advised to be especially concerned with their effort to prevent budgetary excesses which would lead to domestic credit policies inconsistent with long-term monetary and exchange stability.

The importance of avoiding fiscal policies that lead to balance of payments disequilibria may be more acute in the ministates since, as discussed above, they face a more serious need to rely on owned or borrowed foreign reserves in order to smooth the impact of external shocks. This is so because these shocks appear to have a more dramatic impact on the smaller economies. It is only through the implementation of a responsible and well-balanced fiscal policy that the access to an adequate level of foreign resources can be assured.

An additional consideration, which strongly points to the optimality of preserving fiscal balance and even of generating budgetary surpluses in very small open economies arises from their structural combination of factors already discussed. While they have an especially acute need to induce capital investments in a number of dynamic sectors in order to reduce their oversensitivity to external shocks, they also face more serious constraints than other countries in their ability to mobilise domestic and foreign savings owing to the thinness of their domestic financial markets and, very likely, their limited access to foreign financial resources.

Given these factors, there will be a particularly high return to policies which promote the mobilisation of savings. If a smoothly functioning capital market does not exist to deal with this problem, then it should be the responsibility of the government to try to develop one. To do so is generally a long-range enterprise. In the meantime the government has only the option of providing a kind of proxy for the capital market. As stressed by Tanzi[11] this may be a very important function of fiscal policy which has not received the attention it deserves, and it provides an argument for a planned budgetary surplus in the current account, in excess of what the government needs to spend itself for direct investment. In other words, the government should aim to set the tax burden at a level which would leave a surplus that could be made available to the private sector and even to the public enterprises; this would provide the government with an extremely powerful tool which would make possible, to a considerable extent, the allocation of private investment in the desired pattern.

Several surveys carried out in many developing countries have shown, beyond any doubt, that lack of foreign investment and the inability on the part of many enterprises and individuals to obtain credit is a serious obstacle to development. This problem is likely to be particularly serious the smaller the size of the economy. It is, therefore, probable that *credit* incentives will be extremely useful, especially for the creation of new enterprises, an important condition in the process of economic diversification. Although *tax* incentives may also play a role, they are likely to be less effective in the over-all economy. Tax incentives, by increasing the liquidity of the already established enterprises, may facilitate their development, but normally will not help very much the potential enterprises or the individuals who do not have access to funds for the fixed initial investment. Credit incentives, on the other hand, will have an impact in both areas.

Thus, credit incentives financed by surpluses in the government budget should be a crucial component of fiscal policy in very small economies. But, unlike tax incentives, they put in the hands of the government an instrument which is exceedingly flexible. Through the use of this instrument, resources can be channelled toward investments which are considered to have high social significance. In this way the government would in fact be acting as a proxy for the capital market; it would, in addition to increasing the level of savings, affect the quality of investment and may reduce the negative domestic impact of external shocks.

Notes

The views presented are the sole responsibility of the author and do not necessarily reflect any policies of the International Monetary Fund.

1. For a complete model, and a comprehensive analysis of the economics of ministates, see Vincente Galbis, 'Monetary and Related Policies in Ministates'.
2. Vincente Galbis, ibid.
3. See, for example, Whitman (1969) and Galbis (1984).

4. On financial instruments of similar characteristics after adjusting for differential risk.
5. This is the central message of the monetary approach to the balance of payments (see Harry G. Johnson, 'The Monetary Approach to the Balance of Payments', and the International Monetary Fund, *The Monetary Approach to the Balance of Payments*).
6. On this temporary tradeoff between inflation, output, and the balance of payments, see Mario I. Blejer, and Roque B. Fernandez, 'On the Output-Inflation Tradeoff in an Open Economy: A Short-Run Monetary Approach'.
7. For a more detailed and complete treatment of the issues discussed in this section, see Vito Tanzi, 'The Role of Fiscal Policy in Developing Countries'.
8. See Mario I. Blejer, and Mohsin S. Khan, 'Public Investment and Crowding Out in the Caribbean Basin Countries'. The crowding-out effects of public investment in the context of a number of small countries in the Caribbean Basin is studied in Mario I. Blejer, and Mohsin S. Khan, 'Government Policy and Private Investment in Developing Countries'.
9. See Vito Tanzi, 'Fiscal Policy, Keynesian Economics and the Mobilization of Savings in Developing Countries'.
10. See Benito Legarda, 'Small Island Economies'.
11. Vito Tanzi, 'The Role of Fiscal Policies in Developing Countries' and Vito Tanzi, 'Fiscal Policy, Keynesian Economics and the Mobilization of Savings in Developing Countries'.

References

Blejer, Mario I. and Mohsin S. Kahn, 'Government Policy and Private Investment in Developing Countries', *International Monetary Fund, Staff Papers*, Vol. 31, June 1984.
Blejer, Mario I. and Mohsin S. Kahn, 'Public Investment and Crowding Out in the Caribbean Basin Countries', in Michael B. Connolly and John McDermott (eds) *The Economics of the Caribbean Basin* (New York: Praeger Publishers, 1985).
Blejer, Mario I. and Roque B. Fernandez, 'On the Output-Inflation Tradeoff in an Open Economy: A Short-Run Monetary Approach,' *The Manchester School*, June 1978.
Galbis, Vincente, 'Monetary and Related Policies in Ministates', *Savings and Development*, Fourth Quarter, 1984.
International Monetary Fund, *The Monetary Approach to the Balance of Payments* (Washington, DC: International Monetary Fund, 1978).
Johnson, Harry G., 'The Monetary Approach to the Balance of Payments', in his *Further Essays on Monetary Economics* (London: Allen & Irwin, 1972).
Legarda, Benito, 'Small Island Economies', *Finance and Development*, Vol. 21, No. 2, 1984.

Tanzi, Vito, 'The Role of Fiscal Policy in Developing Countries', *Akron Business and Economic Review*, 1971.

Tanzi, Vito, 'Fiscal Policy, Keynesian Economics and the Mobilization of Savings in Developing Countries', *World Development*, Vol. 4, Nos 10/11, 1976.

Whitman, Marina von Neumann, 'Economic Openness and International Financial Flows', *Journal of Money, Credit and Banking*, Vol. 1, No. 4, 1969.

Part III
Central America

9 The Economic Crisis in Central America

Clarence Zuvekas

The focus of this paper will be the macroeconomic situation of the Central American countries, rather than US policy toward this troubled region. The large volume of US economic assistance to the region, of course, makes it impossible to ignore the role of this assistance in the over-all macroeconomic picture. However, it will not be the theme around which I will structure this paper. I will define Central America in the traditional sense, that is, the five countries of Costa Rica, El Salvador, Guatemala, Honduras, and Nicaragua.[1]

INTRODUCTION

The attention given to recent political events in Central America has sometimes obscured the fact that the countries of the region are experiencing their most severe economic crisis since the 1930s. Per capita incomes have fallen significantly since 1978, and this decline continued in 1984.[2]

The causes of the current economic crisis are both internal and external. Internally, armed conflicts in El Salvador and Nicaragua have resulted in considerable destruction of economic infrastructure and productive capacity in industry and agriculture. These countries have also lost valuable human resources, both as direct casualties of the conflicts and through emigration. Costa Rica's growth has been constrained by the burden of large external debts accumulated through excessive borrowing. Guatemala, with relatively little external debt, and traditionally sound fiscal policy, suffered from an unwise spurt of expansionary fiscal policy at the beginning of the current decade. A similar development has occurred in Honduras. All of the countries of the region, to one degree or another, are constrained by policy rigidities which have made it difficult for them to make a desirable adjustment in their trade patterns. Past policies, which have emphasised production for a limited, protected, domestic or regional market, are not appropriate in today's environment. To earn more foreign exchange, the region must expand and diversify its exports to markets outside of Central America.

External events have contributed even more to the economic crisis. The recession in the industrial economies in 1980–82 sharply drove down the prices of the region's primary commodity exports, and also lowered the demand for its actual and potential industrial exports. The second oil price shock of 1979–80 sharply raised the costs of a key industrial input which must be supplied almost entirely through imports, given the region's negligible petroleum production. At the same time, external debt-servicing obligations rose rapidly, partly because of the heavy borrowing done in the mid- and late 1970s to maintain economic growth after the first oil price shock in 1973–4, and partly because of the unexpectedly high interest rates which prevailed in the early 1980s, as the industrial countries adopted corrective policies to achieve their own economic stabilisation. The countries of Central America have also faced difficulties in acquiring new short- and medium-term credit, as banks and other private lenders have become worried about political and economic conditions in the region as well as their own relative portfolio exposure there.

The economic deterioration in the region has caused unemployment and underemployment to rise to alarmingly high levels, and the incidence of poverty has grown. Despite concerted efforts by most governments in the region to deal with their problems through austerity programmes and improved policies, policy reforms have been incomplete and near-term economic prospects are not bright. Economic recovery will be especially difficult for Costa Rica and Nicaragua, which have large external debts, and all five countries face discouraging medium-term price prospects for export crops such as coffee, bananas, and sugar, on which they depend heavily.

THE EXPERIENCE OF THE 1960s AND 1970s

The current economic crisis in Central America contrasts sharply with the generally favourable economic performance of the region during the 1960s and most of the 1970s (see Table 9.1). Between 1960 and 1978, per capita Gross National Product (GNP) grew at an average annual rate of 2.5 per cent, matching the Alliance for Progress target. Over this same period, trade among the Central American countries, stimulated by the Central American Common Market (CACM), grew

Table 9.1 Central America: selected socioeconomic indicators, 1960 and 1978

	Population at mid-year			GNP per capita			Life expectancy at birth (years)		Infant mortality rate[b]		Primary school enrolment ratio[c]	
	Millions		Annual growth rate	1978 US dollars		Annual growth rate						
	(1960)[a]	(1978)	(1960–78)	(1960)	(1978)	(1960–78)	(1960)	(1978)	(1960)	(1978)	(1960)	(1978)[d]
Costa Rica	1.2	2.1	3.0	860	1540	3.3	62	70	80	28	96	111
El Salvador	2.6	4.3	2.9	480	660	1.8	50	63	n.a.	60	80	77
Guatemala	4.0	6.6	2.8	540	910	2.9	47	57	n.a.	77	45	65
Honduras	1.9	3.4	3.2	390	480	1.1	46	57	130	118	67	89
Nicaragua	1.4	2.5	3.1	560	840	2.3	47	55	n.a.	37	66	92
Total/ Average[e]	11.1	18.9	3.0	540	840	2.5	49	60	n.a.	70	65	81

(a) Extrapolations based on growth rate trends reported in this table.
(b) Deaths per 1000 births, ages 0–1.
(c) Number enrolled in primary school as percentage of age group.
(d) Data are for 1977.
(e) Weighted by population.
n.a. not available.

Source: World Bank (1980: Annexe Tables 1, 17, 21, and 23).

from only US$33 million to US$863 million. There were also significant gains in health and education indicators:

Life expectancy at birth rose from 49 years to 60;
The infant mortality rate fell from more than 100 per thousand live
    births to 70; and
The primary school enrolment ratio rose from 65 per cent of the
    primary age group to 81 per cent.

Not all of the socioeconomic in indicators, however, were favourable:

Central America's population, for example, grew during the 1960s
and 1970s at an annual rate of 3.0 per cent, rising from 11.1 million in
1960 to 18.9 million in 1980. A rapidly growing population results in
an age structure heavily weighted toward dependent age groups
(particularly persons under 15 years of age), and this places considerable pressure on governments to increase spending for education,
health, and other social services. Where population density is high,
there are also pressures on the land which result in environmental
deterioration, rural landlessness and near landlessness, and rural-to-
urban migration. Population density is especially high in El Salvador,
about 225 persons per square kilometre (580 per square mile), more
than three times the figure for any other country in the region. One of
the results of this pressure on the land, beginning decades ago, was
considerable migration of Salvadorans across the Honduran border.
This movement of population into the region's poorest (but relatively
land-abundant) country was a major factor in the Honduran–Salvadoran war of 1969, one of the consequences of which was a crippling
of the Central American Common Market, generally regarded as
having had a successful first decade. Population density is also high in
the Guatemalan highlands, though this is masked by a national figure
which includes large stretches of sparsely populated (and not very
fertile) land.

Another serious problem during the 1960s and 1970s was income
distribution. Although it is difficult to determine trends because of the
limited extent and poor quality of the available data, the bulk of the
evidence suggests that income inequality in the region was relatively
high in 1960 and remained so throughout the 1960s and 1970s. This
was true even for Costa Rica, which is often cited as a model of
equitable development. Costa Rica's reputation, nevertheless, is still
well deserved: what income distribution measures did not capture was

a widespread expansion of health and educational services, as well as a degree of equality of opportunity to participate in the economic, social, and political life of the country that was not present in the rest of the region.

THE DIMENSIONS OF THE ECONOMIC CRISIS, 1978–84

The economic downturn in Central America began at different times in different countries. The first sharp decline was in *Nicaragua*, where the Gross Domestic Product (GDP) fell by 9 per cent in 1978 and by 26 per cent in 1979 as a result of that country's civil war. A substantial part of this loss was recovered in 1980 and 1981, but since then the economy has spluttered. Further recovery has been made difficult by a large external debt, the reluctance of the private sector to invest in the face of growing government controls over the economy, and a lack of management and policy-making skills in the new government. The GDP in 1983 was still 18 per cent below the 1977 level, and about 29 per cent below in per capita terms. There is unlikely to be any economic growth in 1984.[3]

El Salvador began its economic slide in 1979, but the really sharp declines occurred in the next three years. There was no further economic deterioration in 1983, but also no improvement. The GDP in 1984 was 23 per cent below its 1978 peak, and in per capita terms the decline has been about 30 per cent. A modest growth rate of about 1.5 per cent was estimated for 1984, despite very high levels of economic assistance from the United States.[4] The Salvadoran business community's outlook is becoming more positive, but a strong revival in economic activity is constrained by the continuing armed conflict, political uncertainties surrounding the 1985 legislative elections, relatively poor price prospects for the country's principal commodity exports, and sharply reduced opportunities to export manufactured products to the other Central American Common Market countries.

In *Costa Rica*, the GDP growth rate fell steadily after 1978 but did not turn negative until 1981. The total decline in economic output in 1981 and 1982 exceeded 11 per cent, and while positive growth was restored in 1983, the growth rate was less than 1 per cent.[5] Per capita GDP, which peaked in 1979, has fallen by a cumulative total of 18 per cent. For the rest of the decade and probably into the 1990s, the principal constraint on Costa Rica's economic recovery will be the country's oppressive external debt burden, one of the highest in the world in per capita terms (more, for example, than Brazil's or Mexico's). Costa Rica borrowed heavily in private capital markets in the late 1970s and early 1980s to finance, not only capital projects, but current expenditures as well. Interest rates on these short- and medium-term loans were contracted on variable terms, so that Costa Rica's interest obligations rose along with world interest rates. In July 1981 the country formally suspended both principal and interest payments on its external debt, and it was not until 1983 that a rescheduling agreement was completed. Further reschedulings will be necessary if the country is to maintain its debt servicing obligations without further restricting imports to what its leaders regard as politically impossible levels.

Although Costa Rica has received substantial economic assistance in the last few years from the United States – which not long ago was considering 'graduating' the country out of its aid programme – a rapid and sustained economic recovery will depend fundamentally on increased exports. Since prospects are not bright for traditional agricultural exports – such as coffee, bananas, and sugar – and markets elsewhere in Central America for Costa Rica's manufactured exports will be slow to recover, there is a strong case for a major push to promote new exports to markets outside the region. Indeed, this applies to all of the Central American countries.

Honduras, which had been the slowest growing Central American country between 1960 and 1978, nevertheless had experienced a dramatic improvement in its fortunes in the mid- and late-1970s. As late as 1979, its GDP growth rate was an impressive 6.8 per cent, the highest in the region. But in 1980 and 1981 GDP growth fell below the country's 3.2 per cent population growth rate, and in 1982 and 1983 it was negative. The cumulative decline in per capita GDP between 1979 and 1983 was 11 per cent and a further drop is anticipated in 1984.[6] Honduras remains the poorest country in Central America, and it has the weakest administrative, managerial, and entrepreneurial skills. It has also acquired an external debt problem, with debt servicing now accounting for close to 30 per cent of export earnings. Still, Honduras's debt problem is not as serious as those of Costa Rica or Nicaragua, and with good management it can be kept from becoming more burdensome.

In the short term, the most serious constraint to sustained economic recovery is a fiscal deficit that the government has been unable to bring under control. In 1983 the total public sector deficit amounted to 12 per cent of GDP, and only a slight improvement is likely in 1984. If the fiscal accounts can be brought closer into balance, and economic management improved in other respects, Honduras has an opportunity to achieve faster economic growth for the remainder of the decade than most other Central American countries.

Guatemala's economic performance since 1978 has been similar to that of Honduras. Per capita GDP peaked in 1980 and since then has declined by 12 per cent. In a departure from its traditionally conservative fiscal policies, Guatemala borrowed heavily abroad to finance fiscal deficits in 1980 and 1981, and its debt servicing obligations are now similar to those of Honduras. Nevertheless, Guatemala's per capita public external debt – about US$200 at the end of 1982 – is still relatively low (Costa Rica's, by way of comparison, is about US$1400).

In summary, all of the countries of the region have experienced declines in per capita GDP of at least 11 per cent and most, if not all of them, will experience further declines in 1984. (See Tables 9.2 and 9.3 for details). Even if per capital GDP can start growing at an annual rate of 2.5 per cent beginning in 1985, it will be, at least, until the end of the decade before previous levels can be attained.[7]

It would take even longer at this rate of growth to reverse the deterioration that has occurred since 1978 in the employment situation. Although data on unemployment and underemployment rates are either unavailable or not very reliable, it is clear that double-digit open unemployment rates are the norm. El Salvador's rate is estimated to be as high as 30 per cent or more. With labour forces in the

Table 9.2   Changes in real gross domestic product in Central America, 1979–84 (per cent)

	1979	1980	1981	1982	1983	1984[a]
Costa Rica	4.9	0.8	− 2.3	− 9.1	0.8	3.3
El Salvador	− 7.1	− 9.0	− 9.5	− 5.4	0.0	1.5
Guatemala	4.7	3.7	0.9	− 3.5	− 2.0	− 1.0
Honduras	6.8	2.8	0.3	− 1.1	− 1.4	1.0
Nicaragua	− 26.4	10.0	8.5	− 1.4	2.9	0.0

(a)   Estimates.

Sources: Official country national accounts statistics as reported in various international agency documents.

Table 9.3   Changes in real per capita gross domestic product in Central
America, 1979–84[a] (per cent)

	1979	1980	1981	1982	1983	1984[b]
Costa Rica	2.1	−1.5	−4.6	−11.4	−1.6	0.7
El Salvador	−4.1	−10.5	−11.0	−7.0	−2.2	−0.8
Guatemala	1.7	0.8	−1.9	−6.3	−4.6	−3.8
Honduras	3.5	−0.3	−2.8	−4.2	−4.4	−2.2
Nicaragua	−28.1	7.4	6.0	−3.8	0.5	−2.3

(a)   Population figures are from IDB (1984) except for El Salvador, where
I have made adjustments to account for population losses due to war
deaths and emigration.
(b)   Estimates.

Sources: Official country national accounts statistics as reported in various
international agency documents.

Central American countries growing by 3 per cent a year or so, it
takes a significantly positive rate of economic growth – probably
around 5 per cent – just to provide full-time productive employment
to new labour force entrants.

While the economic declines in El Salvador and Nicaragua are
attributable in large measure to the effects of their armed conflicts, for
the region as a whole, probably the most important factor has been
the deterioration in export earnings, which fell from US$4.9 billion in
1980 to US$3.8 billion in 1983 (see Table 9.4), a decline of 22 per cent
in current dollars and 35 per cent after adjusting for inflation.[8] To put
these figures into perspective, the balance-of-payments assistance
provided by the United States to Central America in Fiscal Year 1983
covered only 18 per cent of the gap between the 1980 and 1983 levels
of export earnings.[9] The drop in export earnings reflects a sharp
decline in commodity export prices and the slow recovery in the
industrialised countries from the 1980–82 world recession, as well as
the collapse of trade within the Central American Common Market.
Between 1980 and 1982, exports of the Common Market countries to
each other fell by 31 per cent.

The Central American countries responded to the decline in their
foreign exchange earnings, and to the accompanying blow of the
second oil price shock, by increasing their borrowings from abroad,
particularly from commercial banks. In this way they sought to
maintain the flow of imported inputs needed to keep production from

Table 9.4   Merchandise exports, 1978–83 (millions of US dollars)

	1978	1979	1980	1981	1982	1983
Costa Rica	864	942	1001	1003	871	870
El Salvador	802	1132	1075	798	704	737
Guatemala	1092	1221	1520	1299	1200	1092
Honduras	626	756	850	784	676	704
Nicaragua	646	616	450	500	408	411
Total	4030	4667	4896	4384	3859	3814

Source: International Monetary Fund, *International Financial Statistics* (1978–82 and 1983 for Nicaragua); unpublished preliminary figures for 1983 (Costa Rica, El Salvador, Guatemala, and Honduras government sources).

declining. But they did not foresee the depth of the world recession, or the steep rise in world interest rates that would add to their debt service burdens. Public and publicly guaranteed debt contracted by the Central American countries rose from US\$5.2 billion at the end of 1978 to US\$11.8 billion at the end of 1982 (see Table 9.5).[10] Interest and principal payments on this debt rose from US\$453 million in 1978 to US\$711 million 1982, not counting arrears in payments due in 1982, especially by Costa Rica.

As the economic crisis deepened, the Central American countries lost virtually all of their foreign exchange reserves, and on a net basis they moved into negative reserve positions – that is, their short-term foreign exchange liabilities exceeded their foreign exchange assets. Capital flight, of an undetermined but clearly large magnitude,

Table 9.5   Public and publicly guaranteed debt, 1978 and 1982 (end-of-year; millions of US dollars)

	Total		Disbursed	
	1978	1982	1978	1982
Costa Rica	1618	3394	950	2475
El Salvador	647	1335	334	801
Guatemala	745	1510	304	1119
Honduras	976	2044	595	1385
Nicaragua	1199	3472	971	2810
Total	5185	11 755	3154	8590

Source: World Bank (1984).

accelerated the reserve loss. Much of this outflow was motivated by the unsettled political conditions in the region.

Economic stabilisation programmes

With all of the Central American countries having difficulties in meeting payments on their debts, their access to new loans and credits has been greatly diminished, further aggravating their foreign exchange woes. One solution to the problem – albeit an unpopular one – was the adoption of economic stabilisation programmes that would give countries access to the resources of the International Monetary Fund (IMF). An IMF-approved programme, in addition to bringing in the IMF's own resources, makes it possible for countries to begin renegotiating their debts with public and private creditors, and in some cases also facilitates new loans and credits from private sources. The US government has encouraged the adoption of stabilisation programmes, and in some cases has made such programmes conditions for its own sharply increased balance-of-payments assistance to Central America, which rose from only US$10 million in Fiscal Year 1980 to US$363 million in Fiscal Year 1983 and US$480 million in Fiscal year 1984.[11]

All of the Central American countries have signed at least one agreement with the IMF since 1979:

Costa Rica in March 1980 and December 1982;
El Salvador in June 1980 and July 1982;
Guatemala in November 1981 and August 1983;
Honduras in June 1979 and November 1982; and
Nicaragua in May 1979.

These agreements committed the Central American countries signing them to adopt fiscal and monetary restraints, and sometimes exchange-rate adjustments, in order to lower the demand for imports and otherwise to bring their internal and external accounts into balance. Austerity measures are never popular, but as the IMF's Managing Director, Mr de Larosière, has stated,

economic adjustment is inescapable. No country can live permanently beyond its means. ... When a government can no longer resort to the expedient of borrowing abroad in order to postpone adjustment ... what happens if it refuses to take corrective economic action? In such a case adjustment occurs anyway but without outside assistance and in a disorderly manner. Such a process is often characterized by extremely severe import restrictions and by high inflation. Experience has shown that the combination of import restrictions and inflation induced by a lack of fiscal and monetary discipline leads to a continual deterioration of employment and production in these countries.

In other words, Mr de Larosière continues:

while [stabilisation] programs do entail sacrifices, the austerity born of adjustment must be compared to the alternatives.[12]

To correct fiscal imbalances, Central American countries have reduced current and capital expenditures and raised taxes. Costa Rica has been the most successful in this respect, lowering its combined public sector deficit from more than 14 per cent of GDP in 1981 to just over 3 per cent in 1983. Other achievements under the Costa Rican programme have included:

A reduction in the inflation rate from 82 per cent in 1982 to 11 per cent in 1983;[13]

Debt rescheduling agreements with public and private external creditors;

A virtual unification of the foreign exchange market and achievement of relative exchange-rate stability; and

Conversion of a short-term foreign capital outflow into a net inflow.

Elsewhere in Central America, stablisation programmes have been less successful. Honduras and El Salvador have been faced with pressures to increase military expenditures, making it more difficult to reduce the size of their fiscal deficits. The last IMF agreement in Honduras was terminated prematurely, and El Salvador completed its drawings only after a considerable delay. Guatemala's current agreement seems to be in trouble because of disappointing fiscal performance. ∶ ·

Notwithstanding the slow progress towards adjustment in most Central American countries – Nicaragua included – significant expenditure cuts have been made in a number of development programmes. Implementation of many investment projects important for long-term economic growth has been slowed or even halted. Progress in health care and education has also suffered. The quality and coverage of health services, on the whole, has very likely declined. In education, the quality if not the coverage of instructional services has probably deteriorated.[14] Thus both physical and human capital formation have received setbacks from which there can be only partial recovery once economic conditions improve. To varying degrees in the Central American countries, there is some scope for increasing taxes as an alternative to expenditure reductions. But the political support for tax increases has been weak, particularly in view of the depressed economic conditions in the region and the increasing frequency of presidential and legislative elections.

PROSPECTS FOR ECONOMIC RECOVERY

In the absence of major changes in the international economic environment, in domestic economic policies, and in political and security conditions in the region, the prospects for economic recovery in Central America are not especially bright. Some rough projections I made a year ago, with moderately optimistic assumptions about the domestic and international environments, showed an average annual growth rate of GDP of 4.4 per cent between 1984 and 1990. In per capita terms this is a growth rate of 1.6 per cent, well below the 2.5 per cent performance achieved between 1960 and 1978. Such a growth rate would not bring down presently high rates of unemployment and underemployment, and it would permit only slow progress in alleviating poverty.

Economic growth in the industrialised world

One of the most important international determinants of economic growth in Central America is the rate of economic growth in the industrialised countries. During the 1980–82 world recession, the Central American countries suffered considerably from falling commodity prices and a decline in world trade.[15] The recovery in the world economy in 1983–4, on the other hand, resulted in an increased demand by the industrialised countries for imports from developing countries, and world commodity prices rose by 21 per cent from November 1982 to March 1984.[16] Thus, as economist William Cline[17] has pointed out, the benefits of higher-than-expected economic growth in the industrialised countries have more than offset the effects on developing countries of rising interest rates earlier in 1984. However, there are signs that world economic growth is slowing down: since March world commodity prices have fallen by 8.3 per cent; economic growth in the United States slowed to an estimated annual rate of 2.7 per cent in the third quarter of 1984; and other industrialised countries are concerned that their slower economic recovery will be threatened by interest rates that are still very high in real terms.

Short-run changes in world economic activity, as already noted, have a direct effect on the price of Central America's commodity exports. But commodity price movements are also affected by longer-term supply and demand considerations. In this respect, it is noteworthy that coffee and bananas, two of Central America's leading exports, are projected to face falling real prices during the remainder of the 1980s. The outlook for sugar is also poor. Although there is likely to be an increase in the presently very low world market price of about 5 cents a pound – well below production costs – a return to the high sugar prices of a few years ago is unlikely. World sugar inventories are nearly 50 per cent of annual consumption, or about twice as high as is considered desirable. With sugar consumption declining in the United States, the likelihood that Central American countries can secure higher quotas and prices in the more favourable US market – where the price is now about 22 cents a pound – does not appear to be strong. Indeed, the US sugar quota just established for Fiscal Year 1985 is 16 per cent below the previous year's quota. Since sugar, coffee, and bananas together accounted for about 50 per cent of Central America's merchandise exports during the three years 1981–3, their poor price prospects for the rest of the decade constitute a major impediment to rapid economic recovery.

The Central American common market

Another major obstacle to economic recovery is the weakness of the Central American Common Market. As noted earlier, trade among the five Central American countries fell by 31 per cent between 1980 and 1982. Countries with a deficit position in the Common Market as

114 *Economic Crisis in Central America*

a whole, or with some individual countries, lack the hard currency needed to settle their negative balances through the Common Market's clearing house mechanism.[18] Their trade partners are thus reluctant to let existing debts build to even higher levels. Trade had also been disrupted by temporary quantitative restrictions imposed by some countries on imports from their partners. The Central American countries have been seeking external assistance to finance higher trade flows, but in itself such assistance would only be a palliative. Unless the countries of the region undertake fundamental reforms in the areas of tariff and exchange-rate policies, the conditions that have given rise to large intraregional trade imbalances will still be present, and the need for more hard currency through increased exports to markets outside the region will not have been addressed.

The debt service burden

Another major constraint to economic recovery is the region's external debt service burden, which is heaviest in Costa Rica and Nicaragua and lightest in El Salvador. Actual interest and principal payments on the public and publicly guaranteed external debt absorbed 18 per cent of the region's merchandise export earnings in 1982; this does not include required payments that were postponed and later rescheduled. The 18 per cent figure also excludes principal and interest payments of an undetermined amount on the private sector's external debt. High interest rates on debts to foreign commercial banks continue to make it difficult for the Central American countries to meet their debt-servicing obligations, and most observers do not foresee a significant reduction in world interest rates in the near term. An estimated US$4 billion in interest payments are due between 1984 and 1990.[19] Additional debt reschedulings are likely to be necessary, and it is not clear if commercial banks will be willing to make these reschedulings on terms as favourable as those recently negotiated with Mexico. Given these debt problems, the Central American countries will find it difficult to obtain much in the way of new loans from foreign commercial banks until their economic performance significantly improves.

Possible sources of foreign exchange

With relatively limited medium-term export prospects for traditional agricultural commodities, and for a revival of trade in manufactured products within the Central American Common Market, and with only limited opportunities for new borrowings from foreign commercial banks, what other sources of foreign exchange are potentially available to the Central American countries to help them meet their debt service obligations and also increase the flow of imported inputs needed for economic recovery? There are four major possibilities:

private foreign investment;
a return of Central American expatriated capital;
foreign aid from bilateral and multilateral organisations; and
exports of non-traditional products to markets outside the region.

Private foreign investment and the repatriation of capital

Private foreign investment and reflows of Central American expatriated capital have been discouraged by the still troubled political and security environments in the region. Even Costa Rica, which has been largely untouched by armed conflicts or military build-ups, has been affected by a generalised skittishness on the part of many potential investors about anything Central American. In El Salvador, despite a noticeable improvement in the business community's confidence since the summer of 1984, including some softening in its traditional distrust of the incumbent President's economic policies, a number of business executives are reportedly postponing investment decisions until after the March 1985 legislative elections.[20] In Honduras, there is a widespread fear that the country may become more deeply embroiled in conflicts in neighbouring countries. Guatemala is still trying to shed its image as an international outcast because of its human rights record. There is very little private investor interest in Nicaragua, where the state's role in the economy has been steadily growing under the current government.

In short, significant inflows of private foreign capital and returning domestic capital will depend, to a large degree, on a lessening of political and military conflicts. Even under present conditions, however, these capital flows would be larger if the economic policy environment were more favourable. Policy reforms would stimulate investment, not only in existing industries and agricultural sector pursuits, but also in many new products, which since 1984 have been able to enter the United States duty-free under the trade provisions of the Caribbean Basin Initiative.[21]

An improved political and security environment would, of course, significantly accelerate new investments. How soon such an improvement might come about is difficult to predict. In the meantime, foreign aid will probably continue to play a major role in cushioning the region's economic decline and laying the groundwork for economic recovery. In the opinion of many observers and actors on the scene, increased foreign aid would also help make the political and security climate more propitious for investment, both domestic and foreign. This clearly is the assumption made by the National Bipartisan Commission for Central America, or Kissinger Commission, as it is commonly known, although the Commission was careful to point out that US economic assistance should be provided 'in conjunction with social and political change and progress'.[22]

Well before the Kissinger Commission presented its report, there was a quantum jump in the level of US economic assistance to Central America. Total US economic assistance to the region – including Development Assistance funds (for specific project activities), Economic Support Funds (mainly to bolster the balance of payments), and agricultural commodities provided under PL 480 Titles I and II – rose from US$175 million in Fiscal Year 1980 to US$607 million in Fiscal Year 1983 and approximately US$760 million in Fiscal Year 1984.[23] Thus the United States has provided the lion's share of the increased economic assistance to Central America during the current economic crisis. But as noted earlier, US balance-of-payments assistance in Fiscal Year 1983 offset less than a fifth of the real drop in the region's annual export earnings between 1980 and 1983.

Given the prospects for only a modest rate of economic recovery during the rest of the decade, even under moderately optimistic assumptions, the Kissinger Commission called for even higher levels of US economic assistance. Including guarantees, insurance, and other contingent liabilities as well as direct appropriations, the Commission recommended a total package of assistance of US$8 billion over the 5-year period beginning in 1985 (including assistance to Panama and Belize), an annual rate roughly double the Fiscal Year 1983 figure.[24]

The goal of this proposal was to restore 1980 levels of per capita income by the end of the decade. This was said to require GDP growth rates of about 6 per cent or 3 per cent per capita, by the end of the decade;[25] but depending on how quickly such a rate could be achieved, the 1980 levels of per capita GDP still would not likely be regained by the target date in all countries.

The Kissinger Commission was well aware that increased US assistance of this magnitude – even if supplemented by large increases in assistance from other official bilateral and multilateral agencies – would be insufficient by itself to achieve the economic growth targets. As the Commission put it

> ultimately, a solution of Central America's problems will depend on the Central Americans themselves. They need our help, but our help alone will not be enough. Internal reforms, outside assistance, bootstrap efforts, changed economic policies – all are necessary and all must be coordinated.[26]

Exports of non-traditional products

This leads us back to the last item on my list of potential foreign exchange sources, namely, increased exports of non-traditional products to markets outside Central America. In the 1960s and 1970s the Central American countries chose not to follow an export-oriented pattern of development but rather to pursue an import-substitution strategy within the context of their common market. While this strategy was successful in the 1960s, and all countries seemed to benefit from the common market arrangement, the gains were relatively modest.[27] By the end of the decade, new import-sutstitution opportunities were limited by the small size of the regional market, and many existing import-substitution industries remained relatively inefficient, though protected behind the regional tariff wall.

This situation continued to prevail during the 1970s. The industries that did have some success exporting to extra regional markets tended not to be those which got their start by producing for the Central American market, but rather those which had favoured access to the US market under Sections 806.30 and 807 of the Tariff Schedule of the United States,[28] and duty-free access under the US Generalised System of Preferences scheme, which came into effect at the beginning of 1976.

The Caribbean Basin Initiative has provided for duty-free entry into the United States of a number of additional products, but recent studies of Central American industry have concluded that relatively few industrial products are now produced in the region at a low enough cost to be competitive, or even potentially competitive in the near term, in the US market. The best opportunities, rather, are for products not currently produced in the region. Thus export diversification depends more on new investments than on a reactivation of unused productive capacity already in place. While the political and security environment is holding up some new investment, other investment is being held up by domestic economic policies that discourage exporting to markets outside of Central America.

Before looking at these policies, a few words are in order on why an export-oriented strategy would be attractive for Central America.[29] A considerable body of research over the last decade has indicated that an export-oriented growth strategy tends to result in faster economic growth, greater employment creation, and quite likely a more equitable income distribution than the kind of import substitution strategy followed since 1960 by the Central American countries.[30] The most successful countries following an export-oriented strategy have been in Asia, particularly the so-called 'Gang of Four': Hong Kong, Singapore, South Korea, and Taiwan. These countries have been able to cope with the unfavourable international economic environment of the 1980s much better than have the Central American countries.[31]

For some Central American countries, perhaps the greatest economic obstacle to substantially increased non-traditional exports is an overvalued exchange rate. Exporters whose currency is valued at more than it is really worth receive fewer units of their own currency than they should for every dollar or other convertible currency they turn in to their central bank. An overvalued exchange rate also has the effect of encouraging imports, further aggravating the pressures on the balance of payments. An exchange rate adjustment – either through a formal devaluation or through a more temporary arrangement – would create some initial inflationary pressures, but these can be held in check if governments bring their fiscal accounts under control.

The structure of the Common Market, and in particular the region's Common External Tariff, also discourages exporting outside of Central America by making production for the protected regional market more profitable and less risky. A proposal to lower and otherwise reform the Common External Tariff, in order to encourage more efficient production for the regional market as well as production for overseas markets, has been in discussion for several years; but the unsettled political and economic conditions in the region have made countries reluctant to adopt a fundamental policy reform of this type. Even if the existing proposal were adopted, it is not clear that it goes far enough to meet its professed objectives.

Other policy reforms that would encourage a shift into production for overseas markets include a revision of tax incentive structures; easier access to foreign exchange for exporters who need imported inputs; better access to credit; and a reduction in the paperwork associated with exporting.

If these policy reforms were undertaken, the Central American countries have the potential to increase their exports of non-traditional products to markets outside the region by 15 to 20 per cent a year, or perhaps more, provided that the industrialised countries achieve moderately rapid growth for the rest of the decade and do not yield to additional protectionist pressures. The results would not be initially spectacular in absolute terms, since the Central American countries are starting from low bases. But by the end of the decade the cumulative effect of five years or so of rapid non-traditional export growth would provide a strong dynamic impulse to the over-all growth of the region's economies.

In summary, export-led growth, based on Central America's own efforts, can provide a stronger, healthier, and longer-lasting economic recovery than a strategy which leans heavily on foreign aid or debt relief without attacking fundamental structural problems. But an export-led strategy will not automatically produce a more equitable pattern of growth. Thus appropriate safeguards are needed if economic recovery in Central America is to be accompanied by greater equity.

Notes

The views expressed in this paper are my own and should in no way be interpreted to represent the policies of the Agency for International Development or any other part of the US government.

1. Others, including the Kissinger Commission, consider Panama and Belize to be part of Central America (see also the Fiscal Year 1985 Congressional Presentation by the US Agency for International Development).
2. Estimates indicate that this trend continued through 1986.
3. In fact, GDP contracted by 1.4 per cent in 1984 and 2.6 per cent in 1985, while estimates for 1986 indicate little change from the 1985 figure.
4. GDP expanded by 1.4 per cent in both 1984 and 1985. Estimates for 1986 indicate a 0.5 per cent decline from the 1985 figure.
5. Subsequently, GDP expanded a healthy 7.9 per cent in 1984, then flattened to a 0.9 per cent increase in 1985. Estimates for 1986 suggest a modest 3 per cent expansion.
6. Estimates indicate that this downward trend continued through 1986.

7. This trend of declining GDP per capita continued in both 1985 and 1986.
8. The 1983 figure was deflated by the change in the implicit price deflator for GNP in the United States between 1980 and 1983. The decline in the real purchasing power of dollar export earnings has been less because of the appreciation of the dollar relative to other currencies. However, overvaluation of most (and perhaps now all) Central American currencies – which are linked to the US dollar – has made Central American exports less competitive in world markets.
9. In 1983 prices the Economic Support Fund (ESF) assistance to Central America in Fiscal year 1983 was US$363 million. A small portion of this actually was project assistance rather than balance-of-payments assistance.
10. Includes the undisbursed portion of the debt. The disbursed portion only rose from US$3.2 billion to US$8.6 billion.
11. For a discussion of AID conditionality related to this assistance, see Clarence Zuvekas, 'Foreign Financial Assistance, Conditionality, and Domestic Resource Mobilization in the Caribbean Basin: A Perspective on the Agency for International Development's Program Assistance for the 1980s', 1984.
12. See J. de Larosière, 'Does the Fund Impose Austerity?' 1984.
13. December-to-December changes in the consumer price index.
14. The National Bipartisan Commission on Central America (or Kissinger Commission, as it is commonly known), on p. 33 of its report states that 'according to testimony before the Commission, health, nutrition, and educational services that were already badly deficient are declining further'.
15. The dollar value of imports by the industrial countries fell by a total of 12.5 per cent during 1980 and 1983 (*IMF Survey*, 5 March 1983).
16. International Monetary Fund, *International Financial Statistics* (monthly).
17. William R. Cline, 'Benefits and Costs of Economics in Central America', 1984, p. 7.
18. The largest net debtor, by far, is Nicaragua.
19. National Bipartisan Commission on Central America, *Report*, 1984, p. 66.
20. However, any increase in the rate of investment failed to materialise.
21. Since 1976 many Central American exports have already entered the United States duty-free under the provisions of the US Generalised System of Preferences (GSP) scheme. The CBI legislation, which passed in 1983, extends duty-free treatment (for 12 years) to all other commodities except textiles and apparel, footwear, leather goods, petroleum and petroleum products, and a few other, relatively minor, items. (Sugar enters duty-free under the CBI up to the current quota limits.)
22. National Bipartisan Commission on Central America, *Report*, 1984, p. 41.
23. The 1984 figure is a preliminary estimate.
24. National Bipartisan Commission on Central America, *Report*, p. 53.
25. Ibid., p. 64.

26. Ibid., p. 5.
27. See the analysis by William R. Cline, 'Benefits and Costs of Economic Integration in Latin America', 1978.
28. Sections 806.30 and 807 deal with US-supplied components which are assembled abroad and returned to the United States in finished form.
29. For a detailed discussion of the argument in favour of an export-oriented strategy in Central America, see V. Bulmer-Thomas, 'Import Substitution v. Export Promotion in the Central American Common Market [CACM]', 1979.
30. See in particular Anne O. Krueger *et al.*, *Trade and Employment in the Developing Countries: Individual Studies*, 1981.
31. Gary S. Fields points to wage policy as an important factor in the success of the East Asian countries. Specifically, rapid economic growth in these countries occurred in the context of 'strict' wage policies, but nevertheless resulted in greater employment gains and more equitable income distributions over time than in countries where wage policies were 'lenient', and economic growth tended to be slower. Fields, on pp. 81–2 of his article 'Employment, Income Distribution and Economic Growth in Seven Small Open Economies', argues that

> If a country adopts a lenient wage policy ... [which] renders the country's exports unprofitable in world markets, then an export-oriented development strategy may *harm* the development effort. An export orientation may make a bad situation worse. If the wage policy cannot be changed, an inward-oriented trade policy may be called for.

References

Bulmer-Thomas, V. 'Import Substitution v. Export Promotion in the Central American Common Market [CACM]', *Journal of Economic Studies*, Vol. 6, 1979, pp. 182–201.

Cline, William R., 'Benefits and Costs of Economic Integration in Central America', in William R. Cline and Enrique Delgado (eds) *Economic Integration in Central America*, (Washington, DC: The Brookings Institution, 1978) pp. 59–121.

Cline, William R., 'Macro Policy and State Intervention', Paper presented at the XIVth Meeting of the Latin American Association of Development Finance Institutions (ALIDE), Fortaleza, Ceara, Brazil, 14–18 May 1984.

Fields, Gary S., 'Employment, Income Distribution and Economic Growth in Seven Small Open Economies', *Economic Journal*, Vol. 94, 1984, pp. 74–83.

InterAmerican Development Bank [IDB], *Economic and Social Progress in Latin America: 1983 Report* (Washington, DC, 1984).

International Monetary Fund [IMF], *International Financial Statistics*, (monthly).

Krueger, Anne O., Hal B. Lary, Terry Monson and Narongchai Akrasanee (eds) *Trade and Employment in Developing Countries: 1. Individual Studies*

(Chicago: University of Chicago Press for the National Bureau of Economic Research, 1981).

De Larosière, J., 'Does the Fund Impose Austerity?' (Washington, DC: International Monetary Fund, June 1984).

National Bipartisan Commission on Central America [KIssinger Commission], *Report* (Washington, DC, January 1984).

United States Agency for International Development [AID], *Congressional Presentation, Fiscal Year 1985 – Annex III: Latin America and the Caribbean, Vol. II: Central Ameria* (Washington, DC, 1984).

World Bank, *World Debt Tables, 1983–84* (Washington, DC, 1984).

World Bank, *World Development Report 1980* (Washington, DC, 1980).

Zuvekas, Clarence, 'Foreign Financial Assistance, Conditionality, and Domestic Resource Mobilization in the Caribbean Basin: A Perspective on the Agency for International Development's Program Assistance in the 1980s', Conference Paper No. 3, Conference on Financial Crisis, Foreign Assistance, and Domestic Resource Mobilization in the Caribbean Basin, Ohio State University, 30 April–1 May, 1984.

10 Financial and Capital Flows in Central America in the 1980s

Raul Moncarz

INTRODUCTION

Since the end of the 1970s, Central American economic conditions have been characterised by a crisis of the external sector. These difficulties are closely linked with the deterioration of the terms of trade, the increase in the real rate of interest in world financial markets, and further with the more limited availability of grants and other international soft monies. In addition, the relatively high service payments on the external debt, and a diminishing financial and capital flow into the region have exacerbated the situation. Central American external financial flows, until the latter part of the 1970s, were a balancing variable, reflecting growth and relatively free exchange rates. As a result of the current political and economic crisis, as well as the lack of favourable conditions for any of the export products of the region, financial flows into the area have been reduced and drastically changed. In the case of Central America, one has to realize that perceptions and information about a specific subject are being continuously examined and re-evaluated. The recent notoriety of the region has been the subject of a number of studies and commissions seen from the United States perspective on the situation.[1] Previous to this interest by the United States, Central American organisations have devoted considerable amounts of time and funds to study the same problems and conflicts of the area.

Interestingly enough, both have come to similar conclusions in terms of the financial needs of the area. As an example, at least two years prior to the Kissinger Commission report, the Central American Bank for Economic Integration (CABEI)[2] formulated the financial needs of the area to be of the order of about six billion dollars, which is very close to the Kissinger Commission requests.

From an international trade perspective, Central America has been, and still is, increasingly vulnerable to fluctuations in world prices of a few export commodities. These commodities have constituted a rapidly decreasing portion of world trade. In the most recent past the oversupply in world commodity markets of bananas, coffee, and sugar have kept prices depressed since the last Central American boom of 1975, that stemmed from the coffee shortage due to the Brazilian frost of that year. Furthermore, primary commodities that are more directly used in consumption goods, such as Central American traditional products including textiles and their raw materials, tend, as a general rule, to have a rather low income elasticity of demand. Therefore demand for these products often lags behind increases of income levels in the developed countries, which tend to be the main importers of these goods. The evidence of the above is that, since 1970, the mixture of imports of the Organisation for Economic Co-operation and Development (OECD) countries has changed, even though roughly half of the total is still for manufactured goods. A much larger share of their spending goes for importing fuel.[3]

THE EXTERNAL SECTOR

During the last five years the evolution of the Central American economies has been characterised by the deepening crisis of the external sector, on the one hand due to decreased production and internal supply, and on the other hand to the slowdown of demand in the industrial countries. These events have led to an acute shortage of foreign exchange, which has considerably weakened the import capacity for goods and services from the rest of the world, thus precipitating a significant slowdown in economic activity, to the point where the area has experienced negative rates of growth in the last three years.[4]

Another key variable influencing the external sector in Central America has been the high international interest rates, with particularly large increases since 1979, caused by anti-inflationary policies in the advanced countries. The nominal London Inter-bank Offered Rate (LIBOR) in 1979–84 was nearly double its 1973–8 value and, if measured in real terms, it moved from a barely positive rate to a positive 5 per cent. Higher interest rates in the United States and Europe, particularly those in the US, were the principal instrument of stabilisation policy, and had the largely unintended effect of strengthening the dollar. The International Monetary Fund (IMF) has estimated that the continuation of high interest rates, falling export prices, and the appreciation of the dollar, had the effect of moving the real interest cost in the majority of the net oil importing countries, from the range of -7 to -11 per cent per annum during the period 1973–8, to a range of $+7$ to $+10$ per cent in 1981.[5] The interest rate shift of this order of magnitude is probably the most significant factor upsetting the previous patterns of world adjustment.

The nature of the crisis

To indicate the depth of the downturn in economic activity and its effect on the sectorial structure, it is important to examine the backward movement of gross domestic product (GDP) and GDP per capita in the region. All countries in the area have moved backwards, in terms of their GDP per capita, having reached their 1984 GDP per capita 20 years ago in Nicaragua and El Salvador, while Costa Rica and Honduras went back to income figures achieved 10 years previously, and Guatemala attained the current level 5 years ago.

The individual productive sectors of the economy followed the same trends. As an example, in El Salvador the agricultural sector is at the same level that it was at the beginning of the 1950s, while in Honduras the building sector is at the same level of activity that it first attained in the early 1950s.

Terms of trade

Theoretically, if one nation is more efficient at harvesting coffee and another better at producing computers, then it would be foolish for each of them to produce both goods. It would be far better to do what each does best, and then to trade the excess.

The evidence for the case of Central America is that for the period 1977–83, the terms of trade have deteriorated by 40 per cent. In part, the above formulation fails to describe the global economy as it actually works. The aforementioned theory of free trade is based on factor endowments. The theory does not fit a world of learning curves, economies of scale, availability of locations, and floating exchange rates. Moreover, it certainly does not look at the fact that today comparative advantage is created, not by markets alone, but by government action as well, for example, the sugar quotas of the US, and the international agreements on coffee and cotton.

The traditional literature on terms of trade and industrialisation has been augmented today by new elements in the developmental process of nations, such as development loans, the incubation of supply with state-seeded demand, and cartels. The inclusion of these elements leads to a fundamentally different strategy of economic growth, one which happens to be attractive to much of the world.[6] These new operational techniques have been very successful for industrial countries such as Japan, but very ineffective for Central America, at least in the short run.

It has to be mentioned that the rise in oil prices in 1979, followed by the collapse of the prices of sugar, coffee, bananas, and cotton, considerably slowed the economic growth of the region and further increased unemployment in economies that already could not cope with an annual increase in the labour force of about 3 per cent. Additionally, the war between the domestic military forces and the guerrillas prevented further investment and resulted, among other things, in a transfer of capital from Central America to the world, estimated at over 500 million dollars annually. This latter figure is greater than the total US economic assistance to the region.[7]

CEPAL (Comission Economica Para America Latina Y El Caribe)[8] confirms that the current crisis is attributable to the fact that, for the first time since 1945, the three dynamic elements that have traditionally been the decisive factors in determining the level of economic activity achieved in the area, exports, industrialisation and total investments, simultaneously experienced recessionary levels.

Foreign trade and the physical balance of resources

Given the deterioration of the terms of trade, industrialisation, investments, and the sociopolitical events in the region, since 1979, the adjustment process has signalled a drastic reduction of imports in all of the countries of the region. This has continued through 1985.

The existing relation between dynamic economic activity and the level of imports has again been demonstrated in Central America. The lowering of imports has also led to a significant downturn in the national product of each country. For Central America it shows, once more, the vulnerability of their economies to the external sector.

According to the governments of the region, the lowering of

imports was necessary to counteract, via the surplus created in the trade balance, the large increase in interest payments due. This increase can be attributed, in part, to the contraction of loans by the international commercial banking sector, and to the other factors already mentioned. In particular, the last coffee boom in 1975 led to an increasing level of deficits and borrowing from the international banking sector, which kept increasing, despite the fact that the favourable economic conditions ceased.

From the macroeconomic side, an excess of imports with respect to exports increases the availability of internal supply, and thus allows consumption and capital formation in aggregate to be higher than the internal product. In the opposite case, an excess of exports over imports decreases internal availability. Consequently, consumption and internal investment are, in aggregate, lower than the amount of the internal product.

In the period 1974–80 the excess of imports over exports reached over one billion dollars. Since 1982 the situation has changed considerably with these balances being reduced by almost one billion dollars a year for the region. Central America faces a unique situation in its history, as these countries of the region are limiting imports in an effort to achieve a trade surplus. They are finding it to be a very painful plight, since these countries have depended on imported capital to sustain economic growth during the past 30 years. Forced to run a trade surplus, the area has now, in effect, become an exporter of capital, building up credits (or reducing debits) abroad. At home, this translates into a capital scarcity, slow growth, high unemployment and, with population expanding at a 3 per cent rate annually, flat or declining per capita income.

SAVING AND INVESTMENT

According to studies made by the Economic Commission for Latin America,[9] in the 1970s, and specifically during the period 1976–80, the investment process was a stronger and more sustained one than in the previous years. At least, in Central America similar rates of growth could only be found during the integration period of the 1960s. However, since the beginning of the 1980s the internal investment coefficients of GDP have shown a significant decline of over 20 per cent for Costa Rica, El Salvador and Honduras, and an almost 50 per cent decline for Guatemala.

Table 10.1   Costa Rican balance of payments. 1977–83 ($ millions)

	1977	1978	1979	1980	1981	1982	1983
Net balance on capital account	363.8	441.1	358.8	826.1	283.2	210.9	300.0
Private capital	236.2	278.6	95.6	416.1	111.3	(2.8)	113.9
Private direct investment	62.5	47.0	42.4	48.2	66.2	30.7	N/A
Private long-term capital	118.7	202.9	54.9	264.3	53.5	(0.4)	N/A
Private short-term capital	55.0	28.7	(1.7)	103.6	(8.3)	(33.1)	N/A
Capital received by the government sector	85.1	171.6	222.7	367.8	159.2	195.5	186.1
Transactions by the monetary sector	42.5	(9.37)	40.3	42.2	12.6	18.1	N/A
Net change in international reserves	(110.8)	(27.2)	119.6	(91.8)	52.2	(118.1)	59.1

Source: Inter-American Development Bank, *Economic and Social Progress in Latin America, 1984 Report.*

It should be noted that the changing international conditions and/ or variations in government policy has strongly influenced the cyclical fluctuations in Central America, as opposed to the traditional view, that investment is the key.[10] Besides the direct and multiplier effect of changes in world prices of exports and imports, changes in world

Table 10.2   Salvadoran balance of payments, 1977–83 ($ millions)

	1977	1978	1979	1980	1981	1982	1983
Net balance on capital account	41.7	369.7	(49.1)	214.5	160.5	279.1	270.4
Private capital	2.6	226.9	(115.1)	(86.3)	(79.6)	(44.4)	(3.5)
Private direct investment	18.7	23.6	(9.9)	5.9	N/A	5.7	(3.6)
Private long-term capital	(2.3)	36.3	5.3	(2.7)	N/A	N/A	N/A
Private short-term capital	(13.8)	167.1	(110.5)	(89.4)	N/A	N/A	N/A
Capital received by the government sector	18.7	139.0	68.2	364.7	250.7	267.0	274.0
Transactions by the monetary sector	20.4	3.9	(2.2)	(64.0)	(10.5)	N/A	N/A
Net change in international reserves	(41.0)	(55.5)	133.7	74.6	48.9	(70.1)	(179.0)

Source: Inter-American Development Bank, *Economic and Social Progress in Latin America, 1984 Report.*

Raul Moncarz 129

Table 10.3 Guatemalan balance of payments, 1977–83 ($ millions)

	1977	1978	1979	1980	1981	1982	1983
Net balance on capital account	241.8	394.9	224.4	(74.4)	290.8	353.4	263.3
Private capital	170.3	283.5	86.4	(242.9)	27.7	188.4	60.8
Private direct investment	97.4	127.5	117.1	110.8	127.6	71.9	N/A
Private long-term capital	33.6	38.6	28.5	29.7	69.4	115.1	N/A
Private short-term capital	39.5	117.4	(59.2)	(383.3)	(169.2)	1.4	N/A
Capital received by the government sector	67.9	110.3	114.0	166.1	269.8	152.0	202.5
Transactions by the monetary sector	3.4	1.1	23.9	2.3	(6.87)	13.1	N/A
Net change in international reserves	(183.2)	(71.4)	25.5	256.7	303.6	34.9	(30.0)

Source: Inter-American Development Bank, Economic and Social Progress in Latin America, 1984 Report.

prices tend to have indirect effects through variations in international reserves and in the level of inflation. Government policy may respond to reserve losses and variations in conditions regarding imported products; in addition, variations in external financing may force changes in monetary emission.[11]

Table 10.4 Honduran balance of payments, 1977–83 ($ millions)

	1977	1978	1979	1980	1981	1982	1983
Net balance on capital account	201.6	154.1	230.8	278.0	237.6	91.5	204.3
Private capital	134.7	126.5	148.1	240.1	195.7	(34.6)	51.8
Private direct investment	8.9	13.1	28.2	5.9	(3.7)	13.8	5.0
Private long-term capital	93.5	111.8	110.4	205.3	185.8	(15.0)	(33.5)
Private short-term capital	32.3	1.5	9.6	29.0	13.7	(33.4)	80.3
Capital received by the government sector	44.2	43.8	54.7	44.6	71.8	112.5	149.7
Transactions by the monetary sector	22.6	(16.0)	27.9	(6.6)	(30.1)	13.6	2.8
Net change in international reserves	(66.3)	(9.4)	(19.8)	77.7	71.8	88.5	8.0

Source: Inter-American Development Bank, Economic and Social Progress in Latin America, 1984 Report.

Table 10.5   Nicaraguan balance of payments, 1977–83 ($ millions)

	1977	1978	1979	1980	1981	1982	1983
Net balance on capital account	194.7	(49.0)	(145.6)	210.9	561.8	383.5	535.9
Private capital	(7.9)	(207.5)	(251.8)	(137.6)	(37.3)	(63.1)	(51.9)
Private direct investment	10.0	7.0	2.8	N/A	N/A	N/A	7.7
Private long-term capital	61.6	12.3	(2.5)	(0.3)	N/A	(14.1)	(39.6)
Private short-term capital	(79.6)	(226.7)	(252.2)	(137.3)	(37.3)	(49.0)	(20.0)
Capital received by the government sector	148.0	109.8	121.1	331.3	517.1	433.9	559.0
Transactions by the monetary sector	54.6	48.6	(14.7)	17.5	82.0	20.4	28.8
Net change in international reserves	(9.1)	83.6	(5.0)	196.6	(57.7)	99.5	(70.5)

Source: Inter-American Development Bank, *Economic and Social Progress in Latin America, 1984 Report.*

Added to the importance that the foreign sector has always had in Central American growth process, is the high level of debt that was acquired in the 1970s. This could not be diminished in the context of the present situation, with low world commodity prices for regional exports prevailing. In addition, the violence in the area has frightened the private sector away from investment.[12] Not only has private investment stopped, but disinvestment resulted in between 2.5 and 3.0 billion dollars having left the region in the period 1979 to 1982.[13]

Internal resources for investments and national savings

The erosion suffered by the national resources of Central America due to the transfers of interest and profits, together with the unfavourable terms of trade and the violence in the region, has affected investment and savings. The data for the area show that there has been a considerable change in the coefficient of gross national savings. Only Guatemala and El Salvador registered a coefficient of gross national savings greater than their internal savings in the last five years, which was due to the effect of the terms of trade and its base year (1975).

It must also be noted that the contribution of the gross national savings went down in all countries, the proportion corresponding to net external financing, in an amount equivalent to the net balance in the current account of the balance of payments.[14] These events have required an increase in the net external financing needed to compensate for the significant increases in the interest payments and transfers of capital.

CAPITAL MOVEMENTS

Long-term loans and investments from abroad, if applied productively, eventually result in an increased flow of output, including exports and import substitutes. Foreign capital thus helps a developing country to prevent inflation, to maintain equilibrium in its foreign balance, and to avoid depreciation of its currency. In the absence of foreign aid or private foreign investment, a country's rate of growth, t, is determined by the proportion of its income that is saved, a, and the effectiveness of investment, or the incremental capital to output ratio, i; simply, $t = ai$. Foreign capital is assumed to supplement domestic savings and leave the effectiveness of investment unchanged, so that the growth rate rises by the amount of ci, where c is net capital imports expressed as a proportion of national income. The rate of growth of national income then becomes $t = ai + ci$.[15]

In this analysis, capital imports are seen as an addition to the physical resources of the developing country and, it is assumed that all of these additional resources are saved and invested. This means that in the absence of capital imports, the growth rate would equal only ai, while foreign investments or aid would allow the growth rate to rise to $ai + ci$.

Adding to this analysis, Chenery and Strout[16] argue that not only do the capital imports raise the rate of investment by the full amount of the foreign assistance, they also lead to a higher rate of domestic savings, a, since the marginal propensity to save is assumed to be higher than the average. Furthermore, others have said that by serving as a transfer vehicle for technical knowledge and organisational ability, capital imports may help to raise the effectiveness of investment i. Just how strong may be the interdependence between c and i is open to considerable debate.

There are a great number of arguments against this approach, from the appropriateness of the transfers to the altering of the composition of investment in favour of large, lumpy, capital intensive projects with long gestation periods. An example of this is the sawmills and dams built in Honduras. This change in the composition of investment, far from raising the incremental output to capital ratio, is likely to lower it, and thereby reduce the rate of growth.[17] The evidence indicates, at least up to 1980, that for all the Central American countries, with the exception of Costa Rica, the capital to output ratio varies positively with the amount of aid received as a percentage of gross national product (GNP). At the same time, increments in the capital to output ratio went hand-in-hand with an increase in the number of unemployed and the expansion of urban slums, with only marginal additional output being generated.

CAPITAL IMPORTS AND DOMESTIC SAVINGS

If one looks at the average rate of growth of GNP over the years, one finds that it is inversely related to the ratio of foreign aid to GNP. The association is rather loose, but the general tendency is that the greater the capital flow is from abroad, the lower the rate of growth of the recipient country. There is absolutely no support for the view that foreign aid accelerates growth. The reason for this is that foreign aid leads to a less desirable composition of investment and hence, a higher capital to output ratio. Another and more important reason is that aid reduces the incentive to save.[18]

In broad terms, once could characterise the Central American situation up to 1980 as one in which growth was occurring, but not development. Honduras remained the poorest nation, while Costa Rica continued to be the economy of the region with the highest standard of living.

Looking at the data from 1977 to 1983 we can notice some significant changes in the Central American financial and capital flows as seen in Tables 10.1 to 10.5. Let us analyse this data through a variety of approaches.

The IDB approach

According to the Inter-American Development Bank (IDB), the virtual stagnation in world trade prevented the recovery of exports in the developing countries. Measured in annual variations, the growth of the GDP and the GDP per capita remained stagnant or negative for all the countries of the region, with the exception of Nicaragua.

One explanation for this is that Nicaragua received almost half of the total capital received by all governments in the region. Furthermore, the amount of direct investment in the region in 1983 amounted to about 42 million dollars, declining markedly from around 100 million dollars in 1977.

The rate of change of imports decreased significantly for all these countries of the region; from − 2 per cent in El Salvador to − 30 per cent in Guatemala. This means that all of the countries in the region, in order to take care of their balance of payment difficulties, on top of the very limited capital inflows, adopted restrictive policies that have substantially reduced the levels of investment and production. The prospects for an alternative adjustment path, that would allow Central America to service its debt through increased exports, are very bleak for the next few years, given the nature of its products. According to the IDB,[19] only if the debt burden can be reorganised in accordance with the countries' capacity to pay, and ways to attract a fresh inflow of foreign capital can be found, will it be possible for the countries of Central America to begin to recoup the losses in per capita income sustained during the last five years.

Private capital

The sum of private direct investment, either private long-term capital or private short-term capital, was about 170 million dollars in 1983, drastically reduced from the figure of about 550 million dollars in 1977. These amounts speak for themselves, and show on the one hand the link between political and economic events, and on the other hand that Central America is deteriorating very rapidly to levels unknown to the majority of its population.

Capital received by the government sector

The balance of payments line that allows the economies to maintain, at least, a survival level, is the funds received by the government sector. This has gone from approximately 366 million dollars in 1977 to 1.3 billion dollars in 1983, with Nicaragua receiving approximately half of this amount.

Capital flight

Capital flight is one of the least tractable of modern economic occurrences. Many problems are involved for developing countries in regard to the inflow of foreign capital, such as the utilisation of these funds, and the service of the debt. But an outflow of funds is still a more serious matter.

The phenomenon of capital flight from Central America reinforces, more powerfully than almost any other evidence, the contention that domestic conditions favourable to saving and investment of domestic capital are absolute prerequisites for foreign capital to be attracted, and for it not to be offset by a reverse flow of funds. For some countries in the region, it seems fairly certain that a large part of the new capital funds coming in from abroad are lost due to this reverse flow. It also should be noted that high taxes in most of the region, even though helpful in combatting inflation and maintaining a given level of expenditures by the government, may drive capital abroad. Capital flight is occurring through traditional ways, such as the manipulation of export and import invoices, with the invoices not reflecting the true nature of the transactions. It also leaves through countries of the region without exchange restrictions. In the last few years, a novel way has been found in terms of exchange rates for those countries that have more than one level of exchange rates. It operates in the following fashion: when foreign exchange comes in from abroad it is credited at the official exchange rate, while someone, in fact, gets the higher rate. The margin is left to the person or persons involved in the transaction.

Three periods can be identified corresponding to different levels of the flight of private capital from the region. The first period, 1971–5, corresponds to an outflow, due to capital flight, of 154 million dollars.[20] In the second period, encompassing the years 1976–80, this figure rose to a total of over 1.6 billion dollars and during the last period, 1979–82, to an amount of between 2.5 and 3 billion dollars.[21]

RESTRUCTURING OF THE DEBT

The restructuring of the external debt of Central America during the last two years has considerably decreased the amortisations of the debt, given the lowering of interest rates in the world. In addition to the lower interest rates, there has been a tendency in the international financial centres, to show a better disposition towards new schemes for the restructuring of the debt in terms of amortisations.

These lower rates should enable Central American countries to increase their liquidity, and allow a reactivation of the internal economies. Even though the additional liquidity would lead to the usual stop–go model of development followed by the region for the last 30 years, the nature of the disequilibrium in international payments is such that it does not correspond to internal economic activity and external trade. The high debt is not a transitory phenomenon, but one that has lasted for several years and cannot be resolved with transitionary adjustment programmes.

Assuming that the political conditions can be cited as the main reason for the problems of the area, then one possible answer is to make more funds available to the area. If the US or any other friendly power extended loans or aid, then they would, in effect, be buying time until the political situation changed such that the countries could begin, once again, the path of growth that existed up to 1975.

If, on the other hand, the nature of the problem is an economic one, then what is needed are new alternatives to the whole development strategy and to the international relations of the countries in the area, in order to face a disequilibrium that will be long lasting.

The new development strategy consists of: first, drastic financial reforms that would eliminate the present fiscal and monetary disequilibria, and secondly, a programme for use of foreign exchange according to priorities linked to economic recovery and the possible compliance to the existing external debt. At the limit, the idea is to finance future growth with the area's own resources. If this is the case, then Central America's potential and its capacity to make external payments are sufficient to reinitiate growth, take care of the most urgent social problems and recover international viability.[22]

PUBLIC VERSUS PRIVATE CONTROL

Either through planning or by way of other governmental schemes, such as development companies or banks, the central governments in the area have been a dynamic element in the economies of the region since the early 1970s.

However, neither comprehensive central planning nor government investments in the private sector are necessary for economic advance, and in fact, is much more likely to retard it. The Central American response to the above is that they were faced with population pressures and forces at both sides of the spectrum to diversify and/or to restructure the economy. The intervention of the government in Central America is unique in terms of being very different in each country, but usually adopting the concept of the government and the private sector working together for the benefit of the nation.

From this perspective the private sector could not lose. The government puts up most of the capital and takes the losses, if any; the private sector puts up most of the expertise and gets profit, if any. In other words, socialise the risk, and privatise the gain.

We must add another element to the equation of government–business practices, and that is, corruption, which is an integral element in the process by both actors, in and out of Central America. As Professor Bauer[23] has mentioned with regard to public enterprise, but applicable to all of Central America with the public–private enterprise, the replacement of market processes by political decisions provides power, influence, jobs and money for politicians, civil servants, and business people.

POSSIBLE REMEDIES

1. Short-run instability could be reduced by concentrating on long-term purchase agreements at fixed prices with the major buyers.
2. Agreements should be sought for long-term loans at low interest rates, instead of relying on direct private investment. In addition, it would be beneficial if the loans could be repayable in local soft currency instead of hard currency, and further that negotiations, if possible, should be for grants rather than loans.
3. Confidence will be favourably influenced by a visible US commitment to assist the area, in terms of technical financial flows, so as to at least maintain the countries as viable entities.
4. Rather than relying on capital imports, it might be easier and much cheaper in the long run to accelerate growth by following different domestic policies which as a by-product would tend to discourage foreign intervention.[24]
5. The maintenance of policies that would assure positive real interest rates, realistic exchange rates and reduced bureaucratic controls on credit institutions, so as to encourage return and growth of local savings, would be desirable.[25]
6. The more effective utilisation of the capital and infrastructure

already in existence. The coexistence of idle installed capacity with unemployed labour offers a unique opportunity for Central American countries to get something for almost nothing. In other words, reactivate the economies.[26]

AN ENDING NOTE

Prior to the second oil shock in 1979, and the Nicaraguan takeover of the same year, the Central American economies were highly dependent on a recognisable unstable sector; throughout the years they have been known to have limited capacity to exert any pressure on world prices, and were at the mercy of world market forces.

The deterioration in the terms of trade, and the sudden changes in the price of imported inputs have been a prominent source of unexpected external shocks that either forces the deflation of the economies, if inflation and the status quo are to be kept under control, or forces borrowing and increased expenditures, if recession and unemployment are to be avoided. It seems that the former solution has been adopted, and as a result local entrepreneurs have been constrained by production costs, the contraction of bank credit, and ultimately the possible closing of their enterprises. Another effect is that the freeze on wages coupled with the increase in prices create a severe recession. This drives many domestic companies into severe financial difficulties and lowers the level of aggregate demand even further. This is the famous Pele example of kicking the economy to obtain stability.

If we add to the above factors the increase in the price of oil and the violence in the region with its effect on entrepreneurship, investment, and capital flight, we see that the situation is really a desperate one.

A possible response to this crisis might be a call for more funds. However, this is insufficient, as we are all well aware that more dollars alone are not enough to provide a strong impetus to development. What is needed is both a concerted effort in Central America and in the rich developed countries to find a long-term solution to the present situation.

Notes

1. *The Report of the President's National Bipartisan Commission on Central America* (New York: Macmillan, 1984) pp. 1–126.

2. Banco Centro-americano de Integracion Economica, *La Demanda de Recurses Externes de Centroamerica en la Decade de los 80s*, April 1981.
3. *The Economist*, 23 November 1984, p. 23.
4. Inter-American Development Bank, *Economic and Social Progress in Latin America, 1984 Report*, p. 325.
5. International Monetary Fund, *IMF Survey*, 15 November 1982, p. 36.
6. Robert Kittner, 'The Free Trade Fallacy', *The New Republic*, Vol. 188, No. 12, 28 March 1983, pp. 16–21.
7. Robert A. Pastor, 'Our Real Interests in Central America', *The Atlantic Monthly*, July 1982, pp. 27–39.
8. CEPAL Istimo Centroamericano, 'El Caracter de la Crisis Economica Actual', Los Desafios que Plantea y la Solidaridad Internacional que Demanda (CEPAL/MEX/1050/Rev. 1, 4 June 1981.
9. Ibid.
10. G. Siri, 'A Minimodel of External Dependence of the Central American Economies', in J. A. Hanson and J. Behrman (eds) *Short-Term Economic Policy in Latin America* (New York: National Bureau of Economic Research, 1979) pp. 289–310.
11. J. Behrman and James A. Hanson, *Short-Term Macroeconomic Policy in Latin America* (New York: National Bureau of Economic Research, 1979) pp. 1–38.
12. R. E. Feinberg and Robert A. Pastor, 'Far From Hopeless: An Economic Program for Post-War Central America', in Robert S. Leiken (ed.) *Central American Anatomy of Conflict* (New York: Pergamon Press, 1984) p. 201.
13. Ibid.
14. Inter-American Development Bank, *Economic and Social Progress in Latin America, 1984 Report*.
15. K. Griffin, *Underdevelopment in Spanish America* (London: George Unwin, 1971) pp. 115–30; R. J. Ball, 'Capital Imports and Economic Development: A Paradoxy or Orthodoxy', *Kyklos*, Vol. 15, No. 3, 1962.
16. H. B. Chenery and A. M. Strout, 'Foreign Assistance and Economic Development', *American Economic Review*, Vol. 56, No. 4, 1966.
17. K. Griffin, *Underdevelopment in Spanish America* (London: George Unwin, 1971) pp. 121–30.
18. A. Sengupta, 'Foreign Capital Requirements For Economic Development', *Oxford Economic Papers*, March 1968; L. O. Geller, 'La Ayuda Extranjera: El Case Chileno', *Desarollo Economico*, Vol. 6, No. 24, 1967; H. B. Chenery, 'Trade, Aid and Economic Development', in S. H. Robock and L. M. Soloman, *International Development* (Dobbs Ferry, N.Y.: Oceana Publications, 1966) p. 187; A. Ferrer, 'Deuda Externa y Soberania de America Latina Los Desafios', *Comercio Exterior*, Vol. 34, No. 4 (Mexico) 1984, pp. 343–6.
19. Inter-American Development Bank, *Economic and Social Progress in Latin America, 1984 Report*, p. 185.
20. F. J. Mayorga, 'Crecimiento y Requirimientos Financieros para el Desarrollo en CentroAmerica', in Donald Castillo Rivas, *Centroamerica Mas Alla de la Crisis* (Mexico City: Ediciones SIAP, 1982) pp. 225–60; Luis Rene Caceres and S. F. Seniger, 'Redes Interregionales, Estructuras

Jerarquicas y Fuga de la Riqueza en Centroamerica: Un Analisis de Cadena de Markov', *El Trimestre Economico*, Vol. 49, 1982, pp. 623–44.

21. R. E. Feinberg and Robert A. Pastor, 'Far From Hopeless: An Economic Program For Post-War Central America', in R. S. Leiken (ed.) *Central American Anatomy of Conflict* (New York: Pergamon Press, 1984) p. 201.

22. A. Ferrer, 'Deuda Externa y Soberania de America Latina Los Desafios', *Comercio Exterior*, Vol. 34, No. 4 (Mexico) 1984, pp. 343–6.

23. P. T. Bauer, *Reality and Rhetoric: Studies in the Economics of Development* (Boston: Harvard University Press, 1984).

24. K. Griffin, *Underdevelopment in Spanish America* (London: George Unwin, 1971) pp. 99–139.

25. W. H. Bolin, 'Central America: Real Economic Help is Workable Now', *Foreign Affairs*, Vol. 62, No. 5, 1984, pp. 1096–106.

26. L. R. Caceres, 'Hacia Una Estrategia Para la Reactivacion y El Desarrollo Economico de CentroAmerica', *Boletim De Ciencias Economicas y Sociales*, Universidad CentroAmericana.

11 The Economy of Guatemala: Recent Developments

Alberto Martinez-Piedra

BACKGROUND AND GENERAL OVERVIEW

Guatemala, a country of more than eight million inhabitants, is the largest in Central America.[1] It is favourably endowed with rich agricultural land and extensive petroleum and mineral resources. Given its natural and human resources, its potential for growth is considerable.[2]

For many years Guatemala enjoyed one of the most stable economies among the less developed countries of the world. During the period 1964–75 Guatemala experienced, (1) a stable foreign exchange, (2) one of the lowest foreign debts in Latin America relative to its gross domestic product (GDP), the debt service ratio being less than 10 per cent, (3) a conservative financial public policy with an extremely reduced central government deficit, (4) very low levels of inflation, and (5) a strong participation of the private sector.

It was only after 1978 that Guatemala began to experience serious economic problems and the country entered into one of the longest periods of economic recession in its history.[3] The real rate of growth which, on a yearly basis, had averaged 6.1 per cent during the period 1965–75, plummeted to −3.5 per cent in 1982 and −2.8 per cent in 1983.[4] In 1984 there was a zero growth rate and in 1985 it is expected to become negative again. On a per capita basis the decline of the GDP was even more pronounced. It is estimated that Guatemala's standard of living today has dropped to the level of 1972.

Guatemala's rapid economic decline can be traced to both external and internal factors. Among the external factors, the two major ones were the world economic recession and the political conditions prevailing in Central America.[5] It is accepted generally that the world recession, centred in the Organisation for Economic Co-operation and Development (OECD) countries, has played a major role in the

140

recent reversal in Guatemala's economic fortunes.[6] The rapid fall in the price of Guatemala's basic exports – coffee, cotton and sugar – did not keep pace with the prices of the goods it imported, and as a result the terms of trade turned sharply against Guatemala.[7] Guatemala, being an export-oriented economy that relies heavily on the export of a few basic commodities, soon experienced the crunch of these trends. Domestic income began to contract and a strong disequilibrium in the balance of payments appeared.

The deterioration in the terms of trade also affected the economies of the other Central American countries and, as a result, had a negative impact on the exports of manufactured goods from Guatemala to its neighbours. The shortage of hard currency made it very difficult for the member countries to settle their trade balances within the Central American Common Market (CACM).[8] Thus, in 1981 the volume of Guatemalan manufactured exports to the region declined by 12 per cent in nominal terms, and by another 16 per cent in 1982. Calculated in real terms, the drop was even more pronounced. This trend was particularly harmful to Guatemala when it is considered that in 1979 Guatemala's regional trade accounted for 55 per cent of all manufactured exports and about 10 per cent of manufacturing production.[9]

Political unrest in Central America, especially after 1979, affected, also in an adverse manner, Guatemala's exports, and significantly contributed to the erosion of confidence of the country's business community. This, in turn, brought about a reduction in the level of investment, both domestic and foreign, creating, at the same time, conditions propitious to capital flight.

Furthermore, internal factors compounded an already critical situation. Guatemala has suffered extensively from serious political violence. Armed guerrillas and subversive elements from both the extreme right and left have made it very difficult for the Guatemalans to carry out sound economic policies. This state of internal violence, together with the deteriorating situation in Nicaragua with its perennial threat to the stability of the region, increased the level of uncertainty within the business community and reinforced the decision of foreign investors to halt investment, stop the roll-over of loans, and not to grant further short-term trade credits.

As will be shown later, all of these problems became even more acute as a result of the expansionary fiscal and monetary policies followed by the government. It is generally accepted that the lack of a well-thought-out domestic economic policy that could have helped

counteract the adverse effects resulting from external sources, led
almost inevitably to the economic crisis that Guatemala is experiencing today.

MAIN TRENDS SINCE 1978

Growth rates

As indicated earlier, Guatemala's annual real growth rates declined
significantly after 1978. Table 11.1 shows the rapid fall in per capita
income between 1978 and 1985.

In 1980 quetzales, the per capita GDP declined from a peak of 1085
quetzales in 1980 to 1060 in 1981, 994 in 1982 and 962 in 1983.[10]

The figures shown in Table 11.1 are generally considered to be
rather conservative. Even though the data provided by the Guatemalan government do not always coincide with estimates made by other
organisations such as the International Monetary Fund (IMF) and/or
The United Nations Economic Commission for Latin America
(ECLA), it is nevertheless a recognised fact that Guatemala has
slipped gradually into a recession. The above per capita income
figures clearly reflect the negative growth rates experienced by Guatemala during the last few years. As already indicated, by the end of
1985 the average Guatemalan will see his quality of life set back to the
1972 level.[11]

Production by sector

During the period 1978–85, the structure of the economy remained
almost unchanged, with agriculture contributing approximately 25
per cent of GDP, commerce 26 per cent, and manufacturing 16 per
cent. Between 1980 and 1981, commerce and agriculture tended to
stagnate and manufacturing to decline. After 1981 the decline in real
terms became more acute.

Agriculture

Agriculture continues to be the most important productive sector of
the Guatemalan economy. Its share of GDP, although somewhat
smaller than in the past, still constitutes slightly over 25 per cent of

Table 11.1   Per capita GDP 1978–85

Year	Dollars at 1970 prices	Annual growth rates
1970	439	− 0.7
1980	561	− 0.7
1981	549	− 2.1
1982	515	− 6.3
1983	489	− 5.1
1984[1]	340	− 3.2
1985[1]	332	− 2.4

1   Estimates for years 1984 and 1985 were taken from the Bank of Guatemala.

Source: United Nations, Economic and Social Council, Preliminary Overview of the Central American Economy during 1983, ECLA (E/CEPAL/G/1279) 29 December 1983.

economic activity and engages over 50 per cent of the labour force. In 1981 agriculture employed 54 per cent of the labour force, and accounted for nearly two-thirds of total exports. In terms of its contribution to GDP, agriculture is second only to commerce. In 1981 approximately 55 per cent of total exports were unprocessed and semi-processed agricultural foods.[12]

The decline in agricultural output that began to take place after 1981 was due mainly to the fall in production of the major export crops (coffee, cotton, sugar and bananas) and basic grains (corn, rice and beans). In 1984, however, agriculture showed a slight increase.

Manufacturing

Guatemala, during 1960 and 1970, developed a light industrial base that was primarily oriented toward the domestic and Central American markets. Being the largest and richest country in Central America, Guatemala benefited most from the Central American Common Market (CACM).

The structure of the manufacturing sector has hardly changed during the last five years. Food processing, beverages and tobacco contribute about 45 per cent of value added in the manufacturing sector. On the other hand, clothing, textiles and leather goods contribute about 20 per cent. According to some estimates, real value added in 1983 was 10 per cent lower than the peak reached by the manufacturing sector in 1980.

Estimates made by the Bank of Guatemala indicate that in 1983 the manufacturing sector was operating at 60 per cent of capacity. Furthermore, a number of plants had to close because of the decline in external demand, resulting from the fall in real income and payments problems within the other Central American countries. Available data tend to show that Guatemala's exports of manufactured products, the bulk of which were traded within the regional markets, fell by 25 per cent in 1981–2 in relation to 1980, and by an additional 4 per cent in 1983.

Construction

Construction also fell significantly after 1981. Real value added, which had increased at an annual average rate of 9 per cent in 1979–81, fell by 12 per cent in 1982 and by 29 per cent in 1983. Most of the construction activity is done by the public sector in Guatemala. It accounts for about three quarters of the real value added in the construction sector. With the completion of the Aguacapa hydroelectric power plant, and Puerto Quetzal on the Pacific Coast, and the drastic cut in public investment in 1982, construction activity fell sharply. Private construction has not picked up the lag and has remained depressed since 1980. The real value added in private construction in 1983 was 50 per cent less than in 1979.

Petroleum[13]

During the 1970s high hopes were placed on the production of oil in Guatemala. Production began in 1978 and, once the pipeline linking the Rubelsanto oil field with the Caribbean coast was completed Guatemala began to export oil. Guatemala's production of crude oil increased from 0.2 million barrels in 1978 to 0.6 million barrels in 1979. Production rose to 1.5 million barrels in both 1980 and 1981 reaching a yearly average of approximately 2.5 million barrels in 1982–3. In 1984 production fell to 1.7 million barrels and it is expected to fall even more in 1985.[14]

Guatemalan oil is difficult to refine domestically because of its high sulphur content. Thus, most of it is exported and domestic needs are met by imports. A small amount is consumed locally as fuel by the cement plant and one power station.

Available data indicate that consumption of petroleum products declined by approximately 30 per cent during the period 1979–83. This was due primarily to the slowdown in domestic economic activity, to the completion of Chixoy and Puerto Quetzal, and to some extent to the substitution of hydroelectric power for thermal generation with the completion of the Aguacapa project.

For a number of years Basic Resources was the only company that produced crude oil. It was joined later on by Elf Aquitaine as operator of the contract. Texaco Exploration Guatemala Inc., Amoco, Texaco Canada, Getty Oil, Hispanoil and Braspetro became involved also in oil exploration. However, exploration activity has been relatively limited during the last few years mainly because of the fall in oil prices coupled with a law that is not overly stimulating. Three out of the five areas which had been under exploration by foreign companies were abandoned in 1983. Elf Aquitaine stopped its operations in 1984 and Hispanoil, together with Basic Resources, took over the exploration sites. Most recently Texaco Exploration, as Guatemala operator for Texaco Canada, Hispanoil and Braspetro, closed.

At present Guatemala is experiencing a very serious energy crisis that threatens to endanger the entire growth process. Gasoline and diesel are rationed and some areas of the country are running out of oil. It is a generally accepted fact that at least part of the problem can be traced to public policies related to pricing and investment management. Although the current scarcity of fuel in Guatemala is, to a large degree, the result of the government's inability to pay its oil bill because of a lack of foreign exchange, it is also true that the lack of adequate pricing policy reflecting the true opportunity cost of fuel and oil generated electricity, has been a major contributing factor. Petroleum and fuel are treated as essential commodity imports and these fall under the official 1:1 exchange rate. Gasoline has been kept at the low price of approximately 3 quetzales per gallon ($0.80 at $1 = 3.75 quetzales.[15] Such low price reflects a substantial subsidy in reality too costly to maintain by the public sector. To make matters worse, the Chixoy hydroelectric plant suffered a serious setback when it was not able to start operations as a result of a tunnel collapse. Until the needed repairs are completed, the poorly-maintained and overburdened petroleum-fed generators (coupled with hydropower during the rainy season) are supplying the country.

In September 1983 the Government revised the terms of the 1975 petroleum code as amended by a model contract published in 1978. In accordance with the revision, there took place a reduction in the sliding scale of the government's share in crude production from 55 per cent to 40 per cent, and the deduction of exploration, development and operating costs in the determination of the production level to be shared. At present the newest company to sign an exploration contract is Exxon. It plans to explore in the Central-Western areas of the Peten region.

Employment, wages and prices

Labour force statistics are not very reliable in Guatemala since no labour market census has taken place since 1964. However, all available data tend to indicate that the employment situation has deteriorated significantly during the last few years.

The population of Guatemala was estimated at over 7.9 million inhabitants in 1984 out of which 2.4 million were considered members of the labour force. In other words, approximately 30.5 per cent of the total population is economically active. The ratio between the economically active population and the total population has been decreasing slowly since 1950 when it represented approximately 33.9 per cent.

Agriculture continues to be the sector that provides the highest level of employment. In 1981, approximately 57 per cent of the labour force was employed in agriculture and only 14 per cent in manufacturing. Unemployment figures must also be taken with great caution. Available statistics indicate that the unemployment figures which include both the open and the underemployed have risen sharply since 1980. Total unemployment as a percentage of the total economically active population has increased from 31.2 per cent in 1980 to an estimated 43.6 per cent in 1984.[16] These figures tend to indicate that the country has been using, through the years, a smaller portion of its available labour force. A larger portion of its economically active population has remained idle, contributing very little or nothing to the country's wealth. Such a trend definitely shows a waste of human resources, one of Guatemala's greatest assets.

Guatemala has very little data on wage trends. In 1980, during the Lucas García regime, a minimum daily wage of 3.20 quetzales was established in agriculture.[17] The wage received by the typical worker on the agricultural sector is still significantly lower than the average for the country as a whole. However, it must be remembered that output per worker is higher in commerce and industry than in agriculture. As wages are paid according to productivity, they tend to be lower in agriculture where productivity is not as great. From 1980 on, the year in which the minimum wage for agricultural workers was established, a continued increase in wages occurred. The minimum wage approved in 1980 accentuated the rate of wage increases in both commerce and industry. Between 1980 and 1981 the average wage for the country as a whole increased by 18.5 per cent. This rate of increase nearly doubled in 1982 (35.5 per cent). However, in 1983 there took place a fall in the wage level (−2.9 per cent).[18]

In general terms, it can be said that the real wage did not change significantly for 20 years. From 1977 to 1981 it experienced a gradual but continuous fall.[19] The falling trend continued after 1983 when the situation began to deteriorate rapidly. It is worth noting that real wages hardly ever kept pace with the GDP during the years it was rising. Again, when the GDP was falling in real terms, real wages fell at an even greater speed aggravating the situation of the wage earner.

Prices in Guatemala have been relatively stable over the years. For many years the average rate of inflation had been less than 1 per cent per year.[20] In 1973 prices began to increase. They rose by approximately 10 per cent in relation to the previous year. This was primarily the result of the rate of increase in oil prices, and the rate of inflation abroad.[21] In 1982 the increase in the consumer price index fell to 5 per cent and did not change significantly in 1983 because of the low level of economic activity.[22] Maximum wholesale and retail prices have been established by the Guatemalan government on a number of basic products and fuels. Medicines and other consumer goods have also been regulated. As the economic situation continued to deteriorate in 1984, and the crisis in the external sector became more acute, the value of the quetzal, which for many years had been maintained at parity with the US dollar, began to fall rapidly. As changes in the foreign exchange began to affect market prices, it was not long before the price level began to feel the pressure, putting an end to the long-established stability of Guatemala's price level.[23] In spite of the fact that government agencies were permitted to set prices and regulate profits in many types of economic activity, the over-all general price level continued to increase and the quetzal deteriorated even further. For the first time in a very long time, the danger of an inflationary spiral of unknown proportion hitting Guatemala became a distinct possibility.

Aggregate expenditures

Aggregate demand registered a sharp deceleration after 1979, in spite of the short-lived significant increase that took place in 1980–81. The expansion of aggregate demand occurring in 1980–81 was the result of the sharp increase in domestic expenditures carried out by the Lucas García government to counteract the drastic fall in both private sector investment and foreign demand. With the fall of the Lucas García regime in 1982, the new government of Rios Montt cut back expenditures, particularly in the area of public investment. The Rios Montt government tried to curtail the expansionary fiscal policy carried out by its predecessor, and cancelled or postponed large capital intensive projects. Among the projects cancelled were the national beltway, at a cost of approximately US$1.5 billion, and three hydroelectric projects (Chulac, Santa Maria II and Xalala). The major hydroelectric power projects (Aguacapa and Chixoy) had already been completed.

Most of Guatemala's economy is still in private hands and the country boasts of a highly-skilled business and professional class that can be credited for many of the economic advances that have taken place in the country. Private consumption represented 84 per cent of GDP in 1960 and 82 per cent in 1982. This percentage is much higher than in other Central American countries. In Costa Rica, for example it was 77 per cent in 1960 and 58 per cent in 1982.[24]

Gross domestic investment represented 18.7 per cent of GDP in 1979.[25] The share of the private sector alone was 14.5 per cent of the GDP. The gross domestic investment of the public sector was only 4.2 per cent of GDP. Nevertheless, after 1979 private sector investment began to decrease; its share in the GDP representing only 8.6 per cent of GDP in 1982. It is expected that it will decline to about 6 per cent in 1985.[26] According to available estimates, private investment declined approximately 44 per cent in real terms from 1979 to 1983. The decline in private investment, together with poor capital formation and a continuing balance of payment deficit, were major contributing factors to the decline in economic activity.

On the other hand, the share of public gross domestic investment in the GDP increased to 5.9 per cent and 7.9 per cent in 1980 and 1981 respectively. This was the result of Lucas García's policy of government expenditure, financed through increased fiscal deficits; a policy that had such negative consequences in the years that followed. Gross domestic investment of the public sector as a percentage of GDP again fell, reaching 5.9 and 4.8 per cent in 1982 and 1983, respectively.

The public sector

The role of government prior to 1976 was very small and it was only after 1979, under the presidency of General Lucas García, that government expenditures began to rise sharply. As government revenues did not increase at the same rate, fiscal deficits began to appear. Table 11.2 clearly shows how the deficit of the Central government jumped from 368.5 million quetzales in 1980 to 637.6 million quetzales in 1981. It was only after the fall of Lucas García that the fiscal deficit declined to 410.4 million quetzales in 1982 and 346.6 million quetzales in 1983. It is estimated that the deficit was 291.6 million quetzales in 1984.[27,28] It can also be seen from Table 11.2 how in 1981 the public sector's fiscal deficit reached 7.4 per cent of GDP. However, due to the large curtailments in government expenditures that took place after the fall of Lucas García, budget deficits fell

Table 11.2 Financial operations of the central government 1980–84 (*quetzales millions*)

	1980	1981	1982	1983	1984
Current account	93.2	13.0	19.8	−7.2	−81.3
Revenues	747.3	740.6	729.8	693.8	654.1
Expenditures	654.1	727.6	710.0	701.0	735.4
Capital account	−461.7	−650.6	−430.2	−339.4	−210.3
Revenues	0.7	1.8	1.3	0.6	0.6
Expenditures	462.4	652.4	431.5	340.0	210.9
Overall balance	−368.5	−637.6	−410.4	−346.6	−291.6
Ext. fin. (net)	92.9	102.1	95.2	100.2	45.4
Dom. fin. (net)	275.6	535.5	315.2	246.6	246.1
Of which Central Bank credit	(241.0)	(400.0)	(178.0)	(−)	(−)
Deficit as % of GDP	4.7	7.4	4.7	3.3	3.1

Between 1979 and 1981 the increase in government deficits was covered by larger amounts of internal financing as shown in Table 11.3. Net internal financing reached 6.2 per cent of GDP in 1981. Subsequently it declined to 3.8 per cent and 2.7 per cent in 1982 and 1983, respectively. The Bank of Guatemala was the most important source of internal financing. However, in 1983 the government relied more on domestic non-bank financing for its needs and placed bonds outside the domestic banking system.
Source: Bank of Guatemala and Ministry of Finance.

The Economy of Guatemala

to 4.7 per cent of GDP in 1982, 3.3 per cent in 1983 and 3.1 per cent in 1984.[29]

Table 11.3 also shows how net external financing of the public deficit fluctuated between 1 and 2 per cent of GDP during the period 1979–83. Most of the foreign financing of the government deficit was covered by concessional loans from the World Bank, the Inter-American Development Bank (IDB) and other sources.

The budget deficits of the Guatemalan public sector have increasingly become a matter of concern. It is generally believed that equilibrium in public finances was one of the first casualties of the recession. However, a closer look at the situation tends to indicate that the primary source of the continued deficit is not the recession, but a lack of incentive to private investment and export activity, together with serious inefficiences in the tax system.

Government revenues as a percentage of GDP declined steadily during the period 1979–83. As shown in Table 11.3, total revenue and grants fell from 9.7 per cent of GDP in 1979 to 7.8 per cent in 1983. Tax revenues dropped even more significantly, from 9 per cent of GDP in 1979 to 6 per cent in 1983. This was mainly the result of the fall in foreign trade taxes. The decline in tax revenue was partially offset by an increase in non-tax revenue.

In order to boost government revenue and stimulate exports and domestic output, a tax reform was carried out in 1983. The main feature of the reform was the introduction of a 10 per cent value

Table 11.3   Guatemala: Central Government operations (as percentage of GDP)

	1979	1980	1981	1982	1983
Total revenue and grants	9.7	9.5	8.6	8.4	7.8
Current	9.7	9.5	8.6	8.4	7.8
Capital	—	—	—	—	—
Total expenditure and net					
lending	12.3	14.2	16.0	13.1	11.4
Current	7.7	8.3	8.5	8.1	7.8
Capital	4.6	5.9	7.5	5.0	3.6
Current account balance	2.0	1.2	0.1	0.3	−0.0
Overall surplus or					
deficit (−)	−2.6	−4.7	−7.4	−4.7	−3.6
External fin. (net)	1.7	1.2	1.2	0.9	1.0
Internal fin. (net)	0.9	3.5	6.2	3.8	2.6

Source: Bank of Guatemala and Ministry of Finance.

added tax which replaced the stamp tax. Among other measures taken, the following can be mentioned: a reduction in the progressive scale of the corporate income tax, the phasing out of export duties affecting traditional exports, and the elimination of the stamp tax in bank credits. Also introduced were tax credit certificates (CATs) for exports of non-traditional goods to non-CACM markets. A change in excise taxes from specific to *ad valorem* was also introduced.

The purpose of the reform was to increase tax revenues and improve the incentives for private sector investment and export activity.[30] Anticipated revenue increases failed to materialise due to the recession, and to modifications in the tax legislation. The value added tax was reduced from 10 to 7 per cent and the number of exempted commodities was increased. As a result, revenue from the stamp tax fell by 149.3 million quetzales between 1983 and 1984 and collection from the value added tax only grew by 98 million quetzales. Consequently, the tax reform had a negative effect on revenue growth in 1984, because the increase in revenue as envisaged by the tax reform did not take place.

The external sector

Balance of payments

Guatemala's balance of payments began to deteriorate rapidly after 1979.[31] The cumulative over-all balance of payments deficit during the period 1980–83 reached almost US$1 billion. This includes the accumulation of external payment arrears of nearly US$300 million. During the period 1980–82, the over-all balance of payments deficits averaged US$328 million. These were mainly the result of large trade deficits and rising net factor payments.[32] In addition, net capital inflows were low by historical standards. The current account deficit narrowed in 1983, as a result of a further decline in economic activity. At the same time, because of heavy borrowing by public financed intermediaries, net capital inflows increased. There also took place a sharp decline in private capital outflows. Consequently, the balance of payments showed an over-all surplus of US$31 million in 1983.

Table 11.4 clearly shows how in 1984 the situation deteriorated significantly, resulting in an over-all balance of payments deficit of over US$180 million. This includes the accumulation of US$204 million of external payment arrears. The current account deficit rose

Table 11.4   Summary balance of payments

	1980	1981	1982	1983	Prel. 1984
			(millions of US dollars)		
Current account	−176.4	−572.5	−404.6	−276.6	−396.2
Capital account	−142.3	223.7	88.5	307.7	209.7
Overall balance	−318.7	−348.8	−316.1	31.1	−186.5
Accumulation (+)/re-duction (−) arrears	−	−	288.1	−2.1	204.0
Net official reserves (In-creases −)	318.7	348.8	28.0	−29.0	−17.5
			(As percentage of GDP)		
Current account	−2.2	−6.7	−4.6	−3.1	−4.2
Capital Account	−1.8	2.6	1.0	3.4	2.2
Overall balance	−4.0	−4.1	−3.6	0.3	−2.0

Source: Bank of Guatemala.

from 3.1 per cent of GDP in 1983 to 4.2 per cent in 1984, reflecting a sharp rise in imports and an increase in interest payments of the external debt. In the capital account net capital inflows fell by approximately US$100 million because the drop in net external borrowing by the non-financed public sectors more than offset the net inflow of short-term private capital.

The magnitude of Guatemala's deteriorating economic situation can be seen clearly when analysing the net international reserve position of the country. According to available data, the net international reserves (including external payments arrears) of the Bank of Guatemala dropped from US$398 million at the end of 1980 to minus US$422 million at the end of 1984. These same sources indicate that gross official reserves fell from US$499 million at the end of 1980 to US$360 million at the end of 1984. However, a large percentage of these gross reserves represented non-liquid claims in other CACM countries. Furthermore, gross official reserves which amounted to approximately four months of imports in 1980, represented only three months in 1984.

Table 11.4 indicates that in 1980 a sharp increase in the over-all balance of payments deficit took place. The deficit continued through 1984 with the exception of 1983 when a small surplus of US$31 million appeared. A substantial balance of payment deficit reappeared in 1984 and it is expected that the deficit will be even larger in 1985.

As can also be seen from Table 11.4, the over-all balance of payments deficit represented 4 per cent and 4.1 per cent of GDP in 1980 and 1981 respectively. The small surplus of 1982 was approximately 0.3 per cent of GDP and it is estimated that the deficit of 1984 was around 2 per cent of GDP.

Many reasons have been given for the declining trend in Guatemala's capital inflows which, prior to 1980, had been generally rather large. Among the reasons given the following can be mentioned:

1. The Sandinista overthrow of Somoza in Nicaragua in 1979 and the resulting political destabilisation of the region.
2. The high interest rates prevailing in the world markets in relation to the fixed rates determined by Guatemala's Monetary Junta.
3. The cancellation of private external credits.

The greater yields and the greater security provided in foreign markets, particularly the United States, was probably the most important factor contributing to the flight of capital from Guatemala. This in its turn was a major contributing factor to the substantial deficits in the balance of payments, in spite of the reduction in the deficit that took place in the current account, especially in 1980.

External public debt

Historically, Guatemala has had one of the lowest external debts in Latin America.[33] Guatemala has traditionally followed a very conservative management policy. Most of its outstanding debt had been contracted on concessional terms from unilateral and bilateral sources. However, during the regime of Lucas García, Guatemala began to resort to foreign commercial borrowing, mainly for balance of payment support. The sharp increase in government expenditures for projects that were not always the most productive, contributed in no small degree to the difficulties which soon began to appear in the balance of payments.

As can be seen from Table 11.5, the medium- and long-term external public debt increased from approximately US$700 million in 1980 to over US$1.6 billion in 1984. The sharp increase was due mainly to foreign borrowing by the Bank of Guatemala and COR-FINA. Guatemala's outstanding external debt which had stood at

Table 11.5 Summary of external public debt operations[1]

	1980	1981	1982	1983	Prel. 1984
			(millions of US dollars)		
Outstanding debt (at the end of the year)	689.7	931.0	1 215.4	1 460.1	1 618.5
Debt service payments	74.3	93.8	108.2	153.0	220.5
Amortization	42.5	49.8	57.0	75.1	122.6
Interest	31.8	44.0	51.2	77.9	97.9
			(Ratios in per cent)		
Outstanding public debt/GDP	8.8	10.8	13.9	16.2	17.3
Debt service/exports of goods and services	4.1	6.2	8.3	12.7	17.5

1 Officially guaranteed external debt of over one year; excludes IMF transactions and interest on short-term debt and arrears.

Source: Bank of Guatemala

approximately 1.5 per cent of GDP for many years, suddenly rose to almost 9 per cent in 1980 and 17 per cent of GDP in 1984. Most of the outstanding debt is owed by public financed intermediaries and the Central Government. Guatemala's external debt is still low when compared to that of many of its neighbours in Latin America. However, Guatemala has now a large amount of its external debt with original maturities of one to five years. This type of short-term maturity was almost non-existent before 1980. In 1984 it amounted to over US$400 million. On the other hand, outstanding external debt with maturities of over 15 years remained practically the same between 1981 and 1984 – around US$800 million. A similar thing occurred with respect to outstanding debt with interest rates of over 9 per cent. It rose from US$28 million in 1980 to approximately US$400 million in 1984. Outstanding debt with rates of less than 6 per cent increased from US$380 million in 1980 to US$530 million in 1984.

As a result of the rise in the external debt and the deterioration in the terms of the new borrowing, Guatemala's external debt burden increased significantly. According to available data, Guatemala's debt service payments on medium- and long-term foreign loans rose from US\$74 million in 1980 to over US\$227 in 1984. Repayment on principal also increased from US\$43 million in 1980 to US\$123 million in 1984 and interest payment from US\$32 million in 1980 to almost US\$100 million in 1984. As shown in Table 11.5, the debt service ratio experienced a significant increase, rising from 4 per cent in 1980 to almost 18 per cent in 1984.

Exchange rate policy

For many years Guatemala enjoyed a stable currency and the quetzal was at a par with the US dollar. An exchange rate of one quetzal for one dollar was accepted everywhere, and the Guatemalans had absolute confidence in the stability of their currency. However, as the economic situation began to deteriorate, confidence in the quetzal also began to deteriorate. The exchange rate could no longer be maintained on a one-to-one basis with the dollar.

Controls on capital flow were imposed by the government in April 1980 and on imports in November 1982. As pressures against the fixed rate of exchange began to drain the reserves, controls were put into effect. Although the monetary authorities tolerated the development of a parallel market, at least since mid-1982 only the Central Bank was empowered to deal in foreign exchange. It is estimated that, by June 1982, nearly 40 per cent of all foreign currency operations were handled through the parallel, illegal, market.

It was only in November 1984 that the Guatemalan government approved a three-tier exchange system consisting of (1) an official rate, (2) a free market (parallel) rate and, (3) an auction market rate. The new arrangement did away with the fixed parity system between the quetzal and the dollar which had existed for over 60 years. All import quotas and outward transfers of capital were eliminated. Restrictions on tourist travel were also done away with.

The official exchange rate was established on a one-to-one basis: one quetzal per US dollar. The official rate handled approximately two-thirds of all foreign exchange transactions. Essential imports, mainly gasoline and other petroleum-based fuels, use the official parity of one quetzal = one dollar. Service payments on the external public debt and all other financial transactions of the public sector also use the official exchange rate. Proceeds from traditional exports and official capital inflows finance most of the official market.

The free market rate was determined by market prices. It covered most of the remaining exchange transactions. Non-essential imports and a limited number of exports (primarily coffee and sugar to non-quota markets and non-traditional exports) are transacted in the parallel market.

The auction market utilised proceeds from special foreign loans to the Bank of Guatemala. It was called the 'auction market with borrowed funds' and it was supposed to be used by the private sector to finance certain types of imports at the parallel market rate. Another type of auction market rate received the name of 'auction market with export proceed'. The Bank of Guatemala bought the proceeds of exports from the parallel market at the prevailing rates in that market. Then the Bank would auction the foreign exchange to importers of certain imports, for instance, imports used in the production of exports outside Central America and raw materials for industry. It is estimated that the first type covered less than 3 per cent of total foreign exchange transactions and the second approximately 7 per cent.

In November 1984, the free market rate (parallel rate) was set at approximately 1.45 quetzales = 1 US dollar. It remained almost unchanged during the remainder of 1984. This represented in real terms, a depreciation of about 15 per cent of the quetzal, in relation to the currencies of Guatemala's major trading partners. In 1985 the quetzal deteriorated even more and by October 1985, it had reached almost 4 quetzales per US dollar.

RECENT DEVELOPMENTS

Guatemala entered a new period in its history on 3 November 1985 when presidential elections took place and the country returned to constitutional government the day the new president took office on 14 January 1986. Although it is difficult to make forecasts, it is almost a certainty that significant changes will take place during the coming months. Both internal and external factors are going to help shape the economic policies that are presently under review. With the new government a completely new scheme of forces will enter into play, making it extremely difficult to make any predictions as to what type of economic policy will be implemented.[34]

In April 1985 the government tried to introduce extensive policy changes, covering fiscal, monetary and exchange rate legislation. It is recognised generally that, as a package, they represented a serious step toward much needed structural adjustments.[35]

The policy initiative was short lived, as public opposition, particularly on the part of the private sector, mounted and threatened the government. Unfortunately, austerity measures that the government was willing to take were presented to the public without, or with little, prior consultation. As a result the authorities, isolated on most major issues and without adequate support, were forced to rescind the package several days after it was announced.

Soon afterwards, the government opened a national policy dialogue to evaluate alternative proposals to solve the economic crisis. Most major political groups were invited to participate, including private sector organisations, universities and labour unions. In spite of differences of opinion, a certain degree of agreement was reached and recommendations for policy changes were finally made. Probably the most positive aspect of the national dialogue was the fact that the numerous diverse groups in the economy were able to get together to discuss major issues and air their differences in an open forum.

The 1 July policy package that resulted from the national dialogue represented a compromise among the participating groups. The public sector conceded a 72 million quetzales spending cut up to the end of the year. The private sector agreed to several new taxes, including a 3.5 per cent tax on foreign exchange transactions. In return, there was a commitment from the government to encourage the establishment of trading companies, an open seas and skies policy and the simplification of export red tape. A number of import commodities were transferred from the official to the parallel exchange market.

The culmination of the dialogue process came when the leadership of the different sectors travelled together to Washington seeking sources of external financing for Guatemala.

The optimism surrounding the national dialogue has begun to fade. Guatemalans are realising that the policy changes which cost so much to hammer out did not go far enough to stem the rapid deterioration of the economy. Protests and strikes, a reaction to accelerating inflation, have forced the Guatemalan government into a holding pattern, with additional economic stabilisation measures unlikely in the near future. Needed policy reforms will most likely rely on the initiative of the elected government, which took power in January 1986.

The challenge faced by the new government will be enormous in the fiscal, monetary and exchange areas. However, perhaps one of the most important single factors that will help shape the new economic policy is the service of the public debt. Regardless of which candidate is elected, he will have to face a growing debt, inflation, growing subsidies and controls, and less investment. To make matters worse, in mid-1984 the standby agreement reached with the International Monetary Fund (IMF) lapsed with approximately US$60 million in credits undisbursed. The standby agreements, which the government of Guatemala had negotiated with the IMF in 1983, and which covered the 16-month period from September 1983 to December 1984, simply lapsed because, according to an IMF staff appraisal, Guatemala's progress toward programme objectives had not been fulfilled, even though the government of Guatemala generally met all criteria except the revenue targets.

A new standby agreement with the IMF would be advisable. But the IMF demands certain conditions that the Guatemalan govern-ment must adopt: higher revenues, more flexible interest rates, unifi-cation of exchange rate more in accordance with existing reality, and the servicing of the debt of the Banco de Guatemala – both amortisa-tion and interest payments – particularly with respect to arrears. For reasons previously indicated, the present Guatemalan authorities are not at this time willing to take the necessary adjustment measures that the country requires. Political and social reasons have forced the government into inaction and as a result the new government that came into power 14 January 1986 will have to take the initiative and carry out the economic adjustment measures that are needed to restore confidence in the economy and do the groundwork for future growth.[36]

The newly-established authorities will have to convince the public of the need to establish fiscal and monetary measures which most surely will not be popular in the short run; however, in the longer run these measures will prove to be not only beneficial, but the condition *sine qua non* for the healthy development of Guatemala's economy. The Guatemalan public has become rather sceptical, and is not always prepared to accept at face value many of the adjustments and reforms that the country needs. That is why it is all the more necessary that the government urgently carry out an immediate campaign of public education explaining the reality of the economic situation and the measures that have to be taken in order to reactivate the economy, increase the level of employment, and bring the fruits of growth to all sectors of Guatemalan society, especially to those that are most in need.

A new window of opportunity has been opened for Guatemala. A new era of political and economic freedom is in the making. The Guatemalans are an industrious and hardworking people. The country enjoys the natural and human resources that are necessary for development. What the country needs more than anything else is the will to carry out the objective that all Guatemalans want: the integral development of their country. Thus the most important factor to be reckoned with in any process of development is the will to carry it through. All the other factors – land, labour, capital and entrepreneurship – no matter how important they may be, are not enough if the will is not there to make them work. There is no limit to Guatemala's potential for development as long as there is the will to carry it through. It is necessary that Guatemalans of all walks of life join together in a common effort and back the newly-elected government in its quest for a new and more developed Guatemala, with freedom and justice for all.

Notes

1. US Agency for International Development, *Congressional Presentation Data Sheet for Guatemala*, October 1985 (derived from World Bank economic and social data base).
2. For an excellent survey of Guatemala's economy up to 1976, see World Bank, *Guatemala, Economical Social Position and Prospects* (Washington, DC: World Bank, 1978).
3. Guatemala was not the only country in Latin America that began experiencing sharp declines in its real GDP in 1980 (see Centro de Estudios Monetarios Latinoamericanos (CEMLA), *Sintesis de la evolucion financiera de America Latina y el Caribe en el ano 1982, Boletin*, Vol. 29, No. 3, Supplement May–June 1983.
4. US Department of State, *Quarterly Economic Report*, US Embassy Guatemala, January–March 1984, p. 2 (see also, Centro de Investigacion Economica Nacional (CIEN), *Analisis de la Situacion Economica de Guatemala 1965–1984*, Guatemala, November 1984, p. 5). According to data presented by the World Bank, the average annual growth rate of Guatemala for the period 1960–70 was 5.6 per cent and for the period 1970–82, 5 per cent (see World Bank, *World Development Report 1984* (Oxford University Press, 1984). p. 220).
5. For general overview of the crisis in Latin America, see United Nations, Economic Commission for Latin America (ECLA), *The Crisis in Latin America: Present Situation and Future Outlook* (E/CEPAL/CEGAN.8/L.2) Montevideo, Uruguay, 18–20 January 1984.
6. Agency for International Development, *Guatemala*, Country Development Strategy Statement FY 1986 (Washington, DC: April 1984) p. iii.
7. According to the World Bank, the terms of trade turned decidedly

against Guatemala after 1980. Using 1980 as the base year (1980 = 100) the terms of trade were 71 in 1982. See also, International Monetary Fund (IMF), *Recent Economic Developments – Guatemala*, May 1985, p. 26.

8. For some interesting studies on the Central American Common Market see *Revista de la Integracion y el Desarrollo de Centroamerica*, published by the Banco Centro Americano de Intergracion Economica, Tegucigalpa, Honduras. In particular see the articles, 'Integracion Regional: i puede reactivarse el Mercado Comun Centroamericano?' and 'Centroamerica: asistencia economica externa, reformas a las politicas y mercados financieros nacionales en recupersion economica' by Eduardo Lizano and Claudio Gonzalez Vega, respectively.

9. Agency for International Development, *Guatemala*, Country Development Strategy Statement FY 1986 (Washington, DC: April 1984) p. 6.

10. See International Monetary Fund (IMF), *International Financial Statistics* (Washington, DC: 1984).

11. See also Centro de Investigacion de la Economia Nacional (CIEN), *Guatemala 1984–1987, A Review of the Economy, the Political Spectrum and a Look into the Future* (Guatemala, 31 May 1985). According to the Banco de Guatemala, per capita income in 1985 is at the level of 1972 (Banco de Guatemala, Informe del Departamento de Investigacion Agricola e Industrial, Guatemala, Octobre 1985, p. 2).

12. US Embassy, Guatemala, *US Economic Assistance Strategy for Guatemala 1984–1993*, Paper for Deputy Secretary of State Dam, November 1983.

13. For a more comprehensive understanding of the petroleum situation in Guatemala see 'Actualidad Petrolera en Guatemala', published by the Direccion General de Hidrocarburos of the Ministerio de Energia y Minas, and 'Anuario Estadistico', published directly by the Ministerio de Energia y Minas.

14. It fell to less than 1.1 million barrels.

15. The price of diesel has been kept at the artificially low price of 1.17 quetzales per gallon.

16. Centro de Investigacio de la Economia Nacional (CIEN), op. cit. (note 11) p. 17.

17. Ibid., p. 6.

18. Ibid., p. 20.

19. Ibid., p. 22.

20. The World Bank, *World Development Report 1984* (Oxford: Oxford University Press, 1984) p. 218.

21. For further information concerning the evolution of Guatemala's and other Latin American consumer prices between 1975 and 1983 see the United Nations, Economic Commission for Latin America (ECLA), *Preliminary Overview of All Latin American Economies 1983*, (E/ CEPAL/G. 1279) 29 December 1983, p. 27.

22. Between 1970 and 1982 the average annual rate of inflation was 10.1 per cent (see World Bank, op. cit. (note 19) p. 218).

23. In January 1985, Decree No. 1–85, the Consumer Protection Law, was approved. It not only set prices and regulated profits but also established

fines and sanctions, including the possibility of direct government intervention in running the business.

24. See World Bank, op. cit. (note 19), p. 226.
25. According to the World Bank, gross domestic investment represented 10 per cent of GDP in 1960 and 14 per cent in 1982. However, gross domestic saving was only 8 per cent in 1960 and 10 per cent in 1982. Thus, the resource balance was − 2 in 1960 and − 4 in 1982. See World Bank, op. cit. (note 19), p. 226.
26. It in fact declined to 5.9 per cent in 1985.
27. Early in 1985 the Bank of Guatemala estimated that the deficit of the Central Government would be approximately 352 million quetzales (see *Guatemala 1984–1987, A Review of the Economy, the Political Spectrum and a Look into the Future*, by Staff of CIEN).
28. The deficit from January to November 1984 was 276.2 million quetzales. Estimates of the 1985 deficit indicate a reduction of the deficit to 214.8 million quetzales.
29. See also, US Department of Commerce, *Foreign Economic Trends and Their Implications for the United States, Guatemala* (prepared by American Embassy, Guatemala City) March 1984, p. 9.
30. According to available data, in 1983 the Central American Countries showed the following ratios of tax revenues to GDP: Guatemala .063, El Salvador .112, Honduras .120, Panama .151, Costa Rica .155, and Nicaragua .222.
31. For a more comprehensive view of Guatemala's balance of payments see International Monetary Fund (IMF), *Balance of Payments Statistics, Year Book*, Part I, 1984, Vol. 35, pp. 236–41.
32. It is interesting to note that, according to World Bank data, the average annual growth rate of Guatemala's exports was 9.3 per cent between 1960 and 1970. The rate declined to 5.4 per cent between 1970 and 1982 (see World Bank, op. cit. (note 19) p. 234).
33. According to the World Bank, Guatemala's debt service ratio was 1.4 per cent in 1970. The ratio did not change significantly until the advent of the Lucas García regime.
34. For an evaluation of the present economic situation in Guatemala and some of the proposals made by the Mejia Government in the areas of monetary and fiscal policies, see Consejo Tecnico Banco de Guatemala, 'Evaluacion de la Actividad Economica y Financiera en 1984, sus Perspectivas para 1985 y Propuesta de Politica Monetaria Cambiaria y Crediticia para el Periodo Febrero-Marzo de 1985', Guatemala, January 1985.
35. See US AID Mission (US Agency for International Development) FY 86/87, Action Plan, Guatemala, 1985.
36. In March 1986 the government announced plans that included the following measures: (i) the simplification of the exchange rate system; (ii) the introduction of a 30 per cent tax on exports; and (iii) the investment of 100 million quetzales in road and drainage projects aimed at generating an estimated 40 000 new jobs.

Part IV
Caribbean

12 Financial Deepening, Domestic Resource Mobilisation and Economic Growth: Jamaica 1955–82

Compton Bourne

The economic growth performance of most Commonwealth Caribbean countries has been unimpressive in recent years. Real per capita gross domestic product declined by 5 per cent in Guyana and 17 per cent in Jamaica between 1970 and 1982. The Trinidad and Tobago economy which grew rapidly during the petroleum price boom of 1974 to 1981 experienced decreases in real per capita Gross Domestic Product (GDP) in 1983 and 1984. Barbadian real gross product per capita also declined in 1982 and 1983.

In the continuing search for solutions, official attention has recently been redirected to domestic resource mobilisation. The structural adjustment policy memorandum adopted by the Caribbean Community Heads of Government in Nassau in July 1984 states that 'structural adjustment programmes should also aim at increasing in the medium term the rate of domestic investment and the nationally financed portion of such investment' (Commonwealth Caribbean Community Secretariat, p. 29).

The financial sector is envisaged to play a critical role:

Diversification of the mix of financial institutions and instruments assists in the savings mobilization and efficient resource allocation effort ... Interest rate policy should aim at providing a real return to savers and hence increase the level of national savings (Commonwealth Caribbean Community Secretariat, p. 166).

The new stance on the role of the financial sector represents a rather remarkable shift in policy orientation. It comes after over one decade

165

of conscious financial repression in some countries, notably Guyana, and severe neglect in others. The policy shift provides the stimulus for the analysis of the role of the financial sector in domestic resource mobilisation and economic growth in Commonwealth Caribbean economies. This paper does so by examining in detail the Jamaican experience between 1955 and 1982. This economy experienced contrasting episodes of financial deepening and financial retardation, and economic growth and recession.

The paper is divided into three substantive sections. The first section describes the main trends in economic growth and aggregate investment and savings behaviour. The second section describes and analyses the process of financial deepening and shallowing, and in the third section an attempt is made to analyse the relationship between financial deepening and either aggregate domestic savings or aggregate domestic investment. The main conclusions are presented in the final section of the paper.

TRENDS IN INCOME, SAVINGS AND INVESTMENT

The Jamaican economy grew rapidly between 1953 and 1973. The annual rate of growth of real GDP averaged 6 per cent. As is evident from Figure 12.1, however, growth rates were highly unstable. The coefficient of variation (a summary measure of stability) was 0.9 during this period. No serious inflationary problems were experienced. The mean annual rate of inflation (measured by the implicit deflator for GDP) was 3 per cent. The rate of inflation, however, was quite variable, the coefficient of variation being 0.8.

The growth performance altered significantly after 1973. Real gross domestic product declined at an average annual rate of 2 per cent between 1974 and 1982. Furthermore, greater fluctuations were experienced. The coefficient of variation of the annual GDP growth rate in this second sub-period was 1.4. Inflation was more rapid though less variable. The mean annual rate of inflation rose to 17 per cent, with a coefficient of variation of 0.4.

The economic growth experience reflects savings and investment trends.[2] Jamaican gross investment ratios were an average 23 per cent lower during the economic recession than during the period of rapid growth, that is, gross investment averaged 17 per cent of GDP in the 1974–82 sub-period, compared with 22 per cent in the 1955–73 sub-period. Moreover, the variability of the investment ratio increased

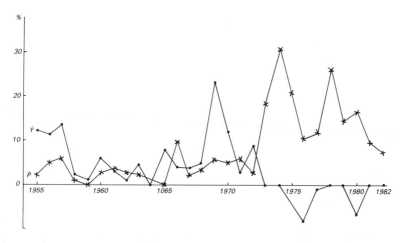

Figure 12.1 Growth rate of real GDP ($\dot{Y}$) and rate of inflation ($\dot{P}$)

from 15 per cent to 20 per cent. The domestic savings ratio decreased by 27 per cent from an average 16 per cent of GDP in 1955–73 to an average 12 per cent between 1974 and 1982. Thus, domestic resource mobilisation was weaker after 1973. It should also be mentioned that, although foreign savings continued to supplement domestic savings, the ratio of foreign savings to GDP decreased from the 1955–73 average of 6 per cent to an average of 5 per cent between 1974 and 1982. Figure 12.2 depicts these trends in investment and savings in greater detail.

The downward trend in the macroeconomic variables depicted in Figures 12.1 and 12.2 signify that policies to raise the domestic savings and investment rates are warranted. A considerable body of theoretical and empirical literature has produced a consensus that financial deepening influences the economic growth rate primarily through its effects on the level and efficiency of savings and invest-ment.[3] It is, therefore, appropriate to proceed to an analysis of the financial deepening process during the periods of growth and decline.

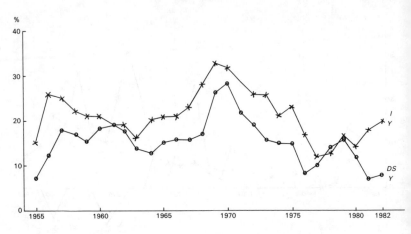

Figure 12.2   Gross investment ratio (*I*/*Y*) and domestic savings ratio (*DS*/*Y*)

FINANCIAL DEEPENING AND SHALLOWING

Financial deepening is a multidimensional concept. It refers to the increasing weight of financial transactions in an economy, as well as to an expansion in the array of financial institutions and instruments. The most widely used indicators are the ratio of real values of financial assets to real income or wealth, the maturity structure of financial instruments, real interest rates, and the ratio of real credit to real income. These indicators will be employed in this study. None the less, it is useful to convey some aspects of the institutional nature of the financial sector.

As in other less developed countries, broad monetary assets (defined as currency with the public plus deposits in financial institutions) are the predominant financial assets in Jamaica. There was a significant increase in the number of depository financial institutions between 1967 and 1974. Nine new commercial banks were established, compared with four banks previously established early in the twentieth century and four banks established between 1959 and 1965.

Some non-monetary institutions and instruments came into existence. For example, a Stock Exchange was established in 1969. Also, the flow of government securities and corporate equity substantially expanded. None the less, currency and deposit instruments retained their predominance. Flow of funds data compiled by the Central Bank reveal that in 1976 broad money comprised 60 per cent of total financial assets held by the household sector. Therefore, the focus on monetary assets is justified.

The ratio of real money balances to real GDP increased unsteadily from 23 per cent in 1955 to 40 per cent in 1971, remained fairly stable at 40 to 43 per cent for the next six years, and then declined to 31 per cent in 1980 as the recession deteriorated (See Figure 12.3). The ratio, however, recovered in 1981 and 1982. On the basis of this monetary velocity indicator, it can be inferred that Jamaica experienced considerable financial deepening between 1963 and 1974, but that the process was reversed between 1974 and 1981.

The literature on financial deepening and other mainstream monetary writings identify two major influences on the growth of demand for real monetary assets. These are the level of real incomes and the

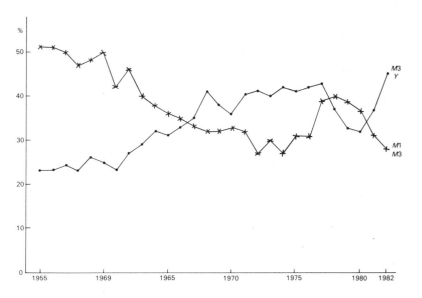

Figure 12.3 Ratio of real broad money stock (*M*3) to real GDP and ratio of narrow money stock (*M*1) to broad money stock

real rate of interest on monetary assets. The real rate of interest, in Fisherine terms, is defined as the nominal rate of interest adjusted for inflation expectations, that is, $r = i - p^e$ where r is the real rate of interest, i is the nominal rate of interest, and p^e is the expected rate of price inflation. The influence of these variables in Jamaica was econometrically investigated with annual data for the 1955 to 1982 period. The nominal rate of interest and the expected rate of inflation were treated separately in order to obtain greater insight into the complementary policies of interest rate liberalisation and price level stability. Expected values of the inflation variable were generated by a first order autoregressive process.

The following is the result of the ordinary least squares (OLS) estimation:

$$\ln M^D = -5.46 + 1.63 \ln Y + 3.64 i_D - 1.48 \dot{p}^e \qquad (12.1)$$
$$ (-7.1) \quad\;\; (13.8) \quad (2.1) \quad\;\; (-2.1)$$
$$\overline{R}^2 = 0.94 \;\; F = 145.3 \;\; DW = 1.76 \;\; RHO(1) = 0.38$$

Where Y is real GDP, i_D is the weighted average nominal interest rate on bank deposits, and $\dot{p}^e$ is the expected rate of change of the consumer price index.

The regression coefficients are all statistically significant and the over-all efficiency of the model is high. The signs of the coefficients conform to theoretical predictions. It can be seen from the direct estimate of the income elasticity of real money demand that demand responds strongly to changes in GDP. In contrast, the computed elasticities for the nominal interest rate and the expected rate of inflation are decidedly weak (0.19 and -0.14 respectively). The level of income has been the main influence on financial asset accumulation. The weak supportive role of nominal interest rates has been almost totally offset by the expected rate of inflation.

In fact, real deposit rates of interest were negative in most years of the entire 27-year period (See Figure 12.4). According to Shaw[4] real interest rates are perhaps the least ambiguous indicator of financial deepening or shallowing. On this basis, some doubt must be entertained about the extent of financial deepening even in the first sub-period for which other indicators suggest substantial financial growth.

Interest rate policy was inconsistent with monetary equilibrium in the post-1973 period. The nominal money stock expanded at an average annual rate of 18 per cent as the government primed the

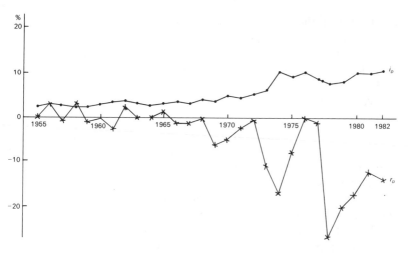

Figure 12.4   Nominal deposit rate of interest (i_D) and real deposit rate of interest (r_D)

pump in an attempt to maintain the growth of public sector real expenditures in the face of declining fiscal revenues.[5] Public Sector net indebtedness to the monetary sector increased from J$98m in 1974 to J$2.5 billion in 1982. The rapid rate of monetary expansion was not warranted in the context of falling real incomes. Granted the expansion of nominal money and the contraction of real incomes, monetary equilibrium required substantial increases in real deposit rates of interest, rather than the decreases which actually occurred.

FINANCIAL DEEPENING AND THE SAVINGS-INVESTMENT PROCESS

McKinnon[6] has outlined a theory of the link between financial deepening and the savings-investment process. The crux of his theoretical scheme is the 'complementarity hypothesis'. By this hypothesis, McKinnon maintains that there is a positive relationship between accumulation of real money balances and real investment under regimes of self-financed investment.[7] Savings takes the form of financial asset accumulation prior to the act of investment. Monetary assets are thus the 'conduit' for investment. As McKinnon[8] shows, the complementarity hypothesis leads to a behavioural specification of the domestic savings rate in which the growth rate of income and the real deposit rate of interest are explanatory variables. With the addition of a Harrod-Domar balanced growth equation, one has a simple formal link between financial deepening and economic growth.

Matters are not so straightforward if more realistic assumptions are made about the functioning of the economy. The household sector and the corporate sector are the main holders of monetary assets.[9] The former are surplus units for which deposits constitute savings at the micro level. The latter are mainly deficit units whose deposit balances are more in the nature of working capital than investment funds. Self-financial investment linked to monetary accumulation is therefore atypical of the Jamaican economy. Because of these behavioural characteristics, Shaw's[10] debt-intermediation approach provides a potentially more illuminating framework for analysing the link between financial deepening and the savings–investment process.

Within the debt-intermediation framework, financial intermediaries are juxtapositioned between micro-savers and investors. The economic sequence is from surplus units (micro-savings) to financial intermediaries (monetary assets) to investment (aggregate savings in the national accounts sense). The strength of the link between financial asset accumulation and aggregate savings and investment depends critically upon the extent to which financial intermediaries transform their liabilities into credit for physical capital accumulation. If the coefficient of transformation is large, that is, close to unity, then one would expect a strong relationship between the determinants of the demand for real money balances and the domestic savings and investment ratios. In other words, econometric estimation of savings and investment functions such as:

$$\frac{DS}{Y} = f_1(\dot{Y}, \dot{r}_D) \tag{12.2}$$

$$\frac{I}{Y} = f_2(\dot{Y}, \dot{r}_D) \tag{12.3}$$

should yield statistically significant positive coefficients.[11]

If the coefficient of transformation is small, there will be a weak statistical relationship between the arguments of the demand for money function and the savings and investment ratios. Furthermore, the coefficient on the interest rate variable may be negative. This can happen if credit flows from financial intermediaries are not allocated to investment expenditures, but are allocated instead to consumption and working capital. In such situations, monetary accumulation is competitive with capital accumulation.[12]

Before examining the econometric evidence, it is useful to consider the behaviour of two financial series which are related to the magnitude of the transformation coefficient. The first is the ratio of narrow money balances, that is, currency plus demand deposits, to the broad money stock. This variable is a measure of liquidity preference. The higher the ratio, the smaller the scope for term transformation by financial institutions. Correspondingly, the lesser is the scope for their financing of investment. Liquidity preference declined in Jamaica until 1974. The ratio of narrow money to broad money decreased from 0.51 in 1955 to 0.27 in 1974 (see Figure 12.3). This trend in liquidity preference was reversed after 1974. The ratio, having increased to 0.31 in 1975, averaged 0.39 between 1977 and 1980. Theoretically, liquidity preference is expected to vary inversely with the level of income and the real rate of interest on deposits. This expectation is supported by econometric evidence. Ordinary least squares regression yielded the result:

$$\frac{M1}{M3} = \begin{matrix} 1.49 \\ (3.0) \end{matrix} \begin{matrix} -0.16 \ln Y \\ (2.2) \end{matrix} \begin{matrix} -1.37 i_D \\ (-2.2) \end{matrix} \begin{matrix} +0.54 \dot{p}^e \\ (2.2) \end{matrix} \qquad (12.4)$$

$$\bar{R}^2 = 0.305 \quad F = 4.8 \quad DW = 2.12 \quad RHO(1) = 0.67$$

However, the sensitivities are weak. The computed elasticities for the three explanatory variables are 0.02 for income and the nominal rate of interest, and 0.01 for the expected rate of inflation. Thus, the behaviour of the ratio of narrow money to broad money is not fully explained by income and interest rate movements.

The second financial series related to the transformation coefficient is the share of real credit allocated to government and personal consumption in total credit. Between 1955 and 1960 the government sector was a net creditor. Between 1961 and 1974 this sector absorbed 15 per cent of total monetary sector credit. Its share rose rapidly to average 65 per cent between 1977 and 1982. The private consumption content of credit decreased substantially over time. The share of personal loans in commercial bank credit fell from average 20 per cent between 1967 and 1975 to average 17 per cent between 1976 and 1980, and 8 per cent in 1982. Compared to these trends in the shares of government sector credit and personal credit, the share of the private productive sector averaged 85 per cent between 1961 and 1974 and 35 per cent between 1977 and 1982. Altogether, it appears that government debt crowded out real credit to the private productive sector in the post-1974 period. None the less, the fact that the private production sector obtained a significant proportion of credit throughout the entire 1955 to 1982 period leaves open for statistical verification the possibility that monetary accumulation was consistent with aggregate savings and investment.

To analyse this issue more closely, savings and investment equations were estimated by ordinary least squares. The savings and investment functions include the ratio of foreign savings to real GDP as an additional determinant to incorporate the negative association of foreign savings with domestic savings, and the positive association of foreign capital with domestic investment.[13] Also, the ratio of real credit to the real productive sector to real GDP $(C)/Y$ is included in the investment function as a separate explanatory variable to allow for credit rationing effects on investment. The regression results are as follows:

$$\frac{DS}{Y} = \underset{(4.1)}{0.15} + \underset{(2.9)}{0.22\,\dot{Y}} - \underset{(-1.8)}{0.75\,i_D} + \underset{(3.5)}{0.60\,\dot{p}^e} - \underset{(-3.7)}{0.53\,FS/Y} \qquad (12.5)$$

$$\bar{R}^2 = 0.525 \quad F = 8.46 \quad DW = 2.22 \quad RHO(1) = 1.3 \quad RHO(2) = -0.5$$

$$\frac{I}{Y} = \underset{(4.1)}{0.16} + \underset{(2.7)}{0.23\,\dot{Y}} - \underset{(-1.8)}{0.78\,i_D} + \underset{(3.3)}{0.60\,\dot{p}^e} \qquad (12.6)$$

$$+ \underset{(3.2)}{0.51\,FS/Y} - \underset{(-0.4)}{0.04\,C/Y}$$

$$\bar{R}^2 = 0.530 \qquad F = 7.08 \qquad DW = 2.22 \qquad RHO(1) = 1.3$$
$$RHO(2) = -0.5$$

In each case, corrections were made for first and second order auto correlation. It can be seen that the equations are efficiently estimated. Only the credit ratio variable in the investment equation is statistically insignificant. The interest rate coefficients are significant at the 10 per cent level, and the others are significant at the 1 per cent level.

The closeness of the estimated equations to each other – compare the coefficients – implies that an independent investment function does not exist. It is sufficient to estimate the savings function in order to explore the connection between financial deepening and economic growth in a model of economic growth. Of particular interest are the coefficients on the interest rate and the expected inflation rate. These are signed contrary to the theoretical predictions of the financial deepening hypothesis. The 'competing asset' effect appears to be dominant. Monetary accumulation, fostered by real deposit rates of interest, does not seem to have been complementary to aggregate savings and investment. When one also considers the absence of any statistical relationship between the credit ratio and the investment ratio, there must be considerable scepticism about the efficiency of the debt-intermediation process in Jamaica.

Despite the non-existence of a strong positive relationship between real interest rates and aggregate savings, there is another possible mechanism linking financial deepening and economic growth. The efficiency of physical capital and labour in the production process varies positively with working capital. Thus, aggregate output varies directly, though not necessarily continuously, with the stock of working capital. In Jamaica, like many other less developed countries (LDCs), corporate enterprises extensively utilise bank credit for working capital. Their demand matches the loan maturity preferences of the banks who make primarily short- to medium-term loans. Monetary accumulation can, therefore, influence the level of growth of aggregate output by facilitating the supply of working capital. Extending the logic one step further, a relationship can be postulated between the real deposit rate and the rate of growth of real gross domestic product. This proposition was tested by the ordinary least squares (OLS) regression reported below:[14]

$$\dot{Y} = 0.007 + 1.249\, i_D - 1.061\, p^e \qquad (12.7)$$
$$\phantom{\dot{Y} = }(2.68) \quad (1.24) \quad (-2.53)$$

$$\bar{R}^2 = 0.3198 \quad F = 7.11 \quad DW = 1.90 \quad RHO(1) = 0.24$$

The signs of the regression coefficients conform with theoretical expectations. The growth rate varies directly with the nominal deposit rate of interest and varies inversely with the expected rate of inflation. However, the interest rate coefficient is not efficiently estimated. Overall, the fitted equation is suggestive of a positive influence of financial deepening on the income growth rate.

CONCLUSIONS AND IMPLICATIONS

The analysis in this study revealed that considerable financial deepening occurred during the period of economic growth and moderate price inflation. The process of financial deepening was reversed in some significant respects during the later economic recession. The behaviour of real interest rates is somewhat at variance with the other financial indicators. Real interest rates were negative throughout the entire period, thereby qualifying the conclusion about financial deepening in the first sub-period. It is to be noted, however, that real interest rates became increasingly negative during the second sub-period when the financial process was unambiguously retarded. Overall, the examination of financial trends leads to the conclusion that the financial sector was an important mechanism for resource mobilisation.

The financial sector functioned passively with respect to resource mobilisation. The main determinant of the growth in demand for real money balances was the level of income. The real deposit rate of interest had a weak, though positive, influence on monetary accumulation. This itself may have been the result of real interest rates being persistently negative.

Resource mobilisation through the financial system does not appear to be associated with changes in the rates of savings and investment. A weak, negative relationship was estimated between the deposit rate of interest and the domestic savings and investment rates. Furthermore, credit to the productive sector as a ratio of total credit was not a statistically significant explanatory variable. The absence of a positive association between monetary accumulation and the savings–investment process may be explained by the asset portfolio behaviour of financial intermediaries. Deposits are not transformed substantially into credit for physical capital accumulation, but are instead directed towards credit for public and private consumption and for working capital requirements of the private productive sector.

The provision of working capital by the financial sector is not without benefit. An adequate supply of working capital improves the productive efficiency of capital and labour. It was shown that financial deepening or shallowing as represented by the real deposit rate of interest does exert a positive, though small, influence on the rate of economic growth.

These conclusions have policy implications. They imply that while a regime of positive real interest rates is likely to strengthen the financial sector and raise the demand for monetary assets, careful attention will have to be directed towards the credit policies of financial intermediaries if financial growth is to have its counterpart in capital stock growth. Some restraint on public sector credit seems warranted. Also, the composition of credit to the private sector will have to be altered in favour of investment credit instead of its presently strong concentration on working capital. Liberalisation of deposit rates of interest needs to be accompanied by policies for restructuring asset portfolios of Jamaican financial intermediaries.

Notes

1. Versions of this paper have been presented at conferences at Ohio State University, Florida International University, and the Bank of Jamaica. I am indebted for the comments of participants. Thanks are due also to James Croal and Arnold McIntyre, who helped with the econometric work.
2. Investment is real gross capital formation. Real domestic savings is estimated as gross capital formation minus foreign savings. Foreign savings is defined as the current account balance in the standard two-gap model.
3. The seminal contributions are by Ronald McKinnon, *Money and Capital in Economic Development* and Ronald McKinnon, 'Money, Growth, and the Propensity to Save: An Iconoclastic View', and Edward S. Shaw, *Financial Deepening in Economic Development*. Important contributions have come from Vincente Galbis, 'Financial Intermediation and Economic Growth in Less Developed Countries: A Theoretical Approach', Maxwell J. Fry, 'Money and Capital or Financial Deepening in Economic Development?' and 'Models of Financially Repressed Developing Economies', and Robert C. Vogel and Stephen A. Buser, 'Inflation, Financial Repression and Capital Formation in Latin America'.
4. Edward S. Shaw, *Financial Deepening in Economic Development*, p. 8.
5. For an analysis of government expenditure and debt policy in Jamaica, see Compton Bourne, 'Government Foreign Borrowing and Economic Growth: The Case of Jamaica'.
6. Ronald McKinnon, *Money and Capital in Economic Development*, and Ronald McKinnon, 'Money, Growth, and the Propensity to Save: An Iconoclastic View'.
7. Ronald McKinnon, *Money and Capital in Economic Development*, pp. 57–61.
8. Ronald McKinnon, *Money and Capital in Economic Development*.
9. At the end of 1982, the household sector held 51 per cent and business firms 21 per cent of commercial bank deposits.
10. Edward S. Shaw, *Financial Deepening in Economic Development*.

11. The saving ratio function is derived by combining a balanced growth equation $Y = S_D/Y \cdot I/V$ with a savings function $S_D/Y + \delta M/Y$ and a money demand function $M^D = F(Y, r_D)$. The investment function follows from the usual national income identity.

12. Ronald McKinnon in *Money and Capital in Economic Development*, pp. 61–2, identifies another reason for this dominant competing asset effect, namely, when the real rate of interest tends towards 'the best marginal and intra-marginal returns to be earned by self-financed investments'.

13. Douglas Dacey in 'Foreign Aid, Government Consumption, Savings and Growth in Less Developed Countries' and Nathaniel H. Leff and Kazuo Sato in 'Macroeconomics Adjustment in Developing Countries: Instability, Short-run Growth and External Dependency' provide recent evidence on these relationships.

14. Maxwell Fry in 'Money and Capital or Financial Deepening in Economic Development', estimated a similar equation for a sample of seven LDCs.

References

Bourne, Compton, 'Government Foreign Borrowing and Economic Growth: The Case of Jamaica', *Social and Economic Studies*, Vol. 30, No. 4, 1981, pp. 52–74.

Commonwealth Caribbean Community Secretariat, Measures for Structural Adjustment of Member States of the Caribbean Community, May 1984.

Dacey, Douglas, 'Foreign Aid, Government Consumption, Savings and Growth in Less Developed Countries', *Economic Journal*, Vol. 85, 1975.

Fry, Maxwell J., 'Money and Capital or Financial Deepening in Economic Development?', *Journal of Money Credit and Banking*, Vol. 10, 1978, pp. 464–75.

Fry, Maxwell J., 'Models of Financially Repressed Developing Economies', *World Development*, Vol. 10, 1982, pp 731–50.

Galbis, Vincente, 'Financial Intermediation and Economic Growth in Less Developed Countries: A Theoretical Approach', *Journal of Development Studies*, Vol. 13, 1977, pp. 58–72.

Galbis, Vincente, 'Money, Investment and Growth in Latin America, 1961–1973', *Economic Development and Cultural Change*, Vol. 27, 1979, pp. 523–43.

Leff, Nathaniel H. and Kazuo Sato, 'Macroeconomic Adjustment in Developing Countries: Instability, Short-run Growth, and External Dependency', *Review of Economics and Statistics*, Vol. 62, 1980, pp. 170–79.

McKinnon, Ronald, *Money and Capital in Economic Development* (Washington, DC: The Brookings Institution, 1973).

McKinnon, Ronald, 'Money, Growth, and the Propensity to Save: An Iconoclastic View', in George Horwich and Paul A. Samuelson (eds) *Trade, Stability and Macroeconomics* (New York: Academic Press, 1974) pp. 487–501.

Shaw, Edward S., *Financial Deepening in Economic Development*, (New York: Oxford University Press, 1973).

Vogel, Robert C. and Stephen A. Buser, 'Inflation, Financial Repression and Capital Formation in Latin America', in Ronald McKinnon (ed.) *Money and Finance in Economic Growth and Development* (New York: Marcel Dekker, 1976) pp. 35–70.

13 Some Warnings Concerning Possible Financial Reform in the Dominican Republic

Andres Dauhajre

One of the recommendations international financial institutions, particularly the International Monetary Fund and the World Bank, often make to less developed countries with severe balance of payments disequilibria, is to increase the rate of interest on time deposits. The experts who work at these agencies, and the technical missions who visit these countries, adopt the theoretical frameworks of McKinnon (1973), Shaw (1973) and Kapur (1976), and consider that the increase in the rate of interest on time deposits will raise the economy's level of savings. This would enlarge the real size of the banking system and, consequently, the net banking credit flow necessary to finance investment.

Kapur goes even further in this line of argumentation and indicates that the increased flow of banking credit to finance investment projects would cause domestic output to rise over the long-term horizon, which, in turn, would reduce inflationary pressures provided that aggregate demand remains unchanged. These considerations are correct within theoretical frameworks designed for developed economies. However, these points are not necessarily valid for theoretical frameworks encompassing the unique features of small open developing economies.

THE EXISTENCE OF A FRAGMENTED FINANCIAL SYSTEM

Van Wijnbergen (1983) has shown that the results obtained by

McKinnon and Kapur crucially depend on a hidden assumption concerning the asset structure of the financial market, an assumption which is never established explicitly. All these authors suppose that the portfolio shift towards savings deposits originates from 'unproductive' assets, such as gold, cash money and demand deposits, which constitute a very naïve simplification of the financial structure of the majority of less developed countries. These countries, which include the Dominican Republic, are characterised by the existence of informal financial markets where the public and the non-regulated financial companies lend directly to business and to farmers. The existence of this alternative asset market, which supplies more intermediation than the formal banking system itself, might change McKinnon's and Kapur's conclusions drastically.

Van Wijnbergen's argument is as follows:

Let us assume the existence of an economy where three financial assets predominate:

1. non-interest-bearing money,
2. time deposits that bear a fixed interest rate in the formal market, and
3. time deposits with a flexible interest rate in the informal credit market.

Let us suppose that the monetary authorities let the formal market interest rate float. Once one lets the informal market interest rate be determined by the forces of supply and demand for loanable funds, the formal market interest rate rises to the level determined by the informal market rate. Thus rates are unified.

However, the point is to determine the impact financial liberalisation will have on the informal market interest rate. The impact on the latter will depend on the behaviour of the financial assets portfolios. If the public reduces its money holdings (cash money and/or demand deposits) in order to increase its term deposits in the formal market, then the informal market interest rate will drop, as McKinnon and Kapur state. Nevertheless, if the resources to increase time deposits in the formal financial system – which are now receiving a higher rate of interest – come from funds that used to go to the informal market, the interest rate of this latter market rises. Competition among financial institutions of both markets for scarce financial funds would cause an increase in the informal market interest rate. This result, which would not come as a surprise to the executives of financial companies that operate today in the Dominican Republic's informal market, and is contrary to McKinnon's and Kapur's postulate, may have very negative effects on economic activity, given the importance of the interest rate for the different economic sectors of a developing country.

An increase in the informal market interest rate is likely to reduce domestic output (as the increase in the informal market interest rate leads to a reduction in the use of working capital by businesses); it will also increase unemployment and accelerate inflation (assuming that the reduction in domestic output level is larger than the drop in aggregate demand).

THE EXTENSION TO AN OPEN ECONOMY

However, van Wijnbergen's theoretical framework defines the behaviour of a *closed* economy with a dual financial system. The majority of less developed countries typically have economies that are highly open to the international flows of goods and services, with a free movement of financial capital throughout the parallel and black markets. This is the case for the Dominican Republic. Consequently, the analysis for an open economy is more complicated, as we have to take into account other factors within the theoretical framework for a less developed country.

The Dominican economy has very peculiar institutional characteristics as far as the financial and exchange markets are concerned. Besides having a fragmented financial system, the Dominican economy also possesses a dual exchange rate system which has enabled the authorities to undertake a selective devaluation process of the local currency. Consequently, we must analyse the potential impact of a financial reform or liberalisation on the Dominican economy, using a theoretical framework which takes into account the characteristics of both markets: the financial and the exchange markets.

To this end we modify Dauhajre's (1983) dual exchange market model with incomplete segmentation in order to allow for the existence of a fragmented financial system à la van Wijnbergen. The most important characteristic of this theoretical framework for the Dominican economy is the one which states that the informal market interest rate will be tied to the international interest rate plus the expectations of depreciation on the parallel market exchange rate.

A MODEL OF A FRAGMENTED FINANCIAL SYSTEM IN AN OPEN ECONOMY

In this theoretical model of the Dominican economy, an increase in the formal interest rate initially reduces the demand for money, if individuals replace their cash and demand deposit holdings with time deposits in the formal financial system. The reduction in money demand creates an imbalance in the money market as the actual money supply is larger than the actual demand for money. This imbalance induces a reduction of the informal market interest rate, so that money demand returns to its initial level.

Nevertheless, the informal market interest rate is tied to the international rate plus the expectations of a depreciation in the parallel market exchange rate, when it is assumed that financial capital is perfectly mobile in this latter market. Consequently, the drop in the informal interest rate generates a capital outflow, and this causes a depreciation in the parallel market exchange rate. The informal market interest rate, however, can only fall below the international interest rate if, and only if, there exists future expectations of an appreciation of the parallel market exchange rate, which implies that the exchange rate of this market suffers an initial depreciation that *exceeds* its new equilibrium level. The parallel market exchange rate overshoots its new steady state value.

The increase in the parallel market exchange rate generates an excess demand for domestic goods as individuals substitute those goods for imported ones. Since in the short run the domestic supply of goods does not respond immediately to a higher level of demand, the price of domestic goods will start rising. Consequently, and even assuming that the informal market interest rate will diminish when the formal rate is liberalised (as McKinnon and Kapur argue), it is possible that such a financial reform generates adverse effects on the economy, due to the particular characteristics of economies such as the Dominican one.

The decision to carry out financial reform should not be made lightheartedly, nor without carefully considering its potential impact. Recent experiences in Argentina and Chile should constitute lessons on the possible impacts that a financial liberalisation process may have. It is not wise to undertake such a venture without first knowing how the financial and exchange markets work, and in particular, their institutional characteristics, as well as the expectations of devaluation and inflation that exist in the economy at the time the financial reform or liberalisation is to be carried out.

The case of Chile

The Chilean case is a fairly good case in point. Financial liberalisation in Chile considerably raised the interest rates. Real rates of interest increased rapidly and started to exceed the normal profitability of productive activities, which then led to a reduction in financial intermediation. Financial cost exceeded, on average, one-quarter of the sales income of corporations during 1981–2. This situation usually ends up sending banks and financial intermediaries into bankruptcy, which gives rise to intervention by the monetary authorities in order to avoid chaos in the financial system.

If we add up the contributions the Central Bank of Chile made to financial institutions in liquidation (after financial liberalisation) between May 1982 and March 1983, and emergency loans and overdrafts granted to the financial system between December 1982 and March 1983, a total amount of 189 billion pesos is obtained, which is more than 15 per cent of the Gross Domestic Product (GDP) for 1982. This gives an idea of the magnitude of the intervention by the Chilean monetary authorities necessary in order to prevent the financial system from collapsing.

The case of Argentina

The Argentine experience is also quite enlightening. Financial reforms were introduced into an economy with high rates of inflation and a considerable degree of uncertainty as to long-term expectations. Both factors had been present in the Argentine economy since 1975, and dissuaded officials from making any attempts to implement financial reforms of great magnitude as long as these factors were not considerably reduced. Nevertheless, the authorities launched a financial reform and eventually an unrestricted financial aperture.

The Argentine economy has been suffering chronic inflation since the Second World War. The real rate of interest fluctuates when changes occur in the nominal interest rate and in expected inflation. The variability of inflation rates is linked to their magnitude, and highly inflationary processes as those of the Argentine economy cause a wide variation in inflation rates. This variability of inflation rates causes fluctuations in the real rate of interest. On the other hand, the possibility of stabilising the real rate of interest depends on the possibility of stabilising the real exchange rate, as the nominal interest rate responds to the expectations concerning the future exchange rate. If the public does not believe in the exchange measures announced by the authorities, the nominal interest rate will fluctuate considerably and thus, also the real rate. This is why, given a climate of uncertainty, lack of confidence in the economic policy, and strong expectations of exchange rate depreciation and inflation, a programme of financial reform cannot have a happy ending. The Argentine experience is evidence of this.

CONCLUSION

Consequently, before implementing a financial reform, the authorities should conduct a careful analysis of its potential impact. In the Dominican Republic, at present, it is not wise to carry out a programme of financial reform. The desirability of such a financial reform might be considered once the authorities have achieved equilibrium in public finances and an orderly exchange rate system. When these two objectives are reached, and the expectations of exchange rate depreciation and inflation are drastically reduced through a coherent economic policy, then the magnitude of the financial reform to be implemented can be determined. In the current conditions of the Dominican economy, financial reform could have negative impacts on the economy, with the living standards of the population deteriorating even further. We must be patient with financial reform. To rush into this delicate area could produce irreparable damage to the functioning of the Dominican economy.

References

Dauhajre, Andres, *Dual Exchange Rate Dynamics with Incomplete Segmentation and Rational Expectations*, unpublished PhD dissertation (New York: Columbia University, 1983).
Kapur, Basant, 'Alternative Stabilisation Policies in Economic Development,' *Journal of Political Economy*, Vol. 84, No. 4, part 1, 1976.

McKinnon, Ronald, *Money and Capital in Economic Development* (Washington, DC: Brookings Institution, 1973).

Shaw, Edward, *Financial Deepening in Economic Development* (Oxford: Oxford University Press, 1973).

Wijnbergen, S. van, 'Interest Rate Management in LDC's', *Journal of Monetary Economics*, Vol. 12, No. 3, 1983.

Part V

Rest of the Caribbean Basin

14 A Venezuelan Paradox: The Prospects for Attracting (or Repatriating) Foreign Investment

Henry Gomez-Samper and Julian Villalba

Venezuela's handsome income from oil exports, a comparatively small population, and freedom from exchange controls have generated something of a paradox. Although it has amassed a huge foreign debt of $33 billion that will tend to absorb a significant share of future foreign exchange earnings, Venezuelan private holdings abroad are estimated to be $34 billion, thus exceeding the value of the nation's foreign debt. Hence a key factor influencing the prospect for restoring Venezuelan economic growth in the mid-1980s is the extent to which foreign-based savings can be repatriated, and/or new investments can be attracted from abroad.

VENEZUELA'S RECORD AS A SAVER

Although Venezuelans have a reputation for profligate spending – particularly according to South Florida bankers, retailers and realtors – the country's capital formation record is impressive. Venezuela's annual gross fixed investment as a percentage of Gross Domestic Product (GDP) reached an astonishing 40 per cent during the height of the petrodollar boom in the 1970s and substantially exceeded the rate recorded by the leading Latin American countries in every four-year period since 1965. Both public and private savings have contributed to Venezuelan investment. Public investment, adjusted for inflation, rose four-fold from Bs (bolivars) 2.9 billion in 1971 to Bs 13.1 billion in 1978, whereas private savings doubled from Bs 9.4 billion to Bs 19.6 billion during the same period.

After 1978, the level of public investment held its own, at least until 1982, but private investment experienced sharp annual declines from the aforementioned Bs 19.6 billion to only Bs 6.9 billion in 1982. This does not mean, however, that savers became spenders. High interest rates available overseas, coupled with low interest rates at home imposed by Central Bank authorities as a means of curbing inflation, encouraged Venezuelans to invest abroad. As oil prices weakened in the fall of 1982, investors wisely predicted that, sooner or later, the bolivar would be devalued. From this point onwards daily capital outflows often surpassed $100 million, and Central Bank foreign exchange reserves dwindled as the investments that Venezuelans acquired in the United States and elsewhere soared.

From an over-all balance of payments standpoint, whether capital is repatriated for investment purposes or new foreign investment is attracted is immaterial, but the prospect for luring either type of capital inflow differs vastly. In each of the two instances, investor decisions are governed by different factors. Let us first consider the prospect for repatriating Venezuelan investments held abroad.

WILL VENEZUELANS BRING BACK THEIR FOREIGN-BASED SAVINGS?

Investor confidence in Venezuela's economy is obviously an overriding factor which will determine whether Venezuelans will choose to repatriate their savings. For four successive years Venezuela's economy has floundered, as GDP has either remained unchanged or declined. In so far as about 70 per cent of the population is under 30 years of age, unemployment has become more widespread as masses of youths have entered the stagnant job market. Also, consumers are becoming increasingly restless over the higher prices of all goods with a significant import content, for Venezuela's currency is now worth only a little more than half of its January 1983 pegged value. In a pluralist political setting such as Venezuela's these factors tend to generate a noise level that handicaps the ability of the authorities to reverse the course of events and to restore confidence in the economy.

The volume of oil exports and the price of oil are Venezuela's economic bellwether, as oil accounts for nine out of every ten dollars earned from total exports. In solidarity with fellow OPEC members who seek to maintain a floor on oil prices, Venezuelan oil production has been cut from 2.3 million barrels per day in 1979 to 1.5 million in

November 1984. Prices obtained for Venezuelan oil exports averaged
$30 per barrel in 1981 and $26 per barrel in 1984. In October of this
year, oil prices weakened and OPEC is currently deploying a strategy
to restore previous price levels, but, even if 1985 oil prices can be
restored to the mid-1984 level, the demand conditions in Venezuela's
principal oil export markets, the United States and other industrialised countries, remain weak. Although economic recovery in the
industrialised world will lead to increased world demand, which will
tend to strengthen oil prices in the coming years, energy conservation
policies pursued by Venezuela's principal customers are expected to
continue to curb dependence on oil imports. Under these circumstances, the most probable scenario to which Venezuela might realisti-
cally aspire would be stable oil export volumes at prices based on the
mid-1984 level. However, given the current rate of world inflation,
even this scenario would, in fact, represent a decline in real earnings.

Other than oil, the factor that could best influence investor confidence and the prospect for repatriating foreign-based savings would
be the tempo of Venezuela's domestic economy. Once trading in
Venezuela's currency was suspended at the fixed exchange rate of Bs
4.3 to the dollar on 18 February 1983, a day now referred to in
Venezuela as Black Friday, the freely-quoted rate rose sharply,
reaching a peak of Bs 17 per dollar in August of that year and levelling
to about Bs 12.4 in recent months. Not surprisingly, the past practice
of vacationing abroad has been choked and a variety of consumer
buying habits have been altered. Happily, the higher demand for
locally-made textiles and processed foods has substantially improved
the market for these industries. On the other hand, certain labour-
generating industries such as construction, which could broaden the
demand for all locally-produced goods by reducing unemployment
among the skilled and unskilled alike, have yet to rebound.

Beyond these fairly obvious considerations regarding the restoration of investor confidence, there remain unanswered questions
concerning investor preference for domestic versus foreign savings.
This is particularly the case as we know little about the various
characteristics of the savers. Certainly the high interest rates currently
obtainable in the US money market, with the added appeal that such
holdings demand little or no investor attention, dampen the prospects
for Venezuelan capital repatriation. Yet, even if interest rates decline,
for many Venezuelans keeping savings abroad is a firmly entrenched
choice.

An almost compelling reason why Venezuelans will probably

choose to keep their savings abroad is the potential threat that exchange controls might some day be imposed in a country that has virtually never known such restrictions. Additionally, the fact of the matter is that many Venezuelans have found a way to maintain their second homes in South Florida or elsewhere. More legitimate motives for keeping savings abroad include provision for the education of Venezuelan offspring studying in foreign colleges and universities, either because the opportunity to specialise in some areas is not available at home, or because of Venezuela's overcrowded educational system. Such factors, among others, limit the prospect for repatriating Venezuela's foreign-based savings, and must be weighed together with other previously mentioned issues that tend to influence investor confidence. Consider now the prospect for attracting new foreign investment.

CAN VENEZUELA ATTRACT FOREIGN INVESTMENT?

Venezuela's richest mineral deposits, including oil, are reserved for development by the state. Andean Pact restrictions, together with other limitations on foreign investment, apply to banking, insurance, transportation, communications and retailing. Accordingly, manufacturing industries account for more than two-thirds of the officially recorded foreign investment made in Venezuela since 1975. Valued at the Bs 7.5 to the dollar exchange rate currently employed for virtually all permissible imports, the stock of new foreign investment in all fields accumulated between 1975 and early 1984 totals a scant $1.3 billion. This figure reflects Venezuela's past attitude of scoffing at the need for foreign investment.

A variety of historical, economic and political factors account for Venezuela's wary and often antagonistic attitude towards attracting foreign investment. Historically, such investments are associated with the 30-year long dictatorship of Juan Vicente Gomez, which brought the international oil companies to Venezuela in the 1920s, and the amply documented abuse of economic power by such companies, which is duly reported in Venezuela's grade school textbooks. The petrodollar boom in the 1970s enabled Venezuela to purchase back the foreign-owned oil producing and refining facilities and to hire four of the major oil companies as consultants during the transition period. Perhaps understandably, once Venezuela became sufficiently affluent to rid itself of the oil companies, there was little political or popular appeal for attracting other kinds of foreign investors. This helps explain why Venezuela has applied Andean Pact restrictions to foreign investment more strictly than other Pact members.

Today, our standstill economy has reawakened interest, among both political and business leaders, in the possibility of attracting foreign investment for agricultural development and export-oriented industries. Successive drafts of new legislation which would regulate foreign investment in the coming years have been actively circulated. Prospective investors, however, should not interpret these developments as a change of heart. Venezuelans are still wary of the potential costs inherent in attracting foreign investment. Moreover, the process of obtaining political support for modified legislation is still under way, for in Venezuela's pluralist democracy all sectors are consulted before major government decisions are made. None the less, the signals are clear: a change is at hand and the stakes are high, for in the Latin American scene Venezuela continues to be a privileged market.

Underlying Venezuela's privileged status are both economic and political considerations. No other Latin American country boasts a relatively assured per capita export income of nearly $1000 per year. Despite Venezuela's substantially smaller population than neighboring Colombia, consumers have a purchasing power that is nearly half the Andean Pact total, and is the most urbanised of Latin American societies. A significant share of the population is foreign-born, and young Venezuelans from all walks of life have had an opportunity to study abroad. Further, no other Latin American market resembles more closely the consumer buying patterns of North America. This enables foreign-based marketers to use essentially the same strategies as those employed at home as new products are introduced. Lastly, notwithstanding the strain on the economy stemming from capital outflows, Venezuela still boasts a free market for foreign exchange.

The current political appeals for investing in Venezuela cannot be overlooked. Although the time-consuming process of consulting all political sectors may appear discouraging to the investor, who anxiously awaits the new legislation to be enacted in order to make a decision, nevertheless, he can be assured that the rules of the game now emerging in Venezuela are backed by a wide political consensus. Such backing represents a guarantee that the new rules will remain in force for some time. Even more significant in the Latin American context, Venezuela has enjoyed a uniquely stable democracy for more than 25 years, and there exists no organised subversive or guerrilla movement anywhere in the country.

As international companies seriously consider the opportunities for investing in Venezuela in the coming years, the aforementioned economic and political stability will undoubtedly bear heavily on investment decisions. No doubt some of the features of the new legislation will prove disappointing and not nearly as attractive as those proferred by some Andean Pact members. There is no provision, for example, for providing special incentives to investors who locate operations in depressed sectors or outlying regions. Neither are current restrictions on investment in the financial sector likely to be relaxed. No consensus has yet been reached for raising the limits on profit remittances, profit reinvestment, or exemptions for the mandatory fade-out of foreign equity. Also, as foreign investors already established in processed foods and other manufacturing activities have learned, competition from established Venezuelan industries can be as formidable and challenging as competition at home.

On the other hand, new provisions have been slated for the registration of investments in foreign currency, which permits repatriation of dividends or equity under reasonable terms. Also, the new legislation will likely open board memberships to non-Venezuelan citizens, as well as permit investment in real estate.

Significantly, new exchange realities render the bolivar an undervalued currency. Hence, for the first time, the potential returns from locating an export-based industry in Venezuela have become promising; and thanks to the expansion of the higher education system and to massive scholarship support for study abroad, few countries within this hemisphere possess a pool of skilled labour as competent as that available in Venezuela at a comparable cost. Considered as a whole, these factors suggest that, in Latin America, Venezuela is emerging as the land of real opportunity when it comes to Caribbean Basin investment. In short, the prospects for attracting foreign investment to Venezuela have never been better; and once in place, such investment could well help spark the economic recovery to which Venezuelans aspire.

15 Comments on the Mexican Economy in 1984

Manuel Gollas

In these brief remarks, I will only describe some important macro-economic variables of the Mexican economy.

THE DEBT

Mexicans often wonder whether there is life after debt. The country's debt was renegotiated in August 1984, and relieved the country of some of the immediacy of an onerous burden. In 1985 the payments for the principal would have amounted to about 10 billion dollars. Under the new agreement the payment on principal will only be 1.9 billion dollars, and interest payments due in 1985 will be 350 million dollars less than they would have been under the previous agreement. This new arrangement gives Mexico some leeway by transferring the burden of the debt on to the next presidential administration.[1] This process may continue for a few generations if no new and imaginative formulas for dealing with this problem are found soon.

GOVERNMENT DEFICIT

It is doubtful whether the government will reach its goal of reducing its deficit to 6 per cent of the Gross National Product (GNP) by the end of the year, since government expenditures are not being reduced drastically nor is government income being dramatically increased.[2] One interesting issue that has come up recently is whether or not the government will pay its debt to the Mexican commercial banks, as the government took over the Mexican commercial banks in 1982.

PRICES

Despite an expected decrease of about 25 per cent in the rate of inflation from the 1983 figure, it is believed that by the end of 1984, the purchasing power of workers will have decreased by 40 per cent. The rate of inflation by the end of 1984 is expected to be more than 60 per cent.[3]

The variations in the growth rate of the Mexican economy depend, to a large extent, on the price of foreign exchange, that is, the exchange rate. The most obvious relationship is that from the effect that an increase in the price of foreign exchange has on the country's capacity to import goods and services needed for growth. The Mexican peso depreciates in relation to the dollar at a rate of 13 Mexican cents a day: this amounts to an annual devaluation of about 27 per cent. This devaluation rate is probably too small. Most certainly, in 1985, the peso will face a more drastic reduction in its price *vis à vis* the dollar.[4] Hopefully this will lead to increases in tourism and exports.

The behaviour of the money supply has been eclectic. Deposits in the banking system have increased, indicating a positive response to more attractive interest rates. The effective rate (the interest rate actually paid on a loan once all fees and commissions have been considered) declined, between January and August 1984, by almost 20 per cent. However, the effective rate in real terms (when inflation rates has been considered) is still high: about 15 points above the rate of inflation. In the summer and fall of 1984, it was still possible to earn a rate of return on bank certificates which was greater than the rate of increase in the consumer price index.

TRADE AND THE BALANCE OF PAYMENTS

Due to the prolonged recession of the Mexican economy and the tightening of import controls, there has been a significant decrease in imports which resulted in a trade surplus of 7 billion dollars during the first half of 1984.[5] However, in an effort to stimulate growth, between July and August of this year almost 3000 tariff sections were lifted in order to facilitate the flow of essential imports. Moreover, almost the same number of export tariffs were lifted, thus freeing more than 80 per cent of total exports from export taxes. The question, of course, is for how long the export advantage due to the drastic devaluation of the peso will last, and whether Mexico will be able to take full advantage of it.

PRODUCTION AND EMPLOYMENT

There is, in the economy, considerable evidence of industrial recovery. Construction, one of the sectors that was badly hit by the crisis, grew more than 7 per cent during the first five months of 1984.[6] In general, it is estimated that GNP will grow between 2 and 2.5 per cent in 1984.[7]

Above and beyond the obvious fact that it is very high, no one can really make an accurate estimate of unemployment.

SUMMARY AND OUTLOOK

Nineteen eighty-four will be known in Mexico's economic history as the year of the rescheduling of the external debt, also referred to by some as the eternal debt. Nineteen eighty-four will also see the reversal of a two-year negative growth trend in the country's GNP. Among trouble spots on the horizon we might mention a stagnant consumer demand, a high rate of unemployment, an unstable government deficit and the fact that efforts to stimulate growth and increase consumption will make the control of inflation more difficult.

Notes

1. In fact, this leeway was insufficient due to declining oil prices. This led to still further renegotiations during 1986, in which nearly US $44 billion of Mexican external debt falling due over 1985–90 was rescheduled. The amortisation period offered on the rescheduled maturities was lengthened to 20 years and the interest rate reduced to a 0.81 per cent spread over LIBOR (London Inter-bank Offered Rate).
2. It, in fact, remained above 7 per cent in both 1984 and 1985.
3. The inflation rate was actually 59.3 per cent in 1984, and increased slightly to 63.7 per cent in 1985.
4. The devaluation of the peso relative to the dollar amounted to over 50 per cent in 1985.
5. This improvement continued in the second half of 1984, so that the trade balance reached a surplus of US 12.9 billion dollars in 1984. Subsequently, the trade balance weakened to a US 8.4 billion dollar surplus in

1985. Estimates for 1986 indicate an even more rapid deterioration than occurred in 1985.

6. Growth in the construction sector for 1984 as a whole amounted to 3.4 per cent, while it weakened to 2.5 per cent in 1985.

7. The expansion was actually stronger than estimated as GNP increased by 3.5 per cent in 1984. However, growth slowed during the following year to 2.7 per cent and 1986 estimates indicate a contraction of about 4 per cent.

16 Inequality and Growth in Mexico

Adalberto Garcia Rocha

INEQUALITY AND PUBLIC POLICY

The topic of inequality and growth in Mexico is a complex one, so I will try and limit my discussion to some of the central issues. The first point is that, although the economic crisis has brought equity issues to the fore, inequality and poverty in Latin America are really very old issues. One could say, very crudely, that the majority of the people of Latin America have lived under a situation of crisis for the last 30 or 40 years (and of course more) during the industrialisation period. We could refer to tables, figures and formulae to describe poverty and inequality, but a very simple description suffices: inequality in Latin America is not like inequality in developed countries; it is not the fact that there are poor, or even an important group of people in a bad economic situation; it is simply the fact that the majority of the population is very poor, and a small minority of people are very rich. In most Latin American countries, the problem has been how to incorporate that large group of poor people into the modern sector. The lack of success of economic policy has been precisely its inability to incorporate the poor, or even a substantial number of poor, into the benefits of economic growth.

It is common knowledge that in textbook economics, inequality depends on the division of income into wages and profits. However, it is not difficult to show that such is not the case in Mexico, where inequality is explained to a very large extent, not by income differences between wage earners and profit receivers, but rather by intrewage and intra-profit inequality. Reducing inequality between wages and profits would not carry us far in reducing over-all inequality, nor in reducing poverty. Although inequality of incomes among profit earners accounts for a large portion of total inequality, wage inequality is, none the less, responsible for a substantial proportion of total inequality.

It is also a fact that a large proportion of the national payroll comes from government wages. In Mexico, the government is the largest single employer. The government is not, of course, a profit-seeking institution. So, wage inequality depends heavily on government policy regarding the salary structure of its employees.

Many policy instruments are intended to reduce inequality. The most often mentioned instrument in this regard is taxation. However, there are a number of fallacious interpretations, of half-truths, regarding the role of taxes in income distribution. Taxes are a reduction of income, not an increase of individual or private incomes. Taxation is a manoeuvre to take income from the people to finance public expenditure. It is generally thought that what remains after taxation is a less unequal distribution of income. This may be misleading as one could, in fact, have greater equality after taxes (in relative terms, that is, putting aside the income level), but the material level of welfare after taxation has to be *smaller* than before taxation, since the average income level is lower after taxation. Reducing inequality through taxation can only be interpreted as 'fairness' in the distribution of a 'punishment', not in the distribution of a benefit. This leads to a simple, common-sense conclusion: it is not meaningful to evaluate the impact on income distribution of taxation by itself. It is necessary to simultaneously assess the operation of both taxation and government spending. The merits of a tax structure in terms of its progressiveness or regressiveness is meaningless by itself, as a country might adopt a very progressive tax structure, together with a very regressive spending scheme, such that the new outcome of public finance is regressive.

There are very few studies on the impact of government taxation and spending on inequality, but research studies on the role of some areas of government spending tentatively indicate that government spending is probably regressive in Mexico. Tax structures are very unlikely to be progressive, in view of the widespread tax evasion in Mexico, particularly among the richest people. The well-to-do have more means to avoid taxation than captive taxpayers who absorb most of the tax burden. Indirect taxes (which in Mexico constitute a sizeable share of total tax revenues) are well known for their regressive impact. This suggests the following hypothesis: tax structures are very progressive (in their legal appearance) because spending is very regressive. The people with high incomes do not oppose paying higher taxes because they know that the return is going to be significant (highways, public services, sophisticated health centres, 'free' higher education, subsidies to production that favour profits).

Thus, the whole process of government taxation and spending has to be taken into account in any evaluation of its impact on inequality. Partial evaluations have little meaning regarding inequality.

THE CORRECT ROAD FOR PUBLIC POLICY

A well-known conservative economist once expressed the idea that one of the most negative consequences of inflation is that it distracts the attention of policy from more important issues, such as unemployment. In the face of serious unemployment, poverty, and the like, price stability is mostly a concern of the well-to-do. Monetary issues, wage bargaining, and so on, are problems typical of the modern sector. In a situation of crisis, the attention of policy moves to such issues because they are politically the most important ones. In a situation of crisis, economic policy is more regressive than under normal circumstances.

It is a big mistake, and a common one, to regard all policy instruments as means to achieve any conceivable mixture of goals. It is thought that if one could have all policies addressed to their specific purposes, and on top of that to reduce inequality and poverty, then economic policy would work better. If every peso one spends for some particular policy purpose, let us say, increasing rural production, is also used to reduce inequality, then apparently the role of the instrument is improved. For example, rural credit allocated with equity norms, or pricing of public goods oriented to subsidising the consumer, would enrich economic policy. However, the results of following such an approach, very widespread in Mexico, are that most policy instruments end up placing all the emphasis on social goals, disregarding their original purpose. Agricultural credit in Mexico used to be granted with social goals in mind. The result was that poor peasants got some benefits to solve their economic problems, but the policy was a total disaster in achieving its original purpose of increasing production.

Evaluating policy in terms of mixed goals is also very difficult. Public institutions tend to hide their failure in achieving economic goals specific to particular instruments, by emphasising spectacular achievements in giving money away. Industrial policy, for example, could be judged as a success in creating some employment, but inefficiency ended up being very high in the long run, and the cause of a practical failure of the policy even in achieving the creation of sustained employment.

Inequality and poverty-reducing goals in terms of public policy should be kept apart. Equity goals should not be artificially added to all instruments. If one wants to reduce poverty and inequality, then one should have specific instruments for those purposes. In this way, one will avoid any confusion in evaluating the results and the effectiveness of a policy. Adding equity goals to instruments designed for other purposes does not make policy more coherent, as many planners claim. Rather, it creates confusion and inefficiency.

Part VI

Latin America (Southern Cone)

17 Latin America and the World Economy

Larry A. Sjaastad

INTRODUCTION

The economic boom that was shared by most Latin American countries in the late 1970s and 1980–81 has collapsed into a deep recession that is, in some countries such as Chile, reminiscent of the Great Depression. From 1980 to 1983, per capita output in Argentina and Venezuela fell 14 per cent; for Brazil the figure is 10 per cent and Mexico 8 per cent. The only Latin American countries of any significance whose per capita income has not fallen since 1980 are Colombia and Paraguay.

External debt service has become a major problem for no less than ten Latin American countries (Argentina, Bolivia, Brazil, Costa Rica, Chile, Mexico, Panama, Peru, Uruguay and Venezuela). Fiscal deficits and inflation have become a great threat to the financial systems of several major countries. In addition, export trade is facing growing import barriers in the industrialised countries. As a consequence, the major internal adjustments that are urgently needed are being hampered by a hostile external environment. Indeed, the discussion with respect to Latin American economic performance has shifted from emphasis on economic growth to one of merely preventing further erosion of real output. A complete economic recovery appears to be well into the future.

THE LATIN AMERICAN RECESSION

There is no single factor that one can identify as the main cause of the major economic downturn in Latin America. In some cases the explanation lies principally in internal developments; Argentina and Brazil are good examples. Perceived risk of devaluation coupled with an open capital market in Argentina resulted in extremely high real rates of interest in that country beginning during the fourth quarter of

1979; by the time the devaluation finally arrived in March 1981, the net worth of private-sector enterprises had been severely eroded. Capital flight financed by public-sector foreign borrowing has resulted in an enormous external debt, the service of which is one of the major factors lying behind the virtual hyperinflation in that country. In Brazil, the measures taken at the end of 1980 to preserve the international reserve position of the Central Bank encouraged foreign borrowing while driving internal interest rates, in real terms, to levels of 40 per cent and higher.[1] Economic activity fell drastically during 1981, and had begun to recover only during the second half of 1984.[2] Country-specific explanations are also applicable to other countries such as Panama and Mexico, where unsustainable expansions of the public sector resulted in current account deficits that could no longer be financed, resulting in a massive contraction.

If there is a common element in this sorry pattern, however, it is the dollar deflation that accompanied the amazing recovery of the US dollar that began in late 1980. That dollar deflation resulted in extremely high real rates of interest on dollar loans, and these real interest rates were transmitted to domestic-currency assets in those countries with open capital markets. In Chile and Uruguay, for example, real rates of interest on domestic credit rose by _30 to 40 percentage points_ from mid-1980 to 1981; nearly all of the increase arose from a decline in inflation rates rather than an increase in nominal rates of interest.

The magnitude of this dollar deflation is readily appreciated. From 1980 to late 1984 the US consumer price index rose by 26 per cent, and the US wholesale price index by 16 per cent. Nevertheless, unit values (measured in dollar prices) of _world_ trade fell by 10 per cent during the same period. The commodity dollar-price index quoted by the International Monetary Fund had fallen by 19 per cent since 1980, the food and metals components of that index declining by 26 and 27 per cent, respectively.[3] All of this has occurred in the face of an average rate of inflation of less than 5 per cent per annum in the US!

As 1980 and 1984 were similar years in terms of the over-all level of economic activity in the OECD countries, one cannot explain the dollar deflation in commodity markets by world recession. The only plausible explanation lies in the dollar appreciation which, in real terms, is roughly 80 per cent with respect to the major European currencies. That appreciation, other things being equal, depressed dollar prices of many internationally-traded goods (while increasing their prices in DM, and so on), thereby transmitting deflationary pressures to countries that trade heavily in those goods.[4,5] With the collapse of inflation in those countries, real interest rates rose accordingly, particularly in countries whose open capital markets insulated their domestic-currency interest rates from internal developments.

The appreciation of the dollar also resulted in adverse changes in the terms of trade for several Latin American countries. Whereas dollar prices of homogeneous commodities respond (decline) almost instantaneously to an appreciation of the dollar, the prices of less homogeneous (industrial) goods are affected only with a lag. As imports tend to be concentrated in the latter type of goods (and exports in the former) in most Latin countries, terms of trade were at least temporarily worsened. In addition, the real rate of interest on debt service rose dramatically. Given that external debt is denominated mainly in dollars and serviced with internationally traded goods (either by fewer imports or more exports), it is the rate of inflation of the dollar prices of internationally-traded goods that is relevant for transforming nominal interest rates into real rates on foreign debt. For many countries, those real rates were negative, sometimes significantly so, during the late 1970s and 1980, but became very substantially positive by 1981.[6] The combination of a steep rise in real debt service and an effective cessation of access to new borrowings in mid-1982 quickly lead to the infamous external debt crisis that still plagues much of Latin America.

The shift from massive external borrowing, at levels that exceeded the sum of amortization plus interest, to actual payments of debt service, requires sharp contraction in domestic spending (relative to output) to generate the requisite commercial account surplus. In some cases, where the debt was owed mainly by the private sectors, that contraction came about quite spontaneously; in others, however, where the debt is largely a public-sector liability – and this is the case for most Latin American countries – the adjustment has taken a different form. In Mexico, for example, the public sector has actually contracted, but in other countries, such as Brazil and Argentina, whatever adjustment that should have taken place in the public sector has been forced upon the private sector, mainly through grotesque increases in the inflation tax, high real interest rates and increased barriers to imports. In short, monetary and commercial policies have been used (erroneously) as substitutes for fiscal policy. As is well known, commercial policy cannot produce commercial-account surpluses unless complemented by expenditure-reducing measures. In Brazil and Argentina those measures have taken the form of very high rates of inflation, and commensurately high real rates of interest. This is surely *not* the way to adjust.

External debt service in Latin America is, for the most part, a public-sector responsibility; indeed, the private sectors of the major debtor countries have large holdings of foreign assets. It is estimated that, taken together, residents of Argentina, Brazil, Mexico and Venezuela have foreign asset holdings to the amount of US$150 billion, while their governments owe approximately US$275 billion.[7] The net debt, then is about US$125 billion, not an impossible or even onerous burden for a set of countries whose combined Gross Domestic product (GDP) exceeds US$500 billion. The catch, of course, is that the debt is *owed* by the public sectors, whereas the foreign assets are *owned* by private individuals. This observation underscores the obvious fact that the debt service is first and foremost a fiscal problem in those countries.

One cannot be optimistic concerning the short-to-middle run economic outlook for Latin America. The external environment is unlikely to improve, given the continuing strength of the dollar (and the protectionism that it encourages in the US) and the 'structural' protectionism of Europe.[8] The unwillingness of the large public sectors in most Latin American countries to adjust to the new reality of the world financial market will prolong recession in their private sectors. The 1980s are beginning to look more and more like the 'lost decade' for Latin America.

Notes

1. The key measure was a requirement that commercial banks limit expansion of cruzeiro credit based upon cruzeiro deposits to only 50 per cent in nominal terms during 1981 – in the face of an inflation of 100 per cent. This measure was designed to force the banks to borrow abroad, thereby ensuring an inflow of reserves for the central bank; an (anticipated?) side effect was to generate an enormous spread between borrowing and lending rates of the commercial banks. The commercial banks profited handsomely from this measure, which was equivalent to the creation of a banking cartel.
2. The recovery has remained strong, with annual growth rates of about 8 per cent through 1986.
3. Commodity prices fell 12.7 per cent in 1985 as the pace of worldwide economic activity slowed. Prices of agricultural raw materials were hardest hit as they declined almost 25 per cent.

4. For a complete development of this phenomenon, see Larry A. Sjaastad, 'Exchange Rate Regimes and the Real Rate of Interest', in Michael Connolly and John McDermott (eds) *Economics of the Caribbean Basin* (New York: Praeger Publishing Company, 1985).
5. In Chile that effect was dramatic indeed. Although there was no change in economic policy (particularly in exchange rate policy), the rate of the Chilean inflation, measured by her wholesale price index, declined from a stable annual rate of approximately 35 per cent that prevailed through the third quarter of 1980, to actual *de*flation by early 1981. This decline coincided exactly with the shift from dollar depreciation to appreciation in late 1980. For more details, see L. A. Sjaastad, ibid.
6. Again in the case of Chile, the real rate of interest on external debt rose from − 12 per cent in 1970 to + 24 per cent in 1982, an increase of 36 percentage points! See L. A. Sjaastad, *op. cit.*
7. See L. A. Sjaastad, 'Where the Latin American Loans Went', *Fortune*, 26 November 1984.
8. The effect of that protectionism is easily exaggerated, however. In 1983, exports of all developing countries (including petroleum exporters) amounted to 25 per cent of all world exports; for non-oil developing countries, the share was 15 per cent. The share of Central and South American countries was just under 6 per cent. While that share is undoubtedly larger for some goods, it still follows that countries with such a small share of the market should not encounter enormous difficulties in increasing that share (Source: GATT, *International Trade, 1983–1984*).

18 The Role of Foreign Direct Investment in Economic Growth: The Brazilian Case[1]

Helson C. Braga

INTRODUCTION

Broadly defined, foreign direct investment (FDI) is the establishment or purchase by residents of one country of a substantial ownership and management share of a business or real property in another country. Most FDI is made by multinational companies as a way to secure the supply of inputs for the parent company and, above all, as an alternative for exports from the home country.

The stock of foreign capital registered in Brazil at the end of 1983 reached US$22.3 billion, almost an eight-fold increase over the corresponding figure in 1971 (see Table 18.1). Approximately one-third of the registered capital belonged to US residents, followed by the West Germans with 12.8 per cent.

In the period 1965–80, Brazil absorbed a growing share of the world flow of FDI: in the sub-period 1965–9 this amounted to 2.6 per cent; during 1970–74, 4 per cent, and during 1975–9, 7.1 per cent. In the two-year period 1980–81, it dropped to 4.7 per cent.[2]

As can be seen in Table 18.2, approximately three-quarters of this capital was invested in the manufacturing sector, although the service sector share has grown considerably in the last 12 years, reaching just over 20 per cent in 1983 (it was 9.5 per cent in 1971). The industries that received most foreign investment were motor vehicle and parts (12.8 per cent), basic chemicals (10.1 per cent) and machinery (9.5 per cent).

The main purpose of this article is to discuss the role of foreign direct investment in the distinct phases of Brazilian economic development (see the second section) and the treatment given to it (see the third section). The final section presents a summary of the main

Table 18.1 Foreign direct investment (and reinvestment) in Brazil, by country of origin, in selected years

Country of origin	1930[a] US$ (million)	per cent	1967[b] US$ (million)	per cent	1975[c] US$ (million)	per cent	1980[c] US$ (million)	per cent	1983[c] US$ (million)	per cent
United States	210	17.2	1 328	35.4	2 295	31.4	5 004	28.6	7 198	32.3
United Kingdom	575	46.6	178	4.8	430	5.9	1 111	6.4	1 133	5.1
West Germany	—	—	517	13.9	871	11.9	2 448	14.0	2 848	12.8
Switzerland	—	—	140	3.8	736	10.1	1 768	10.1	1 938	8.7
Japan			212	5.7	841	11.5	1 725	9.9	2 037	9.1
France	198	8.1	263	7.1	300	4.1	702	4.0	705	3.2
Canada	100	8.0	625	16.8	411	5.6	641	3.7	1 016	4.6
Others	251*	20.1	465	12.5	1 420	19.5	4 073	23.3	5 427	24.2
TOTAL	1 235	100.0	3 728	100.0	7 304	100.0	17 480	100.0	22 302	100.0

*Refers to other European countries (16.2 per cent) and Argentina (4.0 per cent).

Sources: a Wythe (1945) (portfolio investment included).
b OECD (1972) (portfolio investment included).
c Central Bank of Brazil (position on 31 December).

Table 18.2   Foreign direct investment (and reinvestment) in Brazil, equity capital by country of origin and sector – 1983[1]
(percentage)

Receiving sector	USA	West Germany	Switzerland	Japan	United Kingdom	France	Canada	Total
Mining	4.7	1.9	0.1	1.8	2.5	0.5	2.8	2.9
Manufacturing	74.7	89.4	80.3	73.6	56.7	53.6	82.9	73.5
Metallurgy	4.5	9.8	1.4	19.0	2.6	3.0	12.4	7.4
Machinery	11.8	16.1	5.2	8.3	3.4	5.1	16.0	9.5
Electric and computer equipment	9.0	6.2	9.1	12.5	1.1	2.7	8.0	7.4
Motor vehicle and parts	7.8	35.7	20.6	4.0	0.7	1.0	0	12.8
Chemicals (basic)	13.0	7.3	2.2	1.7	10.7	15.3	33.6	10.1
Pharmaceutical products	5.0	4.2	3.6	0.1	1.4	3.9	12.0	4.2
Textiles	1.0	0.1	2.3	7.7	4.1	0.4	0	1.7
Food processing	4.7	0.5	14.4	1.9	0.3	2.6	0.01	4.5
Services	18.7	8.0	17.2	18.5	38.4	42.5	11.3	20.7
Holding companies	9.4	2.7	12.9	3.2	26.6	20.4	10.2	10.8
Other	1.0	0.4	1.3	4.3	1.8	2.0	3.0	1.8
TOTAL	100.0	100.0	100.0	100.0	100.0	100.0	100.0	100.0

1.   Currencies of the different contries were converted into dollars according to the 1983 year end exchange rate.

Source: Boletim do Banco Central, Separata, May 1984.

aspects examined, as well as a prospective analysis of the role of foreign investment in Brazil.

THE ROLE OF FOREIGN DIRECT INVESTMENT IN BRAZILIAN ECONOMY

Foreign investment has assumed distinctive characteristics and played different roles in the recent history of the Brazilian economy. These changes have been connected not only with political and economic changes in Brazil and abroad, but also with peculiarities of specific sectors. In the following subsections these aspects will be examined in a concise fashion, in accordance with the time periods in which these changes occurred.

Prior to 1930

Before the First World War, foreign investment, mainly British, was concentrated in railways, public utilities, and agriculture (see Castro, 1979). Foreign capital's share in the industrialisation boom, which took place in the late nineteenth century and at the beginning of the twentieth (especially in the food and textile industries), was minimal. However, it must be emphasised that almost half of the main 'Brazilian' economic groups that appeared in this phase were owned by immigrants (Queiroz, 1965, p. 57).

Brazilian industrialisation received its first important stimulus as a result of the outbreak of the First World War, which caused foreign supply to be cut off. Almost 6000 firms were created during the conflict, with the value of output rising more than 200 per cent (Baer, 1966, p. 17).

By the end of the war the industrial structure had undergone important changes in the sectoral distribution of output, as well as in the capital ownership. This was a consequence of the increased foreign investment in the manufacturing sector, and the fact that foreign and Brazilian investment were no longer concentrated in textiles and food, but rather in chemicals, metallurgical products, mechanical products, and so on (Evans, 1982, pp. 103–4). Nevertheless, the 1920 industrial census showed that the textile (28.6 per cent) and food industries (22.2 per cent) were still responsible for half the value-added of the industrial sector. This combined participation decreased to 45.6 per cent and to 39.7 per cent, respectively, in the 1940 and 1950 censuses (Baer, 1966, p. 18).

In the 1920s, many of the firms established during the war were suffocated by the resumption of imports. Concentrating on the protection of coffee production, the government did not adopt a policy aimed at protecting the initial industrial basis that had been formed. It was at that time, however, that some American firms entered into automobile assembly, and record and gramophone manufacture.

The first estimate of the distribution of foreign investment in Brazil, by country of origin, was made by Wythe (1945) and refers to the year 1930. He found that Great Britain accounted for 46.6 per cent, the United States for 17.2 per cent, France 8.1 per cent, Argentina 4 per cent, and other European countries the remaining 16.2 per cent (see Table 18.1).

From 1930 to 1945

The depression of the 1930s considerably increased the stimulus to Brazilian industrialisation. The value of exports dropped from US$445.9 million in 1929, to US$180.6 million in 1932, drastically reducing Brazilian import capacity. This constraint, coupled with the income support policy for the coffee sector – which implied maintaining the level of aggregate demand – represented a powerful incentive to raising production in industries that competed with imports. As a result, industrial production which had decreased for three consecutive years, by 1933 had already recovered to the 1929 level, and rose another 60 per cent by the end of the decade (Baer, 1966, pp. 21–5).

The Second World War brought about a decisive impetus to the consolidation of the industrialisation process. The lack of available products in the countries involved in the conflict and maritime transportation difficulties practically eliminated foreign competition faced by industry.

From 1930 to 1945 foreign capital played a secondary role in the industrialisation effort (Newfarmer and Mueller, 1975, p. 96). In particular, US investment remained fairly stable throughout the period. Between 1929 and 1943 the Canadian and West European share of US foreign investment rose from 26.7 per cent to 30.2 per cent and from 18.0 per cent to 26.1 per cent respectively, while the

Latin American share dropped from 46.7 per cent to 35.6 per cent (Doellinger, 1975, p. 250).[3]

From 1946 to 1961

Between 1946 and 1955, the stock of US direct investment increased significantly from US$323 million to US$1115 million.[4] During the last year of the period, 1955, capital invested in industry reached half the total value of investment (it was 39 per cent in 1946). It is interesting to note that this expansion occurred despite several experiments with exchange and profit remittance controls that characterised this period.[5]

The period from 1955 to 1961 was extremely favourable to the inflow of foreign capital. In the first place, the 1955 Superintendency of Exchange Operations (SUMOC) Order no. 113 allowed foreign companies to import capital goods without exchange cover, thus establishing the precedent of a policy clearly receptive to foreign capital in Brazil. In the second place, protection for the domestic market that had been provided primarily by exchange restrictions, started to be ensured also by *ad valorem* tariffs.[6] Simultaneously, import policies were simplified (the five import categories were reduced to two), but the products supplied by the domestic industry could only be imported under the 'special category' label, at an exchange cost higher than that of the 'general category' (Baer, 1966, pp. 56–8).

Apparently the Brazilian authorities had chosen the conscious promotion of industrialisation as an economic development strategy, in which foreign investment would play an important role, especially in the most modern manufacturing sectors.[7]

Between 1955 and 1962 the investments made in the framework of SUMOC Order no. 113 reached US$511.2 million (more than half of it directed to the automotive industry), the biggest share coming from the United States and West Germany (Gordon and Grommers, 1962, p. 71). Morley and Smith (1971, pp. 123, 126–49) estimated that from 1949 to 1962, 33.5 per cent of the total industrial output growth and 42 per cent of the output of import substitution industries were due to foreign companies.

We must bear in mind that the presence of foreign companies, especially in the second half of the 1950s, went along with a vigorous expansion of state investments in the economic infrastructure, particularly in the energy, transport, iron and steel, and oil-refining sectors. Such investments were part of the Target Plan for the period 1957–60, which, according to one statement, was the 'most solid conscious decision in favor of industrialisation in the country's economic history' (Lessa, 1981, p. 27).

As a result, Brazilian industrial output increased 9.6 per cent yearly in the period 1947–61 (12.7 per cent in the sub-period 1956–60, the period of the Kubitschek Government), while the national product increased 5.8 per cent (Furtado, 1965, p. 84).

From 1961 to 1965

The dynamism which had characterised the Brazilian economy in the previous phase (especially in the second half of the decade), as a result of an expansive macroeconomic policy associated with a massive inflow of foreign investments, started to weaken in the early 1960s. The economy's growth rate, which had reached 7.7 per cent in 1961, dropped successively to 5.5 per cent and 2.1 per cent in the subsequent years. At the same time, the inflationary process gained momentum: 37 per cent in 1961, 61 per cent in 1962 and 73 per cent in 1963. The growth model based on import substitution industrialisation gave clear signs of exhaustion.

As a consequence of the economic and political problems and the severe limitation on profit remittances imposed by the Goulart Government, the inflow of foreign investment in 1962 was only US$9 million, as compared to an average of US$110 million in the four previous years. Similarly, US government official loans dropped to US$140 million (1962–3 average) from US$1909 million (1950–61 average), due to the leftist tendency of Brazilian foreign policy.[8]

The new administrators who emerged from the 1964 military coup radically changed economic policy in order to face the crisis. Orthodox measures to control the money supply, public expenditure and wages were taken to correct the domestic imbalances. To curb the balance of payments deficit, the cruzeiro was heavily devalued, and restrictions on profit remittances were eliminated. The ensuing recession lasted until 1967 (during which time time average increase in per capita income was 0.7 per cent) and inflation was reduced to 40 per cent.

On the other hand, foreign direct investment rose from US$22 million (the 1962–4 average) to US$73 million (the 1965–7 average).

Moreover, in the two years following the military coup, average official borrowings doubled (US$289 million) as compared to the average of the two previous years.

It is worthwhile to analyse the take-over of domestic firms during this time period, because it was the main form of foreign investment in Brazil. Obviously this was not a recent phenomenon in the history of Brazilian industrialisation. During the first phase of this process, several foreign groups, among them the biggest operating in Brazil, settled in the country through the purchase of national enterprises (Queiroz, 1972, p. 170). In the subsequent industrialisation stages, in which foreign capital was directed mainly towards the sectors where Brazilian capital could not face competition, the expansion of foreign investment did not imply the removal of Brazilian groups. Of course there were exceptions, as in the case of the glass industry, which was thoroughly taken over by foreign companies (Evans, 1982, pp. 104–5).

The economic recession of the 1960s and, above all, the credit squeeze, which was a part of the stabilisation programme embarked on in 1964, made national companies extremely weak, thus greatly favouring their take-over by foreign companies (Ratnner, 1972, p. 165).[9] The problem of foreign take-overs became so serious that it led to the establishment of a parliamentary inquiry committee to investigate the matter. The Committee found that there was a 'fast foreign take-over process going on in Brazil, implying not only the purchase of national companies by foreign ones, but also the control of important sectors of the Brazilian economy by foreign capital' (Medina, 1970, p. 130).[10]

From 1968 to 1973

The exhaustion of the model of growth based on import substitution led people to believe that its undoing had been brought about by the fact that exports had been neglected. It seemed clear that the country needed to expand its exports substantially or else its capacity to grow would be permanently blocked by its restricted import capacity (Simonsen, 1969, Chapter 6). Besides, competition in foreign markets would force the companies to reach and maintain high standards of product efficiency and quality, with positive effects also on the domestic market.

In the literature, several authors have defended the replacement of inward-looking trade policies with outward-looking ones, because often the consequences of the former were the creation of an inefficient industrial sector, characterised by idle capacity, limited job creation, little exchange savings and limited possibilities of productivity growth.[11]

To implement the new development strategy which focused on export promotion, the crawling peg system was adopted and fiscal and credit incentives were created to stimulate the export of manufactures.[12] Favoured by expanding foreign trade and by low rates of utilisation of industrial capacity (83 per cent in 1968), exports of manufactures increased rapidly at the yearly rate of 38 per cent for the period. With an average growth rate of 27 per cent, total exports increased their share in the Gross Domestic Product (GDP) (which grew at the average rate of 11.5 per cent) from 5.2 per cent to 7.6 per cent between 1968 and 1973 (Peñalver, *et al.*, 1983, pp. 6–7).

Around 1972 it seemed obvious that the continuing expansion of exports would depend on the growth of productive capacity, as 90 per cent of the installed capacity was being used. For this purpose, the 'Befiex Program' was created. This programme increased fiscal incentives (such as import duty exemption or reduction, and tax exemption or reduction for manufactured products and their circulation, for firms whose imports did not exceed one-third of the company's average exports) and permitted the import of capital goods without the need to prove that there were no similar Brazilian products. The basic prerequisite for the granting of benefits was the company's commitment to reach a certain minimum amount of exports (decided case by case) during a short-term period (usually 10 years).[13]

Although the benefit could be extended to foreign as well as to Brazilian companies, the former were the main target of the programme. In the first place, it was due to their greater ability to shoulder long-term commitments as a consequence of greater familiarity with foreign markets and of being able to determine trade flows by means of intracompany transactions. Secondly, as the Program allowed the importation of second-hand capital goods, the foreign companies could also take advantage of the intra-company transfers in order to reduce depreciation and obsolescence costs.

Until the end of 1980, 41 out of 100 companies that had their export programmes approved were foreign. These companies accounted for 61.8 per cent of investment (US$7026 million), 58.2 per cent of export commitments (US$25 180 million), 47.1 per cent of trade surplus (US$4997 million) and 61 per cent of direct jobs created (45 769) by those 100 companies. In 1980 the Befiex Management Committee estimated that the Program's share of total exports was 22 per cent and its contribution to export growth was 31 per cent for the year.

The post-1974 period

In the opinion of most analysts, the first oil-shock in 1973–4 marked the end of the 'Brazilian miracle', as the 1968–73 period is known, during which the GDP expanded at a yearly average rate of as much as 11.5 per cent. The value of oil imports increased more than six-fold between 1972 and 1974 when it reached US$2960 million. However, the Brazilian government – either because it underestimated the real extent of the crisis or simply because it decided not to bear the political burden of frustrating people's expectations of continuing growth – dismissed the strategy of adaptation to the new conditions determined by the loss in terms of trade, instead choosing to keep intact the incentives to economic activity.

To face the pressure on the balance of payments that this decision would inevitably bring about, the government decided to raise the tariff and non-tariff barriers for imports, resorted to foreign borrowing, and conceived an ambitious substitution programme for basic inputs and capital good imports. Thus, in the 1974–80 period, the domestic product grew at an yearly average rate of 7.1 per cent, while the industrial sector and manufacturing industry grew at 7.7 per cent and 6.8 per cent, respectively.

During this phase a new type of foreign investment, in which multinationals supplied technology, and had a minority holding in joint undertakings with private and state-owned national companies, developed. This tripartite association, which was formerly used in establishing the petrochemical industry, was regarded by the Second National Development Plan (1975–9) as the ideal strategy for making expensive and technologically advanced investments work, avoiding foreign take-overs and an excessive state expansion into the economy.

To strengthen the capital structure of Brazilian private companies in these undertakings, the National Bank for Social and Economic Development (BNDES) created three subsidiaries which, besides offering very favourable financing terms, had minority holdings in the capital of the national companies involved. By the end of 1979, the three BNDES subsidiaries had invested US$1150 million, that granted them a 16 per cent share in the stocks with voting privileges, and 31 per cent of the preferred stock of the 35 aided companies. One-third of these resources were invested in capital goods industry projects and approximately half was directed to basic inputs and semi-finished goods (cement, fertilisers, pulp and mining products).[14]

The best results of the tripartite model took place precisely in the industry which pioneered its application – petrochemicals – as it fulfilled two basic conditions for its success. The first was the dominant position of PETROQUISA – a subsidiary of the state monopoly (PETROBRÁS) – for the production of the basic raw material, through which the government implemented a firm strategy for the expansion of the industry. The second was the fact that this government's goal coincided with the interest of multinational companies from several countries (especially Japan) involved in the keen competition for the petrochemical technology market. This made the Japanese adopt more flexible positions in the transfer of technology. Soon afterwards, in order not to lose a share of the market (a typical motive of oligopolistic competition), multinational companies from other countries decided to participate in the tripartite association (Guimarães, *et al.*, 1982, p. 65; Sorensen, 1983, p. 52).

Another state company – Vale do Rio Doce, which mines ore and exports minerals – was in a more advantageous position in its associations with multinational companies than PETROQUISA. The main reasons were that the raw materials it controls are Brazilian (in contrast to PETROBRÁS/PETROQUISA, which strongly depends on external supply), and the technology for extracting and working ores is known (that eliminates one of the major sources of control that the multinational companies often possess).[15] Vale do Rio Doce's basic motivation in these partnerships, usually with its foreign clients, was to ensure a market for its exports. It is worth noting that the Vale do Rio Doce did not adopt the tripartite model in its joint undertakings. It not only stopped including Brazilian partners in its projects, but also competes with some of them in specific sectors.

The pharmaceutical industry is the third example – when the state does not have any power over the multinational company, and the Brazilian private companies are not strong enough from the financial viewpoint – to characterise the success/failure of the tripartite model. In this case, not only are the important raw materials imported, but further, they are supplied by the multinational companies themselves. Moreover, these companies thoroughly control the new technology. Finally, there were no Brazilian companies – private or state-owned – as large as the multinationals.

The attempt to create a state company (the Drug Agency) in 1971, to make use of the productive capacity of some 20 public laboratories, did not last five years: in the middle of 1975 the company was dismantled and divided into two parts distributed between different ministries.[16] In this sector the predominance of multinational companies is absolute. Objectively, they do not have any interest in associating with the remaining Brazilian companies.

The three examples given – PETROQUISA, Vale do Rio Doce and the Drug Agency – show that the feasibility of the tripartite model as a kind of enterprise organisation depends on a few very restrictive conditions; it cannot be thought of as a general purpose strategy. In the first place, a strong bargaining power is needed on the part of the state partner (to face the multinational company). This has been mainly based on the supply of essential raw materials. In the case of absence of this countervailing power and technology, the predominance of multinationals will be unavoidable.

Only as a consequence of the oligopolistic competition fostered in specific markets, are gaps opened for the participation of multinational companies in joint ventures supplying technology. Otherwise, these companies prefer to set up branches in which they have majority holdings or to sell technology.

These examples further suggest that room for the Brazilian private partner depends on a certain balance between the other two partners. Whenever there is a clear predominance of one of the partners, the attraction of the Brazilian private partner will not be necessary. As was the case in the petrochemical sector, the government must be determined to strengthen the financial structure of the Brazilian entrepreneur so that he becomes an important ally.

Therefore, it is no wonder that the tripartite model was a success in the petrochemical industry, at least during its implementation phase. People went so far as to think it was not only an all-purpose solution but also a stable one.

However, there are signs that this stability is being threatened. First, because there was an excessive splitting up of companies, thus not taking advantage of the agglomerative economies that characterise this industry. Such a splitting resulted, to a great extent, from the need to limit the size of investment in order to make possible the participation of the Brazilian private partners. This was the case despite the effort to strengthen their capital structure.

Secondly, some foreign partners have become more and more interested in withdrawing from the association. The whole of the investments (at the São Paulo, Bahia and Rio Grande do Sul petrochemical poles) were calculated for an expanding domestic market, which at present absorbs only 70 per cent of its output, the remainder being exported.

As a result, it is evident that there is a fairly widespread situation of financial weakness in domestic private corporations, especially among those belonging to the Rio Grande do Sul petrochemical pole. The suggestions most frequently presented to solve this problem are mergers of companies and raw-material suppliers (naphtha) at preferential prices, as occurs, for instance, in Japan.

TREATMENT OF FOREIGN DIRECT INVESTMENT IN BRAZIL[17]

Two basic legal texts deal with the treatment of foreign capital in Brazil: Law no. 4390 of 11 September 1964, which provides for profit remittance abroad, and the Normative Act no. 15 of 11 September 1975, issued by the National Institute for Industrial Property concerning technology transfer. This section will show that foreign capital is given a discriminatory treatment pursuant to many other legal texts and some unwritten rules adopted by government agencies.

Registration of foreign direct investment

Foreign capital is generally free to directly invest in any kind of legitimate venture in Brazil. It is only necessary to follow the same procedures required to set up a domestic corporation.[18] However, there are many exceptions to this rule. First of all, like most of the countries in the world, the Brazilian Government retains for itself some sectors considered as sensitive. Oil exploration, prospecting and drilling[19] and public utilities such as electricity, telecommunications, railways and ports are good examples of this.

Secondly, legislation bars foreigners from the communications media, coastal shipping companies, domestic airlines and highway transportation companies. Although there is no law preventing foreign banks from opening branches in Brazil, the Central Bank – which issues permits – not only has denied registration to foreign banks but also has prevented foreign banks already operating in Brazil from increasing the number of their branches. In 1980 a system of market reserve was imposed on data processing and related fields. The Special Secretariat for Computer-Related Activities (SEI), set up to manage the system, has reserved the mini- and micro-computer industries, as well as testing and measuring instrumentation systems for Brazilian firms.

Lastly, until the mid-1970s Brazilian legislation did not provide for prior approval of the acquisition of Brazilian firms by foreign corporations. As we have seen in the second section, this was the procedure of choice for firms entering the Brazilian market.

However, the new 1976 Corporation Law included a provision to the effect that the take-over of any company quoted in the stock market depends on the previous approval of the Securities Commission.[20]

Except for these cases, where there are restrictions to the inflow of foreign capital, foreign corporations in Brazil are free to do what they want with the returns on their investment. However, to make a legal remittance of profits abroad or to repatriate capital requires registration with the Central Bank (this aspect will be dealt with shortly). However, it is thought that a substantial amount of foreign investment in Brazil has never been registered with the Central Bank.

Among the possible reasons for this are:

1.   the impossibility of proving the foreign origin (total or partial) of investments made before 1962 when the registration was effectively enforced;
2.   the acquisition of assets abroad in larger amounts than those registered;
3.   INPI's refusal to register technology or industrial property rights; and
4.   the conversion of foreign currency at black market rates more profitable than the official ones.

The profit remittance law

The first attempt to regulate the flow of foreign capital and earnings in Brazil took place in 1946, through Law Decree no. 9025. The amount of capital that could be repatriated in any year was limited to 20 per cent, and profit and dividend remittance was restricted to 8 per cent of the foreign capital duly registered with the Exchange Division of Banco do Brasil. As was expected, these regulations provoked strong reactions from the foreign investment community, especially because they did not permit the addition of unremitted earnings to registered capital in order to build up the remittance base.

This regulation was short-lived: 'Due to the favorable conditions on the exchange market', it was revoked six months later and there was no charge until 1962,[21] when Brazil enacted a very restrictive Profit Remittance Law.[22]

This statute limited capital repatriation to 20 per cent of registered investment and yearly profit remittance to 10 per cent (remittances above this amount were considered as capital repatriation). In addition, its regulatory decree[23] banned the inclusion of reinvested earnings to registered capital in order to increase the remittance base.

One of the first steps taken by the administration which took power after the military coup of April 1964 was to eliminate the restrictions on capital repatriation (since then, it has been totally free) and on profit remittance. As regards the latter aspect, the former prohibition was replaced by a supplementary progressive income tax (in addition to the 25 per cent normally charged – 15 per cent if there is a double-taxation agreement with the country from which the capital originates over remittances made to non-resident individuals and corporations) whenever the average remitted over a three-year period surpasses 12 per cent of registered investment and reinvestment.[24]

Foreign transfer of technology

Until 1958 the technology and technical assistance license agreements with foreigners were not subject to any kind of restriction in Brazil. In spite of the frequent delay in granting patent or trademark registrations, the royalties could be freely remitted. However, that year limits were set for royalty payment on patents and technical assistance (ranging from 1 to 5 per cent, depending on in which group the patented product was placed) and trademarks (1 per cent of gross sales).[25]

These restrictions were later incorporated into the 1962 Profit Remittance Law as profit remittance limits. According to this law, if the foreign licensor controls the Brazilian licensee directly or indirectly, all royalty payments for patents and trademarks are both non-remittable and non-deductible for income tax purposes. The payments for technical assistance can still be made, but they are considered as distributed dividends and must, therefore, be included in the 12 per cent limit over the registered capital.

Today, the most important regulation pertinent to the registration and approval of technology transfer agreements is the Code of Industrial Property, administered by the National Institute for Industrial Property (INPI),[26] by a government agency set up in 1970.[27] Unless a technology transfer agreement has been registered with INPI, the Central Bank will not authorise remittance of royalties abroad nor will the Ministry of Finance allow tax deductions on the corresponding payments. Registering with INPI is also necessary to ensure legel protection to the right of industrial property.

INPI will not approve technology agreements which impose restrictions on product manufacturing, marketing or exportation or on the importation of intermediate inputs required for their manufacturing. Nor will INPI accept contracts requiring the licensee to use only the licensor's trademark.

An evaluation of the Brazilian regulatory scheme

A set of often conflicting objectives can be identified in Brazil's regulatory scheme on foreign investment:

1. balance of payments adjustment;
2. preventing foreign capital from taking advantage of domestic coporations, which are supposedly weaker;
3. inducing foreign industries to set up operations in Brazil; and
4. stimulating the development of domestic technology.

The task of simultaneously achieving these objectives is extremely difficult and complex, and it is only natural that many of the compromise solutions adopted have frequently brought about dissatisfaction among the parties involved, or have seemed to produce a negative net effect.

However, we are convinced that the positive aspects have outweighed the negative ones. In this evaluation we do not intend to put forward arguments in support of this view.

What we intend to do, instead, is to identify possible distortions prevailing in the scheme that can be improved, both from the legislative and the operational point of view, in the institutions involved. We should consider the following aspects:

First, Brazilian legislation encourages foreign investors to register their investments as debt instead of equity, unnecessarily aggravating Brazil's foreign debt problem. In fact, while interest income is only taxed (25 per cent) when it is remitted to the foreign lender, dividend income is doubly taxed: through the regular corporate income tax (35 per cent) and again by 25 per cent over the remaining 65 per cent, when remitted to the foreign investor. Besides, in the case of exchange control, Law no. 4131 provides for restrictions on profit and dividend remittance, but imposes no restriction at all on interest remittance. Finally, in view of the 12 per cent limit imposed on the profit and dividend remittance, and of the fact that the interest income is determined by market conditions, the behaviour of foreign interest rates may determine the benefits of registering an investment as a debt or as an equity. For instance, in 1980–81, when the interest rate fluctuated between 18 and 20 per cent, capital inflow in the form of loans was strongly stimulated; since 1983, with the interest rate lowered, this tendency has been reversed.

It seems evident, therefore, that there should be a reversal – or at least an equalisation – in the treatment given to both kinds of investment. Among the possibilities to consider are a reduction of the ratio of profit and dividend remittances to registered capital for supplementary tax application purposes, and to make the 12 per cent limit more flexible. This might be set as equal to London Inter-bank Offered Rate (LIBOR) plus a margin to stimulate the conversion of debt into equity.

Secondly, the Profit Remittance Law does not provide for any indexation to make up for the devaluation of the currency in which the capital registration has been made. Although on a decline, inflation is a more or less generalised phenomenon in the major capital-providing countries. Therefore, it would be reasonable to allow this conversion so that earnings do not incur supplementary tax liability as a mere consequence of nominal increases.

Thirdly, the setting of a single ceiling for the percentage remittance over the invested capital implicitly presupposes that the gross earnings (as regards capital and risk intensity) of different activities do not show significant variations – this is simply not the case.

The more obvious examples are service firms (where capital tends to be quite low in relation to their net earnings), and firms engaged in oil drilling and mineral exploration, where risks are fairly high. Some flexibility to take these differences into account would be technically recommended.

A final recommendation is related to the institutional framework for control of foreign capital in Brazil. As it is difficult to rely on uniform regulations enforced by a single institution, efforts should concentrate on the following practical objectives: to promote better co-ordination between the different government agencies involved (INPI, CACEX, SEI, and so on), more stable rules of the game, and fewer possibilities for arbitrary decision.

CONCLUDING REMARKS

Foreign investment has undeniably played a prominent role in the Brazilian economy's recent development. This role, as well as the actual nature of foreign investment, has gone through significant changes during the different phases of this process. It is also undeniable that participation of foreign investment occurred in an environment which was characterised by ambiguity and contradiction, producing in many analysts the conclusion that it had a negative net impact.

These forms of participation involved undertakings wholly controlled by foreign companies – above all in the period prior to the First World War, in which these companies were basically 'service workers' – the selling of technology by means of licensing trademarks and patents and the associations (joint ventures) with Brazilian companies – private and/or state. The most recent version of these associations, gathering the three types of agents (the 'tripartite' model), after an initial success in the establishment of the petrochemical industry, went on to be incorporated into the government's development strategy itself for certain sectors. However, experience has shown, that not only did its success depend on the convergence of very restrictive factors, but also in the petrochemical industry, the model even started to show clear signs of weakness.

Brazilian policy regarding foreign capital cannot be considered one of the more restrictive ones, even according to the standard of less developed countries. Moreover, Brazilian legislation as regards this subject has been able to show remarkable stability for over 20 years.

However, the magnitude of the country's present foreign debt is posing new questions as to the official position regarding foreign investment. Reflecting a rather generalised tendency,[28] the multinational companies with subsidiaries in Brazil have increasingly started to transfer resources in the form of loans substituting for the equity capital.[29]

Aiming at lessening the interest payment burden implied by the debt, the expansion of official incentives to convert the foreign companies' debt into capital share has been suggested.[30] The main argument underlying this proposal is the discriminatory treatment that fiscal legislation gives to profits compared to interest, the latter being deductible as expenditure in income tax calculations.

Notwithstanding the seriousness of the debt problem, and the important role in fostering Brazilian economic growth that foreign investment will continue to play, there are some doubts regarding, not only the benefits, but also the effectiveness of a more liberal treatment of foreign capital.

The first aspect has to do with the political exploration on an incidental worsening of the conditions governing foreign capital in Brazil and with the increasing risk perceived by investors, which would result from a breach of stability in the rules. Regarding efficiency, one must bear in mind, first of all, that the capital flow compositions is also subject to the characteristics of fiscal legislation in other countries, as well as the existence of double taxation agreements.

Secondly, the preference shown by multinational companies for loan capital seems to be more heavily based on other non-fiscal factors. This is so for two main reasons: the first is that contractual agreements grant an income flow that does not depend on operational performance of the subsidiary, the benefits of which grow in recessive periods. The second reason is that profit remittances and capital repatriation are more subject to governmental control than loan and interest payments. It is assumed that the second possibility, taken to its limit, complete prohibition, would be equivalent to a moratorium declaration and, as a consequence, a confrontation with the world financial community.

In spite of this, there are some technical aspects which could be improved in the regulation of foreign capital. They should be done in a way that would be compatible with the above considerations.

Notes

The author is grateful to Werner Baer, David Denslow, and Keith Rosenn, for the comments they made on a former version of this paper.

1. A substantial amount of FDI has not been registered with the Central Bank and there is not a reliable estimate of this value (see the third section).
2. US Department of Commerce (1984), p. 47.
3. Doellinger suggested that this decrease in Latin American 'attractiveness' had a lot to do with the political and institutional alternations that occurred in the region, including Brazil.
4. A systematic record of foreign capital stock in Brazil was only issued in the early 1970s (see OECD, 1972). Before that, the only available information that referred to US investments was published in the *Survey of Current Business*.
5. See Baer (1966) pp. 46–56.
6. The former specific tariffs completely lost their effectiveness, owing to inflation.
7. The exchange and trade policies were supplemented with easy granting of credit and the expansion of public expenditure, which kept aggregate demand at a constant high level.
8. See Baer and Kerstenetzky (1972) p. 111.
9. From 1965 on, foreign companies could receive from their head offices abundant and inexpensive resources for their working capital, at a time when the Brazilian companies were facing a credit squeeze and high interest rates (Doellinger, *et al.*, 1974, pp. 54–7).
10. The Committee found out that, between 1964 and 1968, foreign capital took over the control of 74 Brazilian companies, among which was a commercial bank and 17 investment banks out of the 27 existing banks. It is obvious that the Committee's conclusions did not influence the government's behaviour, nor was the foreign take-over process interrupted (see Bandeira, 1975, pp. 104–13).
11. See, for instance, Keesing (1967), Hirschman (1968), Baer (1972) and Helleiner (1972).
12. A description of these mechanisms can be found in Doellinger, *et al.* (1974), Chapter 2.
13. Almost simultaneously, another decree-law exempted the importation of whole industrial complexes from tariff duty and the manufactured products tax, since their output was 'essentially' meant for exportation. This incentive, however, did not generate the desired result.
14. See Baer and Villela (1980) pp. 95–107.
15. Evans (1982), p. 218.
16. For the Drug Agency's history and foreign take-over of the pharmaceutical industry, see Evans (1982, pp. 220–5).
17. The analysis in this section concentrates on the principal issues relating to the treatment of foreign investment in Brazil. A more detailed analysis may be found in Rosenn's excellent article (1983).
18. Law no. 4131, Art. 2 of 3 September 1962, provides: 'Identical juridical treatment to national capital under conditions of equality shall be dispensed to foreign capital invested in the country, prohibiting any discrimination not provided for in this law'.
19. Law no. 2004 of 3 October 1952. Since 1976, the Government has allowed foreign oil companies to prospect for oil pursuant to risk

contracts requiring the foreign oil companies to set up Brazilian branches, or subsidiaries.

20. On at least one occasion (Phillips-Consul) the Brazilian Government blocked a foreign take-over of a domestic firm.

21. From 1953 on, however, as a consequence of the aggravation of balance-of-payments disequilibrium, only profit remittances up to 10 per cent of registered capital could be made at the official exchange rate. Anything above that had to be purchased at the free (higher) market exchanges rate (Law no. 1807 of 7 January 1953).

22. Law no. 4131 of 3 September 1962.

23. Decree no. 53451 of 20 January 1964.

24. The marginal rate of the supplementary tax is 40 per cent when the percentage remittance is between 12 and 15 per cent, 50 per cent if it is between 15 and 25 per cent, and 60 per cent if the remittance is over 25 per cent (Law no. 4390 of 11 September 1964).

25. Law no. 3470 of 28 November 1958.

26. Normative Act no. 15 of 11 September, 1975, issued by INPI.

27. INPI has broken down technology transfer into five categories: patent licenses, trademark licenses, know-how licenses, technical-industrial co-operation agreements and specialised technical service agreements. The Code of Industrial Property sets extremely detailed provisions about agreements involving each category.

28. See World Bank (1982), pp. 51–2.

29. In June 1979 it was estimated that 16 per cent of the country's total debt referred to debts incurred by the companies with foreign participation.

30. The Law Decree 1598 of 12 December 1977 granted fiscal incentives to this conversion, which, however, have not produced the expected effects.

References

Baer, Werner, *A Industrialização e o Desenvolvimento Econômico do Brasil* (Rio de Janeiro: Fundação Getúlio Vargas, 1966).

Baer, Werner, 'Import Substitution and Industrialization in Latin America: Experiences and Interpretations', *Latin American Research Review*, Vol. 7, No. 1 (Spring 1972).

Baer, Werner and Isaac Kerstenetzky, 'The Brazilian Economy', in Riordan Roett (ed.), *Brazil in the 1960's* (Nashville: Vanderbilt University Press, 1972).

Baklanoff, Eric, 'Brazilian Development and the International Economy', in John Saunders (ed.), *Modern Brazil* (Gainesville: University of Florida Press, 1971).

Bandeira, Moniz, *Cartéis e Desnacionalização* (Rio de Janeiro: Civilização Brasileira, 1975).

Batista, Paulo N., *Mito e Realidade na Dívida Externa Brasileira* (Rio de Janeiro: Paz e Terra, 1983).

Castro, Ana Célia, *As Empresas Estrangeiras no Brasil: 1860–1913* (Rio de Janeiro: Zahar Editores, 1979).

Helson C. Braga   231

Doellinger, Carlos von, Hugo Barros de Castro Faria, Leonardo Caserta Calvalcanti, *A Política Brasileira de Comércio Exterior e seus Efeitos: 1967/73* (Rio de Janeiro: IPEA/INPES, 1974).

Doellinger, Carlos von, 'Política, Política Econômica e Capital Estrangeiro no Brasil: As Décadas de 30, 40 e 50', *Revista Brasileira de Mercado de Capitals*, Vol. 8, No. 3 (May/Aug. 1975).

Evans, Peter, *A Tríplice Aliança* (Rio de Janeiro: Zahar Editores, 1982).

Furtado, Celso, *Diagnosis of the Brazilian Crisis* (Berkeley: University of California Press, 1965).

Gordon, Lincoln and Engelbert L. Grommers, 'United States Manufacturing Investment in Brazil: The Impact of Brazilian Government Policies 1946–1960', Boston: Division of Research, Graduate School of Business Administration, Harvard University, 1962.

Guimarães, Eduardo A. *et al.*, 'Changing International Investment Strategies: The "New Forms" of Foreign Investment in Brazil', Textos para Discussão Interna No. 45 (Rio de Janeiro: IPEA/INPES 1982).

Helleiner, Gerald K., *International Trade and Economic Development* (Harmondsworth: Penguin Books, 1972).

Hirschman, Albert O., 'The Political Economy of Import-Substituting Industrialisation in Latin America' *Quarterly Journal of Economics*, Vol. 82, No. 1 (February 1968).

Keesing, Donald B., 'Outward-looking Policies for Economic Development', *Economic Journal*, Vol. 77 (June 1967).

Lessa, Carlos, *Quinze Anos de Política Econômica* (São Paulo: Editora Brasiliense, 1981).

Medina, Rubem, *Desnacionalização: Crime Contra o Brasil?* (Rio de Janeiro: Editora Saga, 1970).

Morley, Samuel A. and Gordon W. Smith, 'Import Substitution and Foreign Investment in Brazil', *Oxford Economic Papers*, Vol. 23, No. 1 (March 1971).

Newfarmer, Richard S. and Willard F. Mueller, 'Multinational Corporations in Brazil and Mexico: Structural Sources of Economic and Noneconomic Power', Report to the Subcommittee on Multinational Corporations of the Committee on Foreign Relations, United States Senate (Washington, DC: US Government Printing Office, 1975).

Organisation for Economic Cooperation and Development (OECD), *Stock of Private Investment by DAC Countries in Developing Countries, End 1967* (Paris: OECD, 1972).

Peñalver, Manuel, *et al.*, *Política Industrial e Exportação de Manufaturados do Brasil* (Rio de Janeiro: Fundação Getúlio Vargas, 1983).

Queiroz, Maurício V. de, 'Os Grupos Multibilionários', *Revista do Instituto de Ciências Sociais*, Vol. 2, No. 1 (1965).

Queiroz, Maurício V. de, 'Grupos Econômicos e o Modelo Brasileiro', Tese de Doutoramento (São Paulo: Universidade de São Paulo, 1972).

Ratnner, Henrique, *Industrialização e Conncentração Econômica* (Rio de Janeiro: Fundação Getúlio Vargas, 1972).

Rosenn, Keith S., 'Regulation of Foreign Investment in Brazil: A Critical Analysis', *Lawyer of the Americas*, Vol. 15, No. 2 (Autumn 1983).

Simonsen, Mário H., *Brasil 2001* (Rio de Janeiro: APEC Editora, 1969).

Sorensen, Georg, *Transnational Corporations in Peripheral Societies: Contributions Towards Self-Centered Development?* Development Research Series No. 6 (Aalborg, Denmark: Aalborg University Press 1983).

United States Department of Commerce (International Trade Administration), *International Direct Investment* (Washington, DC: US Government Printing Office, 1984).

World Bank, *World Development Report 1981* (Washington, DC: World Bank, 1982).

Wythe, George, *Industry in Latin America* (New York: Columbia University Press, 1945).

19 Foreign Investment and Development: The Experience of Chile: 1974–84

Andres Passicot

INTRODUCTION

Chile, like all developing countries, needs foreign savings to finance its growth. One way of capturing such funds is to open up the country to foreign capital for the creation of totally or partially foreign-owned enterprises. It is the intent of this paper to describe how this type of investment has worked in Chile over the last ten years, and the impact it has had on the economy. Of course, the process of direct foreign investment cannot be analysed without reference to the laws governing it. Therefore, a brief summary of this legislation will precede comments upon the actual economic aspects.

The story of Chile's experience may be of particular interest because of certain features which caused its economic development policies to markedly depart from those pursued by other Latin American countries during the last ten years. It is thus important to understand these features which led to Chile's different development path.

First of all there was an absence of hostility towards foreign investment during these ten years. To the contrary, Chile has welcomed it, not merely in words, but in deeds as well. For instance, Chile's withdrawal from the Andean Pact – an interregional integration agreement with Bolivia, Colombia, Ecuador, Peru and Venezuela – was largely due to differences of opinion regarding criteria used to screen the entry of foreign investment. In Chile's opinion, Resolution No. 24 would not encourage foreign investment in the countries signatory to the Pact. Interest in foreign investment was further shown by the creation of a special set of rules, with the force of law (Decree No. 600), stipulating the conditions under which foreign investors may enter and work their capital in Chile. Secondly, Chile has continuously used foreign resources to finance its development. Therefore there is no strong competition with domestic savings. Thirdly, during the period in question the economic development policy has been based on a free market system, with considerably lower barriers to foreign trade than other nations in the region and great respect shown for rights of private ownership. Fourthly, since the economic crisis resulting from the unfortunate economic policy of the years 1970–73 was overcome, Chile has had reasonable price stability, sufficient human and energy resources, and adequate infrastructure for transport and communication.

Thus, the case of a developing country which has offered the foreign investor better conditions than at any other time in its history will be examined. These conditions have probably also been better than those offered, on the average, by other Latin American countries. As we shall later see, however, there has been no sizeable inflow of foreign investment. The reasons for this relative failure are both numerous and complex, and cannot, at this point, be set out accurately one by one in this paper. But useful background information for a more in-depth study of this important subject will be found in this paper.

CHILE AND FOREIGN INVESTMENT

Foreign capital has been invested in Chile ever since the end of the nineteenth century. At that time it was concentrated mainly in saltpetre, copper and iron mining, certain transport and communication services, and energy production. Later, and as a result of the First World War, foreign investors entered the manufacturing industry and, between 1920 and 1930, important companies such as Dupont, British American Tobacco, Ford and Parke Davis began to invest in Chile. The 1929 crisis brought on a larger degree of protection for domestic industry and consequently encouraged the arrival of new foreign investment. Between 1931 and 1945, investments were made in Chile by such important companies as Nestlé, Duncan Fox, Phillips and the General Tyre and Rubber Company. We should further mention the three major American companies which started large-scale copper mining and which, by the mid-1960s, were partially bought up by the Chilean Government to be fully nationalised later on in 1971.

Restrictive regulations governing foreign investment prior to 1974

Over the years, foreign investment has been subject to a variety of regulations reflecting the different positions on this question of the authorities of the time. In 1960, the Foreign Investment Statute was promulgated (Law Decree No. 258), replacing the legislation of 1954. The main feature of the laws that came into force in 1960 is the exclusive power of the President of the Republic to decide upon the following matters:

1. Access to the exchange market and the right to repatriate the initial capital investment, its profits and interests.
2. Exemption from customs duties, advance-payments and other restrictions.
3. Tax exemption for export-producing companies or enterprises declared to be of vital importance and not existing in the country as yet.

The preferential treatment granted by the President of the Republic in individual cases was generally valid for a period of ten years, although some could qualify for extension up to a maximum of 20 years.

Since 1961, along with the previously mentioned statute, existed Article 16 of the Law on Foreign Exchange, authorising the Central Bank to sign agreements to guarantee directly-invested foreign capital. Such agreements had to meet the following conditions:

1. The investment should be deemed of national interest by the Bank's Executive Committee and involve a sum not less than US$100 000.
2. The capital could be repatriated after four years, in annual instalments not exceeding 20 per cent.
3. If entered as credit, the capital could bear an interest equal to, but no greater than, the prevailing market rate.
4. The investor had to promise not to use the capital investment to finance imports.

Both sets of regulations clearly gave the President of the Republic and the Central Bank discretionary power to decide upon the entry of foreign investment. Additionally, the existence of a special regulation (Law Decree No. 16.624 of 1967) governing investment in large-scale copper mining augmented discretionary power in regard to foreign investment. This is important to stress because it contrasts so sharply with the non-discriminating nature of the legislation introduced in 1974, and which still governs foreign investment today.

At the end of 1970, the countries signatory to the Andean Pact agreed on a common approach to foreign investment. The policy was enunciated in Resolution No. 24 and, as stipulated under this agreement, the Chilean Government informed the Pact's Secretariat before 1 July 1971 of its acceptance. This called for changes in the Chilean legislation in force (Law Decree No. 258). The common policy agreed upon by the countries of the Andean Pact, and which, but for a few changes, is still pursued today, was highly restrictive of foreign investment. It imposed upon investors few attractive aspects and included limitations, such as ceilings on capital gains and compulsory association with national capital within a specified period of time after entry. Chile withdrew from the Andean Pact in the mid-1970s. Previously, on 13 July 1974, a new Foreign Investment Statute (Law Decree No. 600) had been promulgated, whose contents were, in fact, in contradiction with the prevailing position in the Andean Pact. This new set of regulations and their subsequent modifications in 1977, mark the beginning of a more liberal treatment of foreign investment in Chile.

The more liberal treatment of foreign investment

The legislation governing this matter today is characterised by the following features: First, free access for foreign investors to domestic markets and all economic sectors, subject to the provisions of the laws in force. The foreign investor is free to choose his field of activity, form of organisation, volume of trade, as well as to decide upon possible association with other investors, solely on the basis of his own judgement and considerations of profit and efficiency. Secondly, there is no distinction between domestic and foreign investors. Chilean legislation, regulations and procedures are equally valid for domestic and foreign investors. Thirdly, the procedure for complying with the formalities required of foreign investment is an impersonal and automatic one. The rules and general terms of the contracts are pre-established, as are the rights and obligations of the investor and, further, in practice negotiations between government authorities and foreign investors no longer occur. This guarantees a procedure for authorisation and implementation of foreign investment contracts in Chile, that is expeditious, standardised and efficient.

Capital may enter the country in the following forms:

1. As freely convertible foreign currency, paid up in authorised financial institutions. The exchange rate will be the bank rate.
2. As goods in all forms or states, brought into the country without exchange coverage and valued under the general import regulations.
3. As technology, if susceptible to capitalisation. It may not be transferred independently of the enterprise in which it was brought in, nor does it admit of amortisation or depreciation.
4. As foreign credit accompanying the foreign investment, the financial terms and conditions and general provisions of which must be as authorised by the Central Bank of Chile for all foreign loans raised by the country.
5. Capitalisation of foreign credits and debts in freely convertible currency, contracted with due authorisation.
6. Capitalisation of gains which may be repatriated.

Foreign investment permits are officially stipulated in contracts, drawn up as public deeds, parties to which are the foreign investor, personally, or his legal representative, and the State of Chile, represented by the Chairman of the Foreign Investment Board or the Board's Executive Secretary. It should be pointed out that these contracts have the force of law, that is, they are contracts made by the State of Chile under the law, making certain commitments to the investor which cannot be altered by any future modification of the law. These contracts with force of law are recognised by Chilean law and judicial practice, and no changes can therefore be made unless both parties agree. Basically the contracts consist of standard forms and clauses, specifying the amount and purpose of the investment, the dates on which it was made, and the guarantees that the foreign investor is offered. The period of time allowed for investments is a maximum three years for investments in general, and eight years for mining projects. In the latter case, if preliminary prospecting is called for, the Foreign Investment Board may, by unanimous decision, grant an extension of the deadline up to 12 years, in view of the specific and time-consuming nature of such explorations.

Investors are offered the following guarantees:

1. The right to repatriate capital and net capital gains, without limit or deadline. However, capital may not be remitted until three years after its entry into the country. Capital gains may be remitted any time. In any case, the necessary foreign currency for capital remittances may only be acquired with the proceeds from the sale of stock in the foreign company or from the income produced by its liquidation. The latter is tax free up to the amount of the investment authorised by the Investment Board and effectively brought into the country. Any surplus will be subject to the general tax laws. The exchange rate for repatriation of capital and capital gains is the bank rate for foreign trade transactions, foreign loans and foreign investments. The investor is guaranteed access to the exchange market to buy the corresponding amount of foreign currency and have it remitted abroad.

2. The investor has the right, if he so chooses, to include in his investment contract a clause guaranteeing, for a period of ten years, as of the starting date of his enterprise, a flat tax rate of 49.5 per cent on the income generated from the investment. The investor who has opted for this fixed rate may, only once, waive this right and choose to come under the normal tax regulations, but will from then on always remain subject to the standard tax regulations.

3. The investor has the right to include in his contract a clause stipulating that, for the time it takes to realise the authorised investment, the Value Added Tax (VAT) and tariffs applicable to the import of machinery and equipment will remain unchanged. (This is applicable only to machinery and equipment that the country does not produce and which is included in a special list as mentioned in Article 12 of the VAT law, published in Law Decree No. 635 of the Ministry of Economic Affairs, of December 1976. Under the respective tax regulations, these types of goods are exempt from VAT payment on import, if the goods are on the updated list and a foreign investment contract has been made. Currently, the VAT rate is 20 per cent. On the other hand, under the tariff system, payment of customs duties, taxes, dispatchment fees and other charges paid through Customs, may be deferred. All these costs are stated in US dollars, payable in one single instalment without interest seven years after clearance. Payment must be in Chilean currency, at the exchange rate of the date of payment. The debt is written off each year at the ratio of exports over the total sales of the goods produced by the machinery and

equipment for which duty payment was deferred. The annual write-down percentage may not be higher than 50 per cent of the original debt, nor may it exceed the total f.o.b. (free on board) values of exports over the same period. In practice, this means that projects producing a sizeable amount of goods for export are virtually exempt from import duties. Customs duties in Chile today stand at 20 per cent.

4. Finally, the foreign investor is protected against discrimination. Foreign investment and the enterprises in which it partakes, are subject to the same laws and regulations as domestic investment, and it cannot be discriminated against, either directly or indirectly, with the sole exception being a regulation which could restrict access to domestic credit. However, this restriction has never been put into practice.

A law or regulation is considered discriminatory in a branch of activity, if it is applicable to all but the foreign investor. Since there is no discrimination against any type of foreign investment, it may for instance, profit from legal provisions granted special privileges for certain areas, or branches of economic activity, provided that they comply with the same requirements as domestic investors.

If foreign investors or the enterprises in which they participate, believe that they are being treated in a discriminatory fashion, they may appeal to the Foreign Investment Board for its removal, unless the regulation concerned is more than one year old. If within 60 days of the appeal the Board does not pass judgement on the case, overrule the claim, or decide that the discrimination cannot be removed by administrative measures, the claimants may appeal to an ordinary court of justice for a ruling.

SCOPE AND IMPACT OF FOREIGN INVESTMENT IN CHILE

The main conclusion to be drawn from what has been discussed up to now, is that the policy pursued by Chile with regard to foreign investment can be divided into two clearly different periods. The first corresponds to the years 1961 to 1973, when treatment was discretionary, in that the government, and the President of the Republic and the Central Bank, in particular, were able to negotiate conditions in each case with each investor. The second period, from 1974 to the present, is characterised by a standardised treatment with identical rights and obligations for foreign and domestic investor alike.

It would be interesting to see if there is any significant difference in foreign investment in Chile between the two periods. For the first period we shall consider the ten years between 1961 and 1970, because, although between 1971 and 1973 the foreign investment policy was even more discriminatory, those were years of great political instability and lack of public confidence which make them unrepresentative.

A comparison of the two periods leads to the following conclusions:

1. The number of projects, amounts authorised and effectively brought into the country, increased four- to five-fold, in real terms, under the new legislation.
2. The average size of authorised projects rose from US$8.8 to US$9.9 million.
3. The ratio of effectively entered to authorised investments fell from 38.2 per cent to 27.8 per cent (see Table 19.1).
4. In both periods, realised investment was concentrated in the mining sector. However, whereas under the discriminatory laws, it represented 59.6 per cent, under the new legislation it made up 41.5 per cent.

These figures indicate that the new laws have been successful in encouraging investment. A comparison of the figures in relative terms leads us to the same conclusion. Let us see, for instance, how they compare to the figures of Gross Domestic Product (GDP) and fixed capital investment.

During the ten years immediately preceding 1970, authorised foreign investment represented on average 0.7 per cent of GDP. Of the total authorised, an amount equivalent to 0.3 per cent of GDP was effectively invested. On the other hand, during the ten year period from 1974 to 1983, authorised investments totalled 3.9 per cent of GDP and the effectively invested sum to 1.1 per cent of GDP (see Table 19.2). When comparing total investment in Chile during the two ten-year periods, we also find an increase in the figures. Authorised investment rose from 3.5 per cent to 24.7 per cent of total investment. The amount realised rose from 1.3 per cent to 6.9 per cent (see Table 19.3).

The data clearly shows that during the last ten years Chile has

Table 19.1 Foreign investment*

Year	Number of projects	Amount of investment Authorized (*A*)	Effectively entered (*B*)	(*B*)/(*A*) × 100
1961–70	178	1576.4	602.1	38.2%
1974–83	867	8593.5	2386.0	27.8%

*In millions of 1983 US$.

succeeded in attracting, both in relative and in absolute terms, a larger volume of foreign investment than in the immediately preceding decade. It cannot be said, however, that foreign investment has had a decisive impact on capitalisation in Chile, as the ratio of foreign investment realised to GDP, expressed in percentage terms, amounts to only 1.1 per cent. If all investment authorised had effectively entered during the last ten years, the investment rate would have been almost four times higher. This might have produced an important positive impact.

THE MAJOR REASONS FOR LIMITED FOREIGN INVESTMENT

As we have said earlier, in the course of the last ten years only 27.8 per cent of the authorised investment was actually realised. This could possibly be the prime reason for the relatively small amount of foreign investment that effectively entered the country. Looking at the figures separately, we find that the explanation for the low percentage of

Table 19.2 Gross Domestic Product and foreign investment*

Year	GDP (*A*)	Amount of foreign investment Authorized (*B*)	Effectively entered (*C*)	(*B*)/(*A*) × 100	(*C*)/(*A*) × 100
1961–70	221 545	1576.4	602.1	0.7%	0.3%
1974–83	222 769	8593.5	2386.0	3.9%	1.1%

*In millions of 1983 US$.

Table 19.3   Fixed capital investment and foreign investment*

Year	GDP (A)	Amount of foreign investment Authorized (B)	Effectively entered (C)	(B)/(A) × 100	(C)/(A) × 100
1961–70	44 641	1576.4	602.1	3.5%	1.3%
1974–83	34 816	8593.5	2386.0	24.7%	6.9%

*In millions of 1983 US$.

actual investment in relation to that authorised, lies in the mining sector. Only 15.3 per cent of the authorised investment in this sector effectively entered the country. In the other sectors, the corresponding figure was about 80 per cent.

The reasons for the delay in the large mining projects seem to be of an economic nature, in addition to the time-consuming character of investments of such scope. The prime economic reason is the low price of copper on the world market. During the last ten years the average copper price has been US$1 per pound, whereas during the immediately preceding ten years the average price was US$1.50 per pound, both figures stated in June 1983 dollars. At the time the investment contracts were signed, the price of copper was below a dollar per pound. Today it is down 40 per cent and there is no clear indication that this situation will improve in the near term. The second economic reason is the high international interest rates which, alone, make many investment projects unprofitable. The drop in copper prices has exacerbated this situation.

In addition to the previous factors, there are four other reasons which help to explain the relatively modest amount of foreign investment realised in Chile during the last ten years. First, foreign savers prefer to enter funds in the form of loans and not as direct investment. High interest rates and relatively short maturity have made credit a much more attractive vehicle. During the last ten years Chile has received in gross credit five times the amount of direct investment. The average terms were 4.5 years maturity, with 96.7 per cent at a variable rate London Inter-bank Offered Rate (LIBOR), having a 1.3 per cent spread. Secondly, the effects of economic policies hostile to foreign investment, which were so much in favour in Latin

America some years ago, and reached their peak in Chile between 1971 and 1973, have been slow to wear off. These policies caused the Overseas Private Investment Corporation (OPIC) to stop its operations in Chile in order to protect American investors from political risks. OPIC did not resume its activities in Chile until 14 February 1984. Thirdly, excess liquidity on the world market, especially during the first part of the period under study, made it relatively easy to obtain foreign financing in the form of loans. This explains why Chile, and probably other countries as well, have failed to be aggressive in their attempts to capture foreign investment. Finally, world recession during the second half of the period in question caused the level of investment to drop significantly. In times of recession, firms must do all they can to use their installed capacity to the fullest extent and do not embark on new investment projects.

A LOOK AT THE FUTURE

In the coming years, Chile, and probably other developing countries as well, will have to attach more importance to attracting direct foreign investment. We must improve our attitude towards the foreign investor and prepare ourselves for the changes that the more limited availability of credit will bring.

Direct investment should acquire greater importance, mainly for the following reasons:

1. Over the last few years we have seen loan capital better rewarded than risk capital. This situation should be corrected by the lowering of the interest rates.
2. Some foreign creditors will want to, or have to, capitalise part of their loans owing to the debtor nations' difficulties in making repayment.
3. Investment opportunities with high rates of return should be more available in developing rather than in the developed countries.
4. Within a short period of time tax reforms will be implemented in Chile, offering tax cuts to business enterprises.

Chile's attitude towards foreign investors is bound to improve, for the following reasons:

1. Chile, and Latin America as a whole, have learned the hard lesson of borrowing at high interest rates. Now that a significant percentage of Chile's exports goes towards payment of interest, she is in a better position to realise the advantages of associating with foreign capital, rather than in just obtaining loans.
2. The size of Chile's debt is such that its economy has few possibilities left to attract foreign savings in the form of loans. She no longer has the choice between encouraging growth by means of foreign credit or direct foreign investment. The only alternative to a serious setback in development is growth through direct investment.
3. Technology is an increasingly important variable in economic growth. Its incorporation into Chile's economy through direct foreign investment should be valued more highly in the future.

Finally, Chile should prepare herself to live in a period where risk capital becomes more important than finance capital. This involves challenges, in the following areas:

1. In the structure of the financial system, where traditional banks will have to make room for investment banks. It also means that longer-term savings should be encouraged, and that it will be more important to investigate a project's expected return rather than only its creditworthiness.
2. Development policies should gradually move away from protectionist practices, in favour of more agile financial and commercial markets.
3. Chile should conduct a steady economic policy, instead of the constant experiments which have caused so much harm to development. This is particularly true in the case of Chile, where during the last 25 years many different approaches have been attempted. When the rules of the game keep changing, foreign investment is hard to attract.

Many of these ideas will probably take time, but it seems that Chile is moving in the right direction. Above all, she should fully commit herself to this task.

Index